Children dissolve in the rain

A story about parenthood and playwork

Adele Cleaver

Meynell Games Publications

ISBN 9781898068082

Published by Meynell Games Publications, Eastbourne, UK

Contents

Part 4 - Can I bring my baby?

What if societies just accepted that babies came along for the ride?

Part 5 - When parents play

What if we pay attention to ourselves as much as we pay attention to our children?

Part 6 - Wearing my playwork hat at home

What if we stop trying to control our children?

Para a minha flor,

While you're still young,

Find your heart and find your soul.

The Cat Empire

Acknowledgements

Well, this has been quite a process! First and foremost, I'd like to show some huge gratitude to Mr Lowprofile for doing far more than his fair share of bedtimes so I could escape motherhood and get lost in my thoughts and notebooks. I've been saying 'I promise I am nearly finished' for months and months and months! I don't think either of us really anticipated how time-consuming this little project of mine would become so, meu amor, your patience is, as ever, appreciated. During this writing journey we celebrated ten years together; thank you for believing in me and trusting me to share our personal life. Obrigada.

Although I revelled in escaping to a quiet corner of our home to write, read and re-write, the whole process was at times lonely so thank you to Amber, Abi, Jono and Daisy who read this very early on and encouraged me to keep going. Natalie Koussa from Uncommon People helped me with accountability and kept me on track in the middle stages. And when I decided to self-publish, Judy Tweddle gave me invaluable editorial advice, Justyna A Bielecka from JAB Proofreading has been a huge help in getting through this final hurdle and Wendy Russell provided such a wonderful Foreword. Thank you all.

Then there's all the Brummies! Where would I be without my Brummies?! But particularly, Jen & Aunty Britt, Sara & Uncle Mike and the radical women of community play – El Dorada, Agent Garnham, Simbi, Sandra, Carol and the Seven

Up mums; you have no idea how much you taught me about raising children well before I anticipated having my own.

Thank you to Patrick Morrow, the host of The Parent Journey podcast, for helping me to find my voice through podcasting. I think the conversations that took place over the twenty or so episodes are truly precious, and I am not just saying that because I like listening to a Brummie (and their mate) talk about childhood and play! The recordings helped to gather my thoughts, provoked new thinking and boosted my confidence to keep on writing.

All our villagers in Bournemouth – you know who you are – biggup yourselves and thank you for being part of our life. A special thank you to Teresa and Helen for reaffirming my belief in sisterhood, and to Natasha and Assis for creating spaces for human connection through movement. One special 'Ta Bab' to Dani, founder of First Friends, the most inclusive preschool in Bournemouth. You have been an absolute wonder woman for many local families and super generous and flexible with extra childcare for us when there were simply not enough hours in the day to finish and publish this book.

There's a whole gaggle of playworkers... all my colleagues in Brum, the youth workers in Westminster (I truly cherish some of those epic Saturday adventures with Des driving the minibus). A huge, huge thank you to the Thursday morning Reflective Practice gang – effectively a group of strangers who really got me through the bizarre unfoldings of 2020 and inspired me with new insight, so much knowledge, and gave me a generous space to untangle some of my perceptions, curiosities and challenges of play and being a playworker. A special thanks to Penny for inviting me along in the first place and to Meynell for helping at the publication stage. I can't wait to meet you all in person; what a surreal thought.

Last but not least my faaaaaaamily. My wonderful sibs, our lovely padres, and our growing brood to whom we pass our playful baton. I love you all.

Playful People

I reached out and asked for 50 friends to come forward and help soften the financial blow of self-publishing by buying a copy of my book waaaay before it was done and ready. Your generosity and trust was much appreciated. It was also a great motivation to finish the task in hand.

A massive thank you to Becka White, Kellie Cash, Vero Leopoldino, Tante Britt, Christine Jameson, Natalie Koussa, Zietta Rosie, Irene Cleaver, Karen Stone, Tia "Frank-sense" and Tio Cheikh, Abby Perrins, The Urwins, Lisa May, Jenny B, Karen Stone, Sophie Leon, Helen Gialias, Sachels n' Keitles, Susie & Evie, The Pearsons, Meriel Camara, and the rest of you who preferred not to be named.

xi

Foreword

Thank you, Adele, for this treasure of a book. It had me at times laughing, weeping, nodding in recognition and disagreeing, probably all in equal measure and often all at the same time. It is an eloquent and deeply personal account of exploring what playwork – and other forms of non-judgmental support for things that matter – has to offer being a parent. Given its personal nature, often my response to the book was to reflect on my own experiences. I too was a playworker before I was a mother, and the skills I learned served me well both as a parent and as a daughter supporting both my parents through dementia in later life. I have often wondered if I would have been a different kind of playworker (or parent) if I'd had my children before discovering playwork. I've also often thought that it would be a brilliant research project to talk to the children of playworkers, many of whom will now be parents and grandparents themselves. The Maya Angelou of the children's workforce is how you describe playworkers, adapting 'Still I Rise' with impunity: 'does my playfulness offend you?'

Even though the experiences of being a mother you recount are located firmly in the 21st century, there are, despite your frequent descriptions of differences between the generations, many parallels with my own experiences of motherhood in the 1980s and 1990s. You talk much about the village you gathered around you to raise your child. I think I did something similar, although of course not in exactly the same ways. One of your stories that resonated with me was the hiring of a dance studio. I too was part of a group that hired a hall like you did, providing somewhere for us to be together with our children – although this was unceremoniously called 'the dump', since half the parents would stay and the other half would leave their children and have a couple of hours off. Whilst both aspects (time with other parents and children and time away from the children) were valued, the name describes it perfectly. As you say, if you don't look after yourself, you are not so well placed to look after others.

Actually, 'the dump' was a group where fathers *were* involved in caring for their children, in contrast to your experience of your parents' generation, where this was not the case. In my own family, I was the one that went back to work and my male partner did the bulk of the daytime childcare for many years, although there was a stretch of about three or four years where we ran a co-operative catering company together with friends of ours and shared both the work and the childcare across both families. More than three decades later, those children are still firm friends and our original extended-but-not-related family (why is there no name for this fairly common phenomenon?) group of 8 is now 18, although we have also sadly lost some along the way. My son now works part time and shares equally in the childcare for his own daughter, but that has all been during the pandemic lockdown, so the whole thing has been weird.

It got me thinking about how attitudes towards women, mothers and children don't progress in an orderly manner along a neat, straight line towards what some might call equality or justice. The same is true for other forms of injustice and the intersections between them. The 1980s were the tail end of three decades or more of strong civil rights activism, including the powerful second wave of feminism. We did our best to live our lives according to our values, something that was not always easy. We felt we were breaking new ground, doing things differently. It pulled me up a little short to read your experience of feeling that in involving your husband in the childcare you were also doing something radically new. But what this highlights is the complex and non-linear ways that issues of equality, diversity and justice change over time.

I could say the same about playwork too. In my early playwork days, we were very well funded, there were more of us, most of us worked full time and so it was much easier to have a local village of playworkers – others that we could meet up with regularly and chew the fat and reflect on what we did. We even ran a housing co-operative for play, youth and community workers, creating veritable villages in the council housing stock deemed unfit for families. Now, after decades of sustained neglect and funding cuts, we are arguably better at articulating what it is we do, but no-one seems to be listening, at least not the people with money. Our village though has changed and grown to a digitally enabled global village and we can learn from each other in many different ways. Still we rise indeed.

If you went back to Lisbon now, Adele, I could put you in touch with a fantastic playwork organisation that you would immediately feel an affinity with. Looks like you were there at the wrong time, and possibly also at GOSH at the wrong time too. Moments of could-have-beens. But who needs could-have-beens when you describe the present with such immediate power, detail, wit and honesty. Still you rise, bab.

Dr Wendy Russell, April 2021
Independent researcher in children's play and playwork
Visiting Fellow at University of Gloucestershire

mom

[mom] noun

One's mother. In Brummie. Also American.
See also: mum

Prologue

The house lights dimmed in the theatre where we had sat our bums on the unsteady temporary tiered seating. My finger hovered over the mouse when I'd sat looking at the booking system a few weeks earlier. After too much internal deliberation over whether it was best to sit closer to the exit, or on the back row as far away from the rest of the audience as possible, I opted to sit with my friends. I deliberately chose the aisle seat, a few rows back from the double doors, should I need to make a swift exit.

Twenty minutes earlier, as I stepped through the automatic sliding doors of the main entrance, I felt like a regular; it was an arts centre I'd frequented many a time before. In the theatre I'd seen a handful of shows and in the community dance studios on the other side of the building I'd often attended dance classes. Yes, I was definitely a regular, but on this occasion, I felt irregular.

I held back as the crowd shuffled from the foyer to the theatre with their miniature bottles of Blossom Hill and plastic cups in hand. Bodies were already cluttered with heaps of coats and scarves folded over their arms, but they hastily took a programme and exchanged tickets for stubs from the smiling ushers at the door. It was a normal show, but I was still adjusting to my new normal.

Typically, Papa was on a late shift on the one night I wanted him home. I *needed* to go to that show. I'd been spoiled with multicultural arts my entire life.

Opportunities that I took for granted in Birmingham were few and far between when we settled on the sleepy south coast of England. The performance was only fifty minutes long so it seemed more trouble than it was worth to express a load of breastmilk and book a babysitter who would only fret about all the bottles and cups that would be refused until I came home.

And of course, buying the ticket was a bit of a treat at sixteen quid, plus the extortionate town-centre car-park fee, so paying a babysitter on top of that just made seeing a show really, really expensive – too expensive for my maternity allowance budget, especially for less than an hour's entertainment, so I decided to take her with me.

Upon arrival all the fellow humans – ticket holders and staff – had cooed at my bright-eyed cherub dangling from my torso. They had smiled and nodded at me in what I interpreted as approval when we were out in the foyer, but as we took to our seat I was nervous. Of course, I hid my unease behind the incredible little human I had on my lap and treasured the sanctuary of my sisterhood at my side. I was among friends: mostly fellow amateur dancers, mothers and grandmothers with whom I had grooved throughout my pregnancy. They were used to seeing our daughter out on the community arts scene with me. But I really didn't know how the strangers in the audience would react to sharing their night at the theatre with a baby.

The auditorium doors closed and the stage lights darkened. As one silhouette took to the stage in silence, I cradled my daughter close and popped my nipple into her mouth. She obligingly sucked, but I had, very naively, never expected the opening scene from an African dance company to be a cappella. That's what I love about the arts: we can't predict another person's creativity.

Motherhood is also full of surprises: that night the sheer volume of my nine-month-old daughter's suckle took me by surprise.

'How had I never noticed the noise of her gob slapping against my boob?' I asked myself, starting to panic.

As she enthusiastically gulped at my breast I broke into a violent sweat. Maybe it was the synthetic fabric on the pull-down seats, or maybe it was because THE AUDITORIUM WAS FILLED WITH THE ACOUSTICS OF MY NIPPLE.

Each slurp was followed by a satisfying nasal inhalation while her equally vigorous exhalations bounced off the long black curtain at each side of the stage where a beautiful piece of choreography was unfolding. How could her neat button nose be making such a racket? My body started to rise out of my seat as panic told me I needed to leave.

Simultaneously my daughter and my friend stopped me in my tracks. Just as my instinctive little child raised her hand and placed it on my chest to feel my palpitations, the friend occupying the not-so-sweaty seat next to me felt my hurry to leave. She carefully grabbed my arm, the one that wasn't cradling my baby, and hissed firmly, 'Stay!'

I sat with gritted teeth, flaring nostrils and a clammy back, desperately waiting for the silent scene on the stage to be over.

The figurine continued to move with robust elegance against an intense-orange-lit backdrop. My body burned.

Before long an inviting percussion ensemble kicked in. It was so sudden that my almost sleeping babe was called to attention. Never one to miss out on the action, she stood, present and correct, on my lap for the duration of the spirited, dynamic performance.

My dad is the only white man I know with a record collection of bands from Congo, Senegal, South Africa, Mali, Ghana, etc. For as long as I can remember I have been magnetised to these flamboyant rhythms. And there, in the darkness of the theatre, my baby daughter was connecting with them too.

Her childhood was only just beginning while the soundtrack of that show brought memories of mine flooding back. Amongst the shadows of the dancers on stage were joyful images of my childhood in Birmingham and the colourful citizens that lined the streets of our second city. I saw the faces and the spaces of the place where I'll probably never reside again but will always call home. My upbringing by a liberal duo afforded me healthy doses of unfamiliar cultures, community arts festivals and being dragged to gig after gig after gig with songs that were often not sung in English.

Our summers were spent roaming around in a rusting Ford Transit which was converted into a holiday home for six. From dawn to dusk, in British and European countryside my three siblings and I played freely amongst ourselves and with children who were drawn to our clan. Through the global language of play we connected with our peers; moving sand around for hours, running barefoot in fields and making things to play with from whatever we scavenged while our parents embraced a timelessness that didn't exist in their working lives back home.

My dad's vinyl, lovingly recorded onto ninety-minute blank cassettes, were my soundtrack to these summers. As he drove us from concrete to countryside, his wedding ring tapped against the vibrating steering wheel, mimicking the rhythms that were blaring from the mediocre speakers.

The same rhythms were floating about the stage in front of me while I was now holding his fifth grandchild. Barely blinking, she remained fixated on the colourful action unravelling beneath the bright lights of the stage. She bounced and yelped in unison with the audience's laughter and cheers.

She reached out to hold the movement of her ancestors close.

Her intrigue and curiosity, and my enjoyment of a fiercely entertaining show, both reinforced that I could, and would, bring my baby wherever I bloody well pleased. Since the mid-1980s I have been growing a healthy addiction to play: I couldn't suddenly give it up the moment I gave birth to an incredible human who required my care. With babe in arms it became very clear to me that I *needed* the freedom of choice and the intrinsically motivated decision making I've developed from living playfully. Muddling through these first three years of her life has given me a newfound appreciation of living a life full of play.

Part 1 - Born to play

What if we listen to our children?

Since I had a baby and found myself, day in day out, chatting about our children's play with the mamas and papas of baby Joe Bloggs in the park, I started to realise just how much my playwork career had taught me. With closer mama friends we'd talk for hours about the nuances of their play, what was happening inside our babies' incredible brains and, of course, we'd daydream collaboratively about how we could ditch the kids and go get lost on a dancefloor to rekindle some of that brilliant juicy good stuff we knew our brains also needed.

When I started sharing that I was writing a book about play, well-meaning people have started introducing me as a 'play' pause 'expert? specialist? consultant?' Playworker doesn't seem to cut it.

'Children are the experts of play. I am a playworker,' I said to a colleague when she asked me if she should introduce me as a Play Expert in a meeting with local artists.

'Yes, but you have to think about the connotations of the word "worker". It is low-grade, poorly paid, you deserve more. I mean you have worked at Great Ormond Street Hospital after all.'

Bang! There it was again, those few months of employment that keep coming back to haunt me. Everyone sees the playwork of world-renowned Great Ormond Street Hospital (GOSH) but no one sees 'the experts' at play every single day. I guess that is what has geared me up to write this book.

I was appointed as a hospital playworker at Great Ormond Street Hospital (GOSH) in the early summer of 2012. Just a few weeks later the world was entertained with hundreds of gowned children dancing in illuminated hospital beds and roller-skating healthcare professionals parading in celebration of our beloved NHS. When Danny Boyle put nine children from Great Ormond Street in the spotlight of the London Olympics Opening Ceremony I sobbed on my sofa with pride. He hit a chord. My GOSH ID badge attached to my pot of hand gel dumped on the coffee table in a Friday night slump was a teeny tiny validation that I was part of that spectacular. I was playing my part in that heroic workforce.

When I received the call to congratulate me on succeeding in the interview I thought I had 'made it' in the world of playwork. I hadn't. Life at GOSH hit me hard. Their approach to play was miles off the wonderful baptism of fire I had experienced in the underground network of inclusive community play in Birmingham.

My job interview had been at the end of a warren of dark corridors where the play office was tucked away. The old building was worlds away from the new modern annexe that screamed world-class health innovation and pioneering science. The old building was a reminder of the hospital's institutional history of well-meaning philanthropists. The location of the play team HQ, however, was a statement in itself: play is not a priority here. The experienced, wiser me would have taken the role with caution.

Just as the GOSH playworkers' office was tucked away in the dark ages, so were the playworkers. The woman I was instructed to shadow used a high-pitched, soppy voice every time she spoke to a child. Everything was 'Awwwwwwww how

3

lovely' and 'awwwwwww he's so cute' and 'awwwww she's so sweet'. I found it patronising and she really pissed me off.

I've always wanted to empower children, not fuss over them. I've dotted around quite a few childcare settings now and, in each setting, I have noticed a tendency amongst adults to change our voice when we speak to children. Tone change is often necessary; pitch, on the other hand, grates on me. The piercing shrill of that well-meaning, kind and compassionate young woman still haunts me. It is by no means her fault that she speaks to children like that; it is probably how the adults in her life spoke to her. Worse still, she was permanently smiley and sociable and apparently liked around the workplace; I felt I had to act like her to be accepted. It was not really me. The real me was utterly lost in this play setting.

After a couple of weeks I ditched Miss Shrill and her colouring sheets and her spoon-fed, manufactured craft packs from Baker Ross and I introduced play the way I knew how: by building dens with hospital bedsheets, junk modelling with medical supplies and playing with Doctor's torches in semi-darkened rooms to create shadow puppets. I was slowly reuniting with my Brummie playworker mojo and I thought maybe there was hope after all. When I created enriching, uplifting, a little less ordinary experiences for children wired-up in bed I was taken to one side by my line manager.

She was smiley and enthusiastic and I thought she was going to commend my creativity and encourage more. The entrepreneur in me has a tendency to run away, quickly scheming new ideas and projects. In split seconds I saw waiting-room colouring sheets replaced with large pieces of foam;

huge, lightweight, infection-control-compliant building blocks for big open-ended child-led play for families awaiting the unknown.

I thought about bringing long pieces of gutters to bed-bound patients for exploring moving objects or even water. Ideas were flashing in front of me and I smiled. And then a pinprick burst my bubble as I was politely told that I could not initiate that kind of play here. Each patient's isolation room was a goldfish bowl with a large window into the central corridor. It was perceived as unhelpful for the medical team and raised concerns around safeguarding to have patients hiding in dens and dimly lit rooms.

The patients were CHILDREN.

I wish now that I had been more gutsy and had the vision that I do now: that we should all prioritise play. All children, no matter what shit life throws at them, have the right to play; real meaningful play. Just as other healthcare professionals had advocated for protected meal times so patients could eat their meals in peace, I wish I had advocated for protected play time for children to play in peace. After all, Article 31 of the United Nations Convention on the Rights of a Child specifies that all children should engage in play. I just found it a travesty that in a world-leading centre of excellence, a place of groundbreaking research on children's health, colouring sheets were accepted as meaningful play.

Play is a universal phenomenon. Our experiences of play are unique: what is meaningful play to one human could possibly be meaningless to another. It is really quite tricky to find one phrase that defines what play is. Sometimes I describe play as what children do when adults don't interrupt, and equally what adults do when capitalism doesn't interrupt! I see signs of play unfolding here, there and everywhere. Play is inherent to humans and our ways of play evolve through the exploration of our own unique environments.

Most adults associate play with their childhood. Those of us fortunate to avoid the ills of play deprivation will fondly remember numerous ways we played; we look back on our childhoods as a time of freedom. Adults don't have those same freedoms.

In my playwork training in 2009 I was introduced to the Playwork Principles.[1] The non-conformist part of me winces at information that suggests we should do as we are told so I had mixed feelings about them then when I began my career and I still do now. But if these Principles give playworkers a bit of kudos and help outsiders make sense of the most wonderful part of human nature then I am all for a bit of organising.

One of the eight Principles uses the description 'Play is a set of behaviours that are freely chosen, personally directed, and intrinsically motivated.' So, with my playworker hat on (and apparently I never seem to take it off…!), any time a human is free to trust themselves and do as they please with no outside pressures influencing their actions, they are indeed engaging in play.

1 Playwork Principles Scrutiny Group (2004) Playwork Principles. Cardiff: Play Wales. www.playwales.org.uk.

We play here

When I was twenty-two, living back in my childhood home in Birmingham, childless, single, raving to drum n bass in Digbeth at weekends, lapping up Monday night reggae at JamJah in Moseley, nodding along with the hip hop hedz wherever the Heducation DJs did a set and working as a play-worker most of my working week, I was happy. Like really happy: good company, optimistic and energetic. I was physically exhausted at the end of some days, but these were my favourite days. Not because I have the work ethic of a red ant, but because the physical days were mostly spent outdoors and that kind of work gives a really satisfying fatigue.

Those outdoor days were when the biggest resources built a bright skyline of colours and textures and movement on weekend and summer-holiday afternoons. Sometimes we took over large public concrete spaces, other times we relished in secret sanctuaries of green, hidden away from the city's hustle and bustle and the deprivation of inner-city Brum, and sometimes we played in Kings Heath Park, one of my childhood stomping grounds.

Somewhere between the tea rooms and the playground I had once learned to balance and glide on a red-and-white BMX. It was the park where I had been punched by a school bully and the space where I sat with a few girlfriends after our last GCSE exam. That afternoon when I was sixteen we sprawled in utter anticlimax because not all our friends had finished their exams yet. The four of us picked at daisies and pondered our futures with the Foo Fighters playing quietly on an older sister's Minidisk player and 'compact' speakers.

A few years later, on the same grassy expanse, small balls of cotton wool formed sumptuous beds for tiny dreaming fairies and beards for kids wanting to impersonate their grandad. Disco balls prompted giggling mums to point their right fingers up out towards the sky and back down across their bodies to the floor, while curious toddlers chased the accidental projections of rainbows that flickered on the bushes near the Saturday Night Fever dancelawn.

My playworker colleagues and I pegged huge tarpaulins to a slope on the lawn and soaked the surface with a hose pipe to make an enormous waterslide. On top we threw huge sponges, bubble bath and large inflatables.

Our Playteams were dedicated to advocating for the importance of play, pushing the boundaries and stretching possibilities all the way to Timbuktu. We dedicated our thoughts, our creativity and our innovation into planning opportunities for play but we could never ever plan the play that would unfold. That's the best bit about the job: children at play never failed to amaze me with their creativity and innovation.

With canes, fabric, pegs, tape and string children built and rebuilt their dream dwellings, office blocks and holiday homes. Between trees and on hedges there were large bedsheets; each a blank canvas for collaborative murals and much-needed shelter from firing water pistols and more wet sponges. Den building shaped the landscape marking our territory with the message: we play here.

When I was sixteen I never foresaw that I'd be working with children in that park. *We play here* was certainly not on my radar. I was confident, bright and ready to travel the world. I had my eye on a career in travel journalism. I wasn't interested in England, let alone little Kings Heath in old, familiar Brum. My heart was bursting with curiosity and escapism. I pursued my wanderlust through language classes and borrowed world cinema videos from the library; anything to prepare me until I was off around the globe and away from our village within our city.

Sirens and soil

As a child in our garden I spent hours out of sight of my parents. I would hazard a guess that most adults' fondest, most vivid childhood memories involve some sort of outdoor play or time spent outdoors. And those memories don't include adults watching over. My parents were kind of playworkers because they kept out of the way as much as possible. Playworkers create engaging and safe spaces where children can play freely; my childhood home was a free play environment. I don't remember my folks dictating what I did or how I spent my free time.

Big British cities in the 1990s weren't the obvious places to let children roam free until tea time. I was so lucky to grow up with a biggish, wild garden even if police sirens and accelerating motor vehicles drowned out the bird song. Playing outdoors offers an additional element of spontaneity. Neither parents nor playworkers can plan for the surprises that a natural environment provides; and that is why I encourage as much outdoor play as possible. Particularly in the rain.

My career in playwork all stemmed from an unglamourous cluttered broom-cupboard-sized office in a community centre on my local high street. Dens of Equality is an inclusion development agency which set out to put inclusive play on everyone's doorstep. When I was twenty-two I became the protégé of two radical women who were, and still are, committed to growing communities around forgotten children and bringing desolate, sorry-looking corners of Birmingham to life through child-led play. Under Liz and Laura's mentorship I felt a huge sense of purpose and quickly fell in love with my job.

Early on in the broom cupboard I often heard them say 'children don't dissolve in the rain' when someone was questioning the suitability of doing an outdoor play session on a forecast rainy day. It made me chuckle; I wish more parents would embrace playing in the rain.

As a child, come rain or shine, I loved disappearing down to the overgrown end of our garden: completely hidden from view. A modest apple tree grew next to our large shed. There was a space about 1.5 metres wide between our shed and the neighbours' fence, where a large fir tree grew into our garden. It was the perfect space for a den.

I remember days and days of moving buckets of rainwater, digging in the earth and inhaling the scent of decomposing fir needles which were bouncy beneath my feet while police cars and fire engines raced past, sirens on at full pelt, in the too-near distance, just beyond our row of houses. There was a large scaffolding plank that my older brother had placed high above, across two branches of the apple tree. He and his friends could climb up to the platform using the fence to give themselves a leg up. I couldn't do it.

I was not really confident in my physicality or I was too cautious of what could be if I fell. I loved being outdoors but rarely had the inclination to climb trees, take the fast zip wire or let my bike roll uncontrollably down any of the hills in our local park. I can remember vividly watching my friends, wide-eyed and wild, brave and unbreakable. I was convinced I was going to crack a bone; I am still not sure where that fear came from. My ideas were brave and bold, but my physicality and my Locomotor Play were not in correlation. I was wary; unless water was involved.

Put me in the water and I was unstoppable. I first swam independently in the warm waters of Greece when I was three and a half and that was that. I remember swimming across Coniston in the Lake District when I was eight years old. In Year Eight, on a geography field trip, just a short walk from our school, I was one of only two students that frolicked in the brook, along with a discarded shopping trolley and rusting cider cans. My feet squelched in my wellies on the walk across Billesley Common back to the classroom. I'd had a great afternoon: I'd connected with nature, learned about a local ecosystem, I'd even had fun! But my teacher told me he was 'disappointed' with my behaviour: how dare a twelve-year-old exude enthusiasm for learning by doing.

I've always loved swimming outdoors. I asked my mom how I actually started swimming and she casually retold, 'Oh you were just floating around, playing in the really shallow bit near the shore and then we noticed you were actually

11

swimming, "Oh look she's swimming!" What the actual fuck? So my parents weren't even in reach of me; they just left me to my own survival. I sure hope my older siblings were nearby.

My mom defends herself with her argument that third-borns are the most independent. I also think that parents are way more relaxed, or maybe just too damn tired, by the time the third-born comes around.

One of their favourite stories to tell is when I was in a supermarket with my mom when I was three years old.

'Are you helping mummy?' the check-out lady chimed at me.

'No, I am helping myself,' I asserted back at her.

A passport to play

I was born in Kings Heath, a sprawling neighbourhood in south Birmingham. We boast the longest high street in Europe, pre-Brexit we were the most culturally diverse constituency in European Parliament and the largest public secondary school for girls in Europe (a total of 1600 young women when I was there). All these facts are probably true, but no one really knows where they have surfaced from. Other notable occurrences in Kings Heath include a tornado that swept off the roof of Greggs and neighbouring shops in July 2005. What a catastrophe!

I was in Canada at the time, but when I got home and went up the High Street for the first time, I cried. Like actually really shed tears and wept to my Ma. Not because I was

12

grieving the absent roof tiles on Specsavers, but because Kings Heath High Street is grim. 'It's so ugly,' I sobbed.

I had spent five weeks being stunned by Le Plateau-Mont-Royal in Montreal, Canada. Five weeks is a long time away from home when you are a teenager and I left hungry for more. Le Plateau is a vibrant, multicoloured, lush neighbourhood with generously spaced residential and shopping avenues adorned with street art and higgledy-piggledy fairytale buildings. Stoops, staircases and balconies are trimmed with un-uniform, palatial, wrought iron. There was colour and life and diversity everywhere I looked. It was arty farty with an urban edge and I was hooked.

The streets of Kings Heath, on the other hand, were mostly tightly packed with Victorian terraced houses and cars parked hanging over most of the pavements, and often (illegally) stationed bumper to bumper blocking the corners and making crossing roads for unaccompanied children most parents' nightmare. Back home I never saw residents aimlessly wandering taking in the street art, nor congregating on pedestrianised streets munching on street food unless the pubs had just closed and everyone was heading to King Kebab or rival chip shop Hi Tide located opposite. Cosmopolitan cafes didn't spill out onto pavements for lazy afternoons of people watching and bicycles weren't locked to every spare fence or lamppost. I'd say nearly everyone in our neighbourhood had a garden but in B14 there weren't many tree-lined streets, cycle lanes or guerilla gardening projects on no-man's-land street corners like I spotted in Le Plateau.

Our High Street was painfully polluted with flattened polystyrene Fillet-o-Fish boxes from the McDonalds and nitrogen dioxide from the traffic crawling north to Town and south to the Maypole. But we had independent shops! A whole retail unit full of small businesses selling stuff that no one misses buying nowadays. Our beloved Supashopper was an uncharismatic indoor market that smelt of fry and dog biscuits from the greasy spoon and the pet shop tucked away at the very back. It sat opposite the supermarket formerly known as Safeways, just a stone's throw from my primary school.

Every Saturday the High Street was guaranteed to be heaving. There was no space to stop and talk comfortably without feeling like half of the population of south Birmingham was shuffling past like lemmings, their shopping bags knockin' at ya legs. On any trip to the High Street I was, still am, guaranteed to see a familiar face but it just wasn't, still isn't, the place to stop and exchange anything more than a very quick pleasantry. Conversations were always in competition with someone shoutin' a greeting to Mo across the road or bibbin' their horn in return for an exaggerated wave. It never felt like there was much real human interaction.

On my summer trips to Montreal I absorbed how they used their streets for places to be. One warm afternoon, two guys carried their sofa out onto the pedestrianised stretch of Rue Prince Arthur, between St Laurent and St Denis. Just along from the small round fountain, amongst murals and raised beds of colourful petals and cascading foliage, they sat down on their couch. One sipped a cheeky beer, the other glugged from a huge carton of milk, presumably purchased from the dépanneur behind them. Much to the enjoyment of the passers-by and the cafe-goers sitting out on the terrasse opposite, these two blokes theatrically demonstrated how happy life was on their three-seater.

One would have been forgiven for assuming it was a piece of street theatre or an art installation from one of Montreal's many street festivals. But in between them was a flattened cardboard box with 'SOFA $50 TRES COMFY' scrawled in large block letters with a black marker pen. The opportunistic duo had rustled up their own pop-up jumble sale. When we strolled by an hour or so later, tummies full of all-day brunch, they were gone. I spotted their homemade sign: it was poking out of the neat stack of flattened cardboard boxes in front of the convenience store. What a playful way to sell a sofa.

On my return to Kings Heath I eventually recovered from my melodramatic teenage status. My tears did dry despite the grey concrete, the back-to-back traffic pumping out gut-wrenching smog and the constant stench of grease wafting from McDonald's through the atmosphere towards Iceland. Home sweet home. On subsequent visits to the High Street in August of 2005 I was cheered up by the eye-witness accounts of the tornado from the lady in the Discount Greetings Store next door to Greggs, and the local librarian. A Brummie retelling, or more so singing, a story always brightens my day.

That sobbing sixteen-year-old had forgotten that Birmingham is abundant with beauty and has its fair share of fascinating higgledy-piggledy people. Throughout my childhood I had encountered plenty of characters at community arts events all over the city, mostly through my dad's work in Social Inclusion for community mental-health teams.

These events were full of wonderful, colourful people sharing their culture, their art, their struggling mental health. I learned that deep down it is people that make a place interesting and beautiful; the buildings are merely an aesthetic there to distract humans from connecting with each other. And when we allow ourselves to create places to share stories, that's when the magic erupts and we really start living.

That brief experience of globetrotting around Montreal's melting-pot villages gave me a lust to wander. So, in five years after my sobbing return from Le Plateau-Mont-Royal, through college and university, I waitressed my way around the world. Prague, Warsaw, Reykjavik, São Paulo, Barcelona, Paris, Berlin, Marrakesh, Accra, Ouagadougou, Timbuktu, Dakar, Montreal again and again, New York, Salvador da Bahia, Bogota and many wonderful smaller places in between.

When I came back to Brum at the ripe old age of twenty-two, complete with a gold glowing suntan from Ipanema beach and a new tattoo poking out of my Havaianas, I thought I was noble and worldly. But little did I know that accidentally stumbling into playwork was going to be the best voyage I was ever going to embark on. For most of my youth I had been very serious about globetrotting and internationalism. But as the months in my new job unfolded I felt a very seismic shift. Gone were the daydreams of writing for Guardian Travel and Lonely Planet. I quickly became very serious about playwork.

Safety, love

My childhood best friend was an only child raised by her mom whose family were all back home under rural Scandinavian skies where the northern lights occasionally made an appearance. Their house was a sanctuary of Scandy quiet and order. There was warming pine everywhere. It was a very cosy place. The word 'Hygge' wasn't fashionable back then. But their home was a place of orderly calm with an underlying dedication to nature. I felt all Hyggly there.

Our home, on the other hand, wasn't orderly and even though there was a relaxed ambiance the comings and goings of the six of us and our visitors meant their quiet home felt very different from ours. Unlike my home, everything had its place, it was always tidy and her mom fussed over us in a way my parents didn't. At their house our play was more orderly: board games, baking, craft, outings to the park or the countryside. I loved both homes. Even though their home and their style were a world away from mine, I still felt safe and loved. And that is ultimately what every child needs: to feel safe and to feel loved. If those two feelings are consistently met then, no matter the ambiance of the home, a child's intrinsic motivation to play kicks in and the play comes naturally.

I was given a lot of time to play. A big comfort I found in my own childhood was not feeling that I had to commit to anything extra-curricular. There was encouragement but no pressure. Wait. That is not entirely true; I had guitar and later piano lessons that didn't really inspire me. I wanted to be good at an instrument, but I didn't want to be a

17

beginner. My teachers were uninventive with their repertoire and unplayful in the way they taught music.

I loved music but I didn't like what I could hear when I played. In a city where kids see samba bands collaborating with dhol drummers, steel pans busking calypso renditions of Christmas carols and Irish folk singers belting out sea shanties on concrete shopping streets, music lessons really need to be brought alive. I wanted to sound good, really good, but I didn't want to practise. I did, however, invent my own ways to embrace music through play.

In the solitary comfort of my bedroom I used to play 'being in The Beatles'. I lugged my parents' clunky stand-alone record player with a built-in speaker upstairs to my room. From the front room I carefully selected *Sgt. Pepper's Lonely Hearts Club Band* from their shelf of vinyl above our humble 14-inch television. It is strange to think that our televisions used to be the same size as our records; screens have grown bigger and our music has shrunk so much so that our music collections are now invisible, no longer displayed, taking pride of place in our living rooms.

I gathered the headphones from my Walkman and plugged them into mid-air. I set up my folding music stand from my guitar lessons and propped up the red vinyl sleeve so the black song words were at eye height. I wasn't so fussed about performing or making music videos, I just loved singing in my recording studio and signing autographs in pocket-sized notebooks. When I clocked on to the fact that none of my contemporaries admitted they listen to The Beatles, my game progressed to being Elton John and Tim Rice, the composers of The Lion King soundtrack. It was the first real cassette I was given. It was real because it had not been copied on a double-tape deck; this was the real McCoy and again significantly had the lyrics printed in nearly illegible tiny type on the sky-blue background of the accompanying sleeve.

One weekend afternoon, at the hour when children's programmes were not aired on channels 1 to 4, I found an orchestra playing on the television. I twiddled with the contrast and brightness knobs until the screen had blacked out but the orchestra continued to play. I grabbed a stick, not sure if it was of the garden or the chop variety, and mimicked the conductor. I closed my eyes and replayed the scene I had just blacked out on the telly. I was controlling the string section, the grand piano was the most sparkling the world had ever seen and there were smartly dressed men and women lined up in our front room blowing into clarinets, flutes and oboes. I was in control of them all!

Before long, my older brother charged into the front room where I was blasting Beethoven and teased me. But I really didn't care because I was making music.

Education, education, education

My music lessons were a good example of creativity made dull. The control of creativity can turn children off creativity altogether; in fact, I would go as far as to say that the adult-led agenda of learning can turn children off learning altogether! A lot of the curriculum did not interest me; a lot of our lessons did not feel relevant or only skimmed at the surface where I wanted to dive in deep. I know I am one of the lucky ones that didn't get overwhelmed by the ridiculous pressure of learning outcomes and league tables put on our young. I was academically able and I breezed through without much stress.

On my final day of secondary school our headteacher came over to me to tell me that on my first day in Year Seven I had told her forthrightly that I had found the day 'quite boring'. I think that set the tone for the following five years. Even as a teenager I gathered that there was little room for curiosity, reflection and exploration in the National Curriculum so I accepted that my life beyond the classroom would be where I did my real learning.

Like most teenage girls I had a hearty appetite for conversation. Real conversation. I was drawn to other strong-willed, ambitious and unconventional thinkers who were unafraid to question the norm. At lunchtime and in shared feasts in Food Technology lessons we gave each other the confidence to ask questions. We were misfits but we misfitted together so we didn't mind.

I was coming of age in a multicultural city in a weird bubble where race did not matter to me and my friends, but we knew full well it mattered beyond our friendships. Amongst my friends race and social status were evident but did not divide us; we just sought solidarity in freedom of thought and mutual respect. Swanshurst School afforded me an Outstanding education thanks to the lessons taught by my peers.

Sara (pronounced Sarah, the English way, not Sara, the European or Middle-Eastern way) was Black British whose grandparents were from the tiny Caribbean island of Saint

Kitts while Rachelle's family was from Jamaica and lived up to that Caribbean stereotype of being louder, prouder and sassier than the other island folk.

Rachelle's dad lived on BMT, Black Man Time, so much so they arrived a whole day late to the airport on her first trip to Jamaica when we were fifteen. Even though they, eventually, had a great time, when she came back after the Easter holidays and retold the story we giggled the way school girls do like heckling hyenas. She was vex.

Nikki's parents were English Brummies born and bred, Florence's were Yorkshire folk, Mervette's parents were from Egypt, Nafeesa's parents were Pakistani and Vanessa Sowinski was mixed race and inherited her surname from her Polish-settled-in-Oxford grandfather. He came across as a quintessential English grandfather, with a well-to-do suburban home that reminded me of my maternal grandma's house on a cul-de-sac in Surrey. I remember thinking he was lean, loving and bright-eyed like the grandpa from the Worther's Originals advert 'You know, I can still remember the very first sweets given to me by my grandfather...'. I don't remember him having a Polish accent but the glass bowl of exquisitely wrapped sweets on the sideboard was a disgustingly bitter reminder of his heritage. Van and I both gobbled one each only to simultaneously spit them out again; they were filled with vodka. 'Na zdrowie.' Cheers, Grandpa.

And then there was me; a white British Brummie, with strong affiliations to my international lineage who playfully picked up foreign languages at any given opportunity. Once,

21

when we went to the Bullring market, my mom was gently teased for being 'posh' because she speaks the gentle tongue of Surrey folk. And my dad has a fairly neutral born-in-the-south accent. My parents and grandparents spoke European languages and between my second cousins (lovingly promoted to 'cousins' because we have no first-in-line) and their parents they spoke French, Spanish, Wolof, German, Arabic, Italian. Our family home was, still is, a living museum of trinkets collected from our travels and sent from relatives overseas. We had lodgers from Germany, France, Brazil and Cameroon-via-Paris live with us when I was young. I have never felt English English.

Our almost all white, mostly female troop of teachers did not inspire me the way my peers did. We could see the flaws in the education system back then. The organic curriculum that grew from the youthful melange of our lived experiences offered some balance to the learning objectives we were being fed at the turn of the millennium. My secondary education taught me an important lesson that I carried with me as a playworker and youthworker: when children and young people are empowered to explore without interruption from adults, the most distinguished agendas are brought to the table.

When I was fourteen I was left perplexed by a school trip to a BBC youth conference about multiculturalism in the media held in the then brand new and swanky Millennium Point. Suited and booted BBC officials reported that only 7% of the British population was from an ethnic minority and representation of ethnic minorities on terrestrial television was 2–3%. On the walk across the large square to our coach home, I reported to my teacher that 'they must have got it wrong Miss! Only 7%? But it is so mixed here.' And she explained to me that apart from the pockets of diversity in big cities, everywhere else was very white. 'Think about the countryside, Adele, you don't see any,' she hesitated, slightly jerking her chin as she searched for the most politically correct terminology, then tried not to wince as she continued with 'people with darker skin there.'

'Miss, you can say Black. Or Asian,' I taught her.

It is no real surprise to me that our secondary school friendship group quickly dispersed after our GCSEs; young fierce independent thinkers raised in a system that didn't really push us to our full potential had grown a hunger for moving fast. Wooosh! Off we went.

I like the way you move

I remain forever thankful for that circle of critical thinkers; we learned a lot together. We were ambitious young Brummies who knew there was life beyond Key Stage 4 and we were hungry for a slice of the real world. Our all girls' secondary school was a feeding ground for bitchy behaviour. I fell out with a lot of girls in my year; I'm not even sure why. I was comfortable as me, I liked the person I was so I didn't parrot the popular girls just for the sake of being liked. I guess they found my quietly assertive yet nonchalant attitude threatening so they blocked me out. I found their hostility pathetic so I blocked them out. Despite these differences I held on to the confidence I had built as a child. Free play builds resilient people – more on that later. So, I was a resilient, confident teen. Until it came to dancing.

I was surrounded by a lot of girls who took dancing very seriously. There were also a lot of girls whose cultures took dancing very seriously. I am reluctant to put Morris Dancing in the same category as the movement I saw from my classmates. Despite the odd bandstand waltz with my grandparents on visits to see them in Southend-on-Sea, as a teenager I felt ill-prepared for the lunchtime discos in Upper School Hall.

Yep, lunchtime discos were a thing. A real thing.

What a funny old place. Once a term, in the name of social action and raising (piddling amounts of) money, each form in Upper School was equipped with hi-fi, a microphone and a venue. Lunchtime discos were not perceived as an opportunity for freedom of expression, disguising Physical Education or uniting young women from contrasting cultures in meaningful connection; no, none of that. In the name of social action we paid 25p to attend a disco, at lunchtime, for twenty-five minutes. I couldn't make this shit up if I tried.

Usually on Fridays we were allowed, with the presence of one or two unlucky members of staff, to occupy the hall where we usually ate our packed lunches if it was deemed too wet or too cold to eat outdoors.

'You goin' disco?' we enquired. It was sort of a trick question; no one really wanted to admit they were going. It always took a ring leader, usually with personal affiliations to the MC, to show enthusiasm or downright disgust for the event.

The average attendance was around forty girls which from a population of 1600 pupils was pretty abysmal.

The main lights were turned off, the large curtains drawn and occasionally someone brought in a plug-in disco-ball lamp from home that was too small, and the wire too short to make any sort of ambiance. The whole setup was rather pitiful. Depending on our mood, teenage girls of all shapes and sizes either moved at full pelt or sat on the side awkwardly eating a baguette from the takeaway counter in the canteen.

Inevitably there were always a few girls who stood out from the pathetic excuse for a crowd. The Mistress of Ceremonies was always the mouthiest girl from each form. She bossed about whoever she had declared was her best mate that lunchtime (best friends are interchangeable by the hour in a girls' school) to play the CDs she had stolen from her older brother's bedroom. Predictably Bashment or Bhangra were played at full blast depending if the leader of the pack was Black or Asian. White girls were not leaders of the pack when it came to discos; it was presumed that we liked pop and there was no way the MC was gonna play shitty chart music.

But after a few songs the power shifted from the self-appointed MC and her bitches who were wo-manning the 'decks' as the real Queen B rose from the tantalising shadows, fully charged with her illicit groove. Let me make this clear: she was not a pop star. There was always a Dancing Queen; she could learn any routine from her Dance Academy and shamelessly repeat it to any song until the cows came home.

But her popular routines had nothing on Queen B and every-one knew it.

There was no telling from which section of society the Queen B would rise except that she was never the Dancing Queen. At each disco the excitement of un-uniform movement and loud music in the school hall was elevated in anticipation of Queen B's arrival. Would she rise from the meek Asian girls who loved Bollywood movies but didn't dare reenact their flirtatious love stories in all their glory? Or the more radical Muslims who removed their headscarves to allow unrestricted movement as soon as the house lights turned off? Could it be the Skater girls who mimicked the Goth girls as they parodied the Black girls (accompanied by their non-Black following) all stern-faced as they did the Bogle or the Dutty Wine? Nobody knew.

Not even the Queen B came prepared for her uprising. She was as dubious as the next one paying their 25p at the door. But something about *that* song, something she had not heard before, took over her body in a journey of self-discovery and cultural enlightenment. The blaring unknown anthem caused minuscule vibrations to force through her body. The result was an unforeseen flow of gesticulations; a shimmy here, a sway there, a subtle thrust as her hips hooked from side to side, around and back again.

Her mind was pleasantly lost, separated from her body as it made unimaginable shapes in her jubilant state as she rose to become the next Queen B. There must have been other wonderful things going on in the background of that young woman's life lifting her insecurities and allowing her body to move without constraint. Maybe it was her genuine friendships: a sisterhood protecting her from a bully. Or the moment of eye contact with a boy at back gates earlier in the week. Maybe her homework was completed. Or could it be that her disabled sibling would be away at respite for the weekend. Or that her mom's abusive boyfriend had finally left the scene. Perhaps she finally got her first B in History and a merit for her effort. No one knew what released Queen B, but everyone cheered with their bodies as she basked in her state of euphoria.

If we'd had a lighting rig the spotlight would have found her in the crowd, the flashing lights slowing until all rays were on her. If we were outdoors the dust beneath her soles would have awakened the connection to her ancestors; they would have been proudly cheering her on. If we'd had live music the lead singer would have lost her trail of song, stopped in her tracks and bowed to hail her.

All hail Queen B.

All hail Queen B.

All hail Queen B.

After twenty-three minutes the teacher instructed no one in particular to switch off the hi-fi; it was time for afternoon registration. As the lights flickered on, Queen B vanished and left behind a sweaty young woman. Right on cue, the bell rang for afternoon registration as clouds of smoky Impulse body spray and Sure deodorant attempted to mask our post-disco pubescent body odour. Travel hair brushes and pocket mirrors appeared in front of the more vain amongst us, bottle-green jumpers were put back on (we were thankfully spared of blazers), and the last of Calypso apple juice were scooped up from the edge of the stage and slurped and shared amongst thirsty friends. Like lemmings we flowed through narrow corridors and upstairs to classrooms as if the previous twenty something minutes had not happened. Queen B was obsolete.

In afternoon registration the appointed Disco Committee Chairwoman would count up the coins collected at the door and the Treasurer would take the grand total to the Main Office where a cheque would be written to the RSPCA, Children in Need or any other predictable national charity the form had voted to support. The following Monday an announcement would be made in assembly in recognition of the £13.82 raised from Friday's fundraiser. We obediently applauded their efforts. No one ever mentioned Queen B; her three and a half minutes of glory had passed.

Needless to say, back then I was never Queen B, nor the Dancing Queen, but I've grown to connect with my body. I have always liked exercise. When I was a teenager I didn't worry about the shape and size of my body. I loved wearing belly tops and low-rise baggy jeans. I was not skinny but I was happy in my own flesh, even with the extra bits of puppy fat that generously lurked, I did not ever consider myself fat. I had a very round face and chose terrible glasses. Teenagers have way better specs to choose from these days.

Photos were of the click-and-wait-a-week variety so I actually had very little awareness of what I looked like a lot of the time. One of the most positive factors of growing up in diversity is that very few of my friends looked anything like me so there was very little inclination to even try and look like them. My skin tone, my hair, my abysmal choice of glasses were my own. I didn't spend much energy wanting to drastically change any of it.

But there was one thing I wanted to change about my body: my ability to move it. As a teen I liked exercise. I loved swimming. Being in the water made me feel fit, powerful and strong; it still does. But back in secondary school I did not love PE, neither did I loathe it. Physical Education and Dance were disappointing hours of my timetable each week in that I always wanted to be better: I wanted the lessons to be more dynamic and the teachers to be more passionate.

At a time when we needed to make most sense of our awkward bodies we were pigeonholed into dancing in unison whether we could pick up a routine or not. I've never been one for following suit so sports and dance lessons where we focussed on technique of games such as hockey and badminton rather than free movement felt boring and frustrating. And what is it about forcing young women, with no consideration of the stage of their monthly cycle, into uninspiring sport? I think it should be considered a form of neglect.

I think times have changed. I sincerely hope times have changed. PE in school was elitist in favour of those who had the best trainers (footwear was at the centre of identity for us uniformed femmes) and ironically did very little for the wellbeing of the young women it was trying to serve. There is no joy in exercise when body shaming amongst peers and obligatory communal showers were part of the deal.

Why not start the term with a series of body positive talks with relevant keynote speakers to exemplify the importance of self-respect? Why not start the term with an understanding of different hormones that positively affect physical performance? And explore what else could be happening when we do not feel up to it? Why not let young people choose their preferred course of exercise from three options each term? Motivation and enthusiasm rather than dread would fuel the changing room.

It goes without saying that the playworker in me would like a large loose-parts adventure playground attached to each secondary school because play can be extremely physical. Through age-appropriate play I've seen teenagers find confidence in their bodies and feel empowered to explore their physicality without the toxicity of body image haunting them. Lugging large 4x4 tyres, jumping from height onto crash mats, water fights, racing alongside a friend on homemade go-karts: all evoke exhilaration, relieve stress and burn a few calories. I remember quoting that 'children get 90% of their exercise through play'. Teenagers are indeed still children statistically speaking, but society frowns upon them frequenting playgrounds where younger tots roam. So if there is no adventure playground or youth club with outdoor space in the community where are teenagers meant to play? Jumping and swinging and racing becomes antisocial behaviour if teens are playing in the 'wrong' place.

I think we are a long way off getting adventure playgrounds on secondary school sites but given any opportunity to involve a teenager in empowering playful activity I'll try to lure them in. Teenagers are in a weird limbo: many are deemed to grow up too fast. But then I wonder where they are invited to be kids again?

I sincerely believe that, as play is normalised and encouraged in neighbourhoods either through street play, play rangers regularly visiting parks, play buses doing the rounds or with adventure playgrounds staffed by playworkers, we will raise healthier children. They will become healthier teens and, as history repeats itself, they will evolve into the next generation of playful parents. But I do think we do need to nurture our teens as much as we nurture our pre-teens.

Incredible

Uninspired by the lunchtime discos, throughout my early adolescence I was a dancefloor recluse. At their family parties I watched my Black and Asian friends and their relatives naturally move their hips and swing their arms in effortless flow. In the comfort of my bedroom I tried to embody their freedom but I felt trapped and static.

It wasn't until I was fifteen and got drunk in rock clubs (which probably should have been closed down for permitting so many children through their doors) that I allowed myself to explore movement. I somehow encountered a space of safety on darkened, smoky dancefloors, fuelled by Lambrini we drank on the bus ride into town, on a children's bus fare of course.

Back then I didn't feel very connected to my body. I know I was not alone. I felt embarrassed about my sexual urges, cursed my period each month and didn't really understand the importance of a good diet. Don't get me wrong – I knew the vegetable element of a Greggs Vegetable Bake did not constitute one of my five-a-day but beyond that I didn't really take much notice of what I was putting in my body, or on my skin.

A blessing of maturing out of my teens was the permission I gave myself to move my body. Luckily by the time I was seventeen I had graduated from sticky-floor rock clubs to hip hop nights where dance battles between crews made up of b-boys and b-girls occupied the dance floor. Heducation at the Medicine Bar was my Thursday night study group. In the stylish lakeside setting of the Custard Factory, then Birmingham's leading arts venue, I experienced not one but two musical epiphanies.

Of course, I'd heard plenty of hip hop music before; one of my most treasured birthday gifts in primary school was a recorded cassette of The Score. My classmate Kez, who is still one of my most esteemed friends, lovingly handwrote, and smudged because she is left handed, the tracklist on the cardboard sleeve in a luxurious and almost illegible gold gel pen.

I have since been to a lot of hip hop nights all over the world, but Heducation has always stood out. Maybe I'm just pledging my allegiance to my Brummies, but there was something about the setting; it was so relaxed, friendly and respectful. Intelligent hip hop flowed with a soulful vibe. People congregated, not always to party, but more just to be. Conscious MCs and occasionally live bands took to a small humble stage dedicated to good vibes, freedom of speech and authenticity. Discovering the teachings of hip hop was a gentle epiphany that grew in me over months and years.

I learned that hip hop culture combines visual, auditory and physical communication: it wasn't just about the music. Stories are told through the 5 pillars of hip hop: rapping, DJing, graffiti, breakin' and knowledge. It was impossible for me to ignore the raw expression, sophisticated wordsmithery and explicit respect for one another despite social inequalities. The demand for dignity and respectful treatment of the marginalised rang loud within me. I knew I wasn't marginalised, far from it, but I felt it in my gut that every human deserves respect.

Those nights were such a valuable step in my musical education and my own philosophies; they shaped the way I wanted to socialise. I later realised it was a privilege of coming of age in a diverse city that made that sort of venue so accessible. At such an impressionable age I had matured out of my parents' eclectic but somewhat dated musical encyclopedia and was forming my own library of non-mainstream music. I knew I would never go back to pop-rock clubs.

One night, early on in my patronage at the Medicine Bar, I had the second epiphany. Unlike the first, this one was not gradual. It was a smack in the face, but I didn't get hurt. The last DJ of the night came on and everything changed. He dropped his needle on a record and a husky male voice spat 'Wicked. Wicked. Jungle is massive' with a distinctive high-pitched squeak racing around him.

The energy shifted in an instant. Bodies began to move with a different kinda upbeat flow. There were multiple cheers

33

and hands threw up in the air shouting 'Boyaka Boyaka' over the track. I had no idea what was happening around me but I could sense it was going to be good. Until then the crowd had mostly shown their appreciation through respectful nods and gentle bouncing to the mellow hip hop vibes. But this track took it up a few notches; smiles were shot across the room to no one in particular. They knew what was coming. I had no clue.

Hypnotising syncopated drum loops dropped and suddenly the dudes that had been nonchalantly nodding their heads to velvet-smooth hip hop melodies exploded into part jump, part jog, part seizure while their curved shoulders bounced from side to side or arms pumped at full pelt. I didn't know what it was but I fucking loved it.

There were no rules, no routines, it was a free-flowing expression with a baseline that vibrated deep to my core. Just as I'd taken in the view and joined the madness and movement the DJ stopped the track. Playful DJs don't just play a track from start to finish. They rewind – oh how I have grown to love a rewind! Rewind is an intrinsically motivated technique used by DJs to playfully gather momentum and build a rapport with the folk on the dancefloor. An older Rasta at the bar in Moseley once generously enlightened me that it stemmed from Jamaican soundsystem 'selectors' in the 1960s and still dominates DJ mixes.

Just as everyone got into the groove the DJ took a risk and pulled a rewind. Voices cheered from all corners of the dancefloor and some bellowed 'Puuuuuuulllllll Itttttttttt'.

The record started again from the beginning but this time with a crowd of fully pumped and rhythmically palpitating torsos ready to skank again. And more came flocking in from the bar next door.

I discovered drum n bass when I was seventeen. Technically I wasn't old enough to be out clubbing so technically I also wasn't old enough to know it was really called 'jungle'. But I was old enough to see that it was one of the most wonderful ways to see grown men and women embody real playfulness on a dancefloor.

A friend said to me recently as we raved in her living room on a Friday night, 'I've never known how to dance to drum n bass.'

'Just close ya eyes n move bab. Stop thinkin' about it!' I shouted back at her over the music. Us adults, we even overthink how we dance in our own bloody living rooms. We are looking for rules and direction at every step of our day. Not with jungle! For me it is the most playful way to sway.

When I was younger, my raver friends and I often used to describe some of the dingier drum n bass clubs in Brum as 'moody'. I wasn't put off; I just went to dance. Nowadays when I look beyond the often drug-fuelled screwface ravers I now just see the definition of play: 'a set of behaviours that is freely chosen, personally directed and intrinsically motivated'. When children move for movement's sake with no set of instructions to follow, and no pressure to move in unison, we call it Locomotor Play. And that is exactly what I saw on those dancefloors too. A dancefloor of Oldskool Junglist

35

ravers is just a group of big kids indulging in some intrinsically motivated Locomotor Play. Beautiful.

Rich kids' playground

Six months after graduating from a redbrick university I was employed as a development worker in Birmingham to write bids and work with small parent groups to become constituted committees and apply for charitable status. Even though the application forms were tedious, I loved writing with the purpose to playfully convince the funders that play should be a priority for every community. At the heart of every piece was a heartfelt stark message that less visible children, those living with a disability or living in poverty, were being deprived of their fundamental right to play.

I graduated from the University of Leeds with a degree in 'unemployability studies' in 2008 when the Credit Crunch dominated much of our headlines. Graduate employment opportunities were a national scarcity; I was destined for a future of unemployment. Even after the first term I was seriously questioning what on earth I was doing there. Yorkshire folk were charming but I was milling around in a rich kids' playground where I was ill-inclined to play with my peers.

By day I was being spoon-fed information about colonisation and poverty alleviation by mostly white older men. Cringe. By night I was avoiding anywhere groups of mostly white younger men making a spectacle of themselves on pub crawls, in fancy dress, that ended in all-you-can-drink student nightclubs with revolving dancefloors boisterously rapping to 'The Fresh Prince of Belair'. Double Cringe.

The silver lining was I was reading about a lot of people who were persevering in poverty; grassroots movements challenging dysfunctional capitalist systems and creative education programmes. Humans are designed to survive against the odds.

I had also been able to choose elective modules in Radical Geographies, the Geographies of Childhood & Youth and a sociology module called Race & Ethnicity taught by a more diverse workforce.

I experienced a level of White Privilege that I've not come across anywhere again in my adult life. Just like in secondary school where I had dismissed the influence of my teachers and opted to learn from my peers, the whole time I was enrolled in Leeds I was convinced that I could be learning more out in the real world. I mean how much enriching learning can we really pack into six hours of weekly contact time for a humanities degree? I was academically capable but I didn't want reading lists, nor was I particularly inclined to follow the rules of the Harvard Referencing System. I craved real people and had a hunger for understanding people and their communities through conversations and working together, not so much by other people's research written up in books.

The academic side of my degree wasn't quite what I was hoping for although to be fair when I was seventeen and choosing which city I wanted to live in for three years I was more concerned about the local nightlife and if it was going to feed me sufficient levels of hip hop and jungle. I didn't even go to Open Days of places that didn't host DJs I had grown to love.

For the duration of my course I had good attendance at seminars and lectures because I was acutely aware my parents were paying over three grand for my tuition and that was a lot of money to me. Although I knew that the real world beyond the Parkinson Building steps was what really sucked me in as an undergraduate, I respected the opportunity to learn at a good university so I didn't put my privilege to waste.

Yes, beyond the grandeur of the Brotherton Library I explored lessons in life that didn't require participants to be paying several hundred pounds a year in tuition fees. I volunteered at the Common Place near the outdoor market helping asylum seekers and refugees to learn English and took children tangled up in the care system out to the Yorkshire countryside for a breather. I saved my pennies from waitressing two or three times a week to fund my hearty addiction to international travel: as soon as term was done I was gone.

On campus, my saving grace was that our Student Union was particularly lively and gave me some exposure to the real world I was looking for. Each time in the middle of term when I thought about packing it all in and jetting off to Montreal, the lively opportunities on campus reminded me that it was well worth sticking around. The samba band often took its rehearsals into the courtyard, the Union shop had proudly boycotted Nestlé products, the thirst for peaceful protest and the race to democratically elect student leaders gave me optimism that tiny grassroots movements did indeed empower the voices of minorities and activists, and bring about real change.

Even though my employers in Kings Heath were not specifically looking for graduates, I put lessons learned from my degree to use. I carried with me successful case studies from the impoverished global south: communities can rise like a phoenix. Those three elective modules taught by eclectic lecturers felt so relevant to the dialogues of the broom-cupboard office in Birmingham.

Before going to university I hadn't had any interest in working with children. How different my life would have been if I had heard about the playwork degree on offer down the road at Leeds Beckett University! Beyond my lecture halls and library visits I discovered an untapped intrigue for finding ways to help children escape the stresses of homelife. While studying abroad in Ghana in my second year my eyes opened as children everywhere appeared to have a freedom that brought life and joy to every inch of land their bare feet touched. Even in the most bustling West African cities I spotted groups of children playing wherever they could find a bit of space, with whatever 'toys' they had scavenged, often made of rubbish or deemed 'broken' by a European child. Back in my Leeds in my final year of studies, learning just a tiny bit about childhood in the School of Geography thoroughly drew me in.

I started volunteering with children living in hostels, young carers and the children of asylum seekers. I saw a lot of the shitty bits of childhood. It was a great contraceptive! But the stark inequalities I saw, which contrasted with my own simple, yet enriching, childhood, geared me up to do something about lessening the gap between haves and have-nots.

It was no surprise that upon graduating I would be drawn to advocating for the fundamental rights of *all* children. And so, I worked with all my youthful might to help give the most excluded children in Brum a really playful childhood.

My official graduation

My playwork training in the latter quarter of 2009 was a welcomed distraction from the seasonal turn into darkness. My Fridays were bright and joyous despite my short commute to the dull concrete inner city and potholed car park at the rear of the rectangle block conference centre in Highgate. Along the long corridor were rooms hired for community learning, budget-conscious corporate training and other unceremonious gatherings. Our meeting room was unmemorable except for the large windows that looked out over the arse end of PC World, but inside, our circle was animated and lively. I loved the mix of humans in the room.

Alongside the five years I was studying in college and uni, before I discovered playwork, I was a waitress. From mid-November through to December I used to play 'guess the profession' for any group bookings who had pre-ordered from the Christmas menu. I was non-judgementally judging the group dynamics, the demographics, their attire, their enthusiasm for Christmas-themed banter and/or party games, if they exchanged Secret Santa gifts and who footed the bill, etc. By the end of the meal I'd casually ask 'so is this a work doo?' then 'Ah nice, where do you work?'

There was always one brazen colleague, you know, the one that much to the table's disinterest ordered that extra bottle of wine after desserts, who would give a reply along the lines of 'well I wouldn't be here with this lot outta choice', elbowing their neighbour and laughing at their own humour. Party twat. I had an 80% success rate to which my camp manager told me I should go work in recruitment. 'The commission is much better than the tips 'ere bab.'

Back in that square conference room, there were a bunch from eastern Brum. They spoke of their play space in like it was the centre of the universe and I am sure for the kids that went there, it most certainly was. I hadn't heard of their project, but deciphered from the elaborate descriptions of the risky play, the fire pit, the hand tools for building and the structures they described that it was an adventure playground. Just sitting across the circle from the team made me want to work there. I am pretty sure that prior to becoming a playworker, their little pack would have been in the 20% that I just couldn't place at their Christmas party. Playworkers are typically a misfit bunch.

Yes, they were definitely in that 20%. There was the older white bloke, very Brummie, gentle and practical; a proud dad who brought in toys he'd made when he was a kid, like his peg gun (a nifty arrangement of wooden clothes pegs and elastic bands attached to scraps of timber that could 'sling n fire' small objects quite incredible distances). He'd started out as a sports coach in the 80s, then worked in youth services and was drawn to the anti-establishment side of play.

Sat next to him was an athletically built, mixed-race woman with a fierce demeanour and always immaculately presented with fake nails, a full face of makeup and carefully styled hair. One would be forgiven for assuming she worked in higher-end retail or sales but actually she grew up on the adventure playground and was loyal to the place that let her use her strength to climb to and jump from unthinkable heights. On first impression she held herself like a special-forces recruit, but after a few weeks of our course she let her guard down within our circle of strangers and I could see how her warmth would radiate through any crowd of children or teens.

Next to her was an Asian dude with a fantastic collection of trainers; a fresh pair every week. He was bubbly and chatty and quick to open up about being disowned by his family when he chose to follow a childcare apprenticeship when he was sixteen instead of going to business school. 'My dad wanted me to be an accountant, ennit. But I always loved lookin afta my cousins so obviously I wanna work with kids. So, ya know, he kicked me out for doing woman's work ennit.'

They had nothing in common except their deep-rooted respect for children and a dedication to honour their right to play. In that course we had lively, clashing, eyebrow-raising debates about challenging gender and cultural stereotypes. My memory doesn't serve me well enough to remember all the characters of the rest of the circle but what stood out was that creativity comes in all shapes and sizes. No, we don't present ourselves like a bunch of art school graduates but the

42

school of thought coming from our circle was just as radical, controversial and counter-cultural.

All my life I had been directed through an institution-alised education system fuelled by snobbery where knowledge was to be earned officially only through a hierarchical system of certificates and qualifications. Playwork quickly proved to be refreshingly different. Yes, there are people who dedicate themselves to the research, the policy and the theory but in my playwork training there was no talk of climbing the ladder or the next step in our career development.

I learned early on that playworkers were there first and foremost for the children, to protect their space and keep adults from interfering in matters that only concerned the children. No child was sussing out my academic credentials when they picked me to help them. Any adult can be invited to sit on the dew-soaked grass with a child, or dared to jump in the deepest, darkest puddle, or asked to read a book, or drape a superhero cape, or stick the masking tape there ('no, not there, THERE'), or tie the string in a really tight knot, but children will only invite back the adults who hold children and their play in positive regard.

We playworkers are an optimistic bunch and we roam in a land where children lead and what a wonderful place it is to be where possibility is infinite. Through asking for help in their play children are simply just searching for an adult they can trust. I learned quickly, and probably carried with me from my own childhood, that children trust in adults who trust in children. Trust is built through reciprocal respect and a sense that all involved are being listened to and no length of time spent in a university library, or certificates on the wall matter to a child who just wants a bit of help and the freedom of thought to advance their play.

Through playwork theory and case studies from around the world I got my head around creating and protecting spaces where children could do whatever came to them that was freely chosen, personally directed or intrinsically motivated.

What really mattered to the children I was working with was my respect for their space.

I didn't need to get involved, lead or teach; I knew the children were perfectly capable of following their own agenda. Sure, I met children who had lovely long lists of medical conditions and support needs to accompany their diagnoses but given the right resources these children always showed us they knew how to play. We as playworkers had to create ways for these children to grow and flourish in their own self-directed play, reading their cues (however subtle they were) without us doing it all for them. Through teamwork, sharing experiences and Reflective Practice we always found new ways to follow every child's lead.

Our discussions that winter on Fridays in Highgate went deep and we squirmed in our seats when Sue or Ali, our trainers, gently suggested that what we were describing sounded like an adult-led agenda being inflicted on a group of children.

Were we there to tell them what to do?

Were we teaching children how to play?

Were we employed as a form of supervisory crowd control?

Were we there to protect a space where children could seek safety from the outside world that didn't treat under 18s as equal citizens?

Were we needed to advocate for every child's right to flourish and thrive in confidence to make their own decisions, innovate their own magic and lead their own play?

Through well-meaning smiles of nurturing kindness they forced us to look deep and reflect on what our purpose really was with those kids. No other profession values Reflective Practice as highly as playwork does. I loved the Reflective Practice – it was an opportunity to look inward, be philosophical and hear stories from strangers about their play: past and present.

Sue Smith and Ali Wood had probably over fifty years of playwork experience between them (they'll tell me I'm being polite but one should never give a woman's age away...). I loved how they urged us to think deeper and challenge our collective conditioning. They'd cross-examine us with provocations like 'now was that what *you* were thinking or is that what the child *said* they were thinking?' and 'why do you think *you* responded like that?'

Despite sitting through seventeen consecutive years of education as a capable, high-achieving student I had never been in a learning space that was so open and dedicated to considering *all* the options. There was never just one answer and one size absolutely did not fit all.

From that training I took away the permission to 'just' let them play (and by the way 'just playing' is never *just* playing). I took away the understanding that I only needed to intervene in children's play if someone was at risk of physical or emotional harm; all the other adult butt-ins were unnecessary interruptions. I took away the permission to trust children; we've been conditioned to avoid giving these incredible humans the autonomy they deserve. Needless to say, those weekly lessons in that faceless meeting room in the unsuspecting conference centre left quite an impression on me.

The broom cupboard

There was something very fascinating about watching children take the lead. Throughout my childhood and youth, I'd been told I was a good leader, or a leader in the making, so as a young adult I knew how important it was to pass the baton and let the children lead.

Leading by example meant giving the children the same level of respect we expected of them, as equal citizens. I didn't care that little S's impairment meant he couldn't see me; I saw him as a creative soul with so much curiosity for the world at the end of his fingertips. His ears and his touch receptors did his gazing and it was an honour to hear his view of the world he explored.

I quickly learned that the use of medical diagnoses was pretty useless in learning anything meaningful about a child. Back in the broom cupboard on Kings Heath High Street I spoke to a distraught mom on the telephone for over forty minutes. My manager raised her hands with joy when I eventually hung up, yelling, 'Little One, well done! That woman has been through shit, excuse my French, and you just talked to her about her son like he is a human.'

'How do you know who I was talking to?' Evidently our office was really that tiny. I suddenly felt very aware that she really had heard every single word of the conversation.

Ignoring my question, she continued 'And you know what, Little One, you know what you didn't do?'

'Oh no, what did I forget?'

'You took so much interest in her son, and not once did you ask if he had a disability, and for that reason I want to dance a little bit and make you a cup of tea.' I was getting used to Laura's eccentric outbursts. She wiggled her hips and muttered a line from a song in Spanish that I didn't recognise as she got up from her desk to fill the kettle.

The first time I met Laura she told me about her adventures in Venezuela in the 1970s. After a few months I realised every time she met a twenty-something-year-old she told them about her adventures in Venezuela in the 1970s. It was her playful icebreaker. She diluted lessons on funding applications and charity sector policy with anecdotes about Latin America. I filled in funding application forms where I wrote about play deprivation and all the wonderful sensory experiences we could create rather than listing all the things the children we worked with couldn't do. She encouraged me to paint a picture with words and bring the often-formulaic questions to life by sprinkling descriptions across the PDF.

I also wrote factually, with case studies about the lack of opportunities for child-led free play, particularly for children who didn't attend their local mainstream school. In a city the size of Brum a disabled child could easily spend three hours a day on special needs transport which taxi-ed them across town from their home to their special school. Add in meal times and extended personal care routines, there really was no time to play each day.

The non-disabled children who walked to their local school but lived in overcrowded flats with no garden were scared out of their playgrounds and green spaces because they were frequented by local gang members and drug dealers. The staffed community play centres and adventure playgrounds which thrived in the 1970s, and the Play Rangers that circulated parks around the city in the 1980s and 1990s all ceased to operate because of government funding cuts (and we all know which governments made the biggest cuts to children's services...). So, watching television in the safety of their own home became the easy option for lots of families, and so play time, from one generation to the next, has dwindled quite drastically. It was no wonder we were collecting waiting lists of clinically obese and clinically depressed children. Back then I didn't get bogged down with the science of the play-deprived brain, that only came in parenthood so I'll save that for later.

What really stole my heart was the human connection and the community that organically grew around the places we dedicated to play. Their postcodes and their medical labels defined these groups of humans as poor, but the palatial play spaces we created in these deprived communities were exquisite, rather splendid, bursting with energy that money could certainly not buy. The copious giggles, the sumptuous smiles, the carefree children in all their glory were enriching for me as the experience was for them.

Way before I had considered the prospect of procreation, I saw for myself how family life should be. Three or four generations congregating outdoors with folk from all tribes and arriving on all modes of transport. Groups of neighbours picnicked, babies slept while women chatted, children charged about, teenagers watched from the treetops, spritely grandparents got stuck in while other older adults sat and enjoyed the view. I got an up-close and personal glimpse of how to build village life in cities: invite everyone out to play.

In the park where I had grown up, alongside corners of my city that were totally new territory, with a team of incredible, dedicated humans who prioritised play, I felt proud to be contributing to elaborate village greens: mini festivals where everyone was invited to play as they pleased.

Advocating for play

'What? Like an adventure playground?' My friend asked me when we met one evening at a pub in Moseley. We'd both moved back home and in with our respective parents after uni, and though it had been nearly a year since graduating we hadn't got around to having a pint together.

'No, we move around the city with play resources.' I'd come straight from a networking event with funders of a new healthy-communities initiative. I felt proud and confident as I talked passionately about the need for more inclusive play in parks around Birmingham. I was on fire and felt like I was pitching to a benevolent millionaire about the importance of integrating disabled children to play in their local parks. Playgrounds with fixed equipment are not only predictable for able-bodied children, but point-blank exclude children with limited mobility from engaging in meaningful physical play.

'Just think about how crap it must be for the kid in the wheelchair just watching his little sister whizzing around, goin' up the climbing frame and flying down the zipwire. Or even for that child to watch a tamer child just float away her troubles over on the basket swing. He just has to sit there. Sure, the fresh air and change of scene is better than stayin' home all day, but it ain't very stimulating.' I took a sip of my half pint. Ever since coming back from Brazil where larger bottles of ice-cold beer were shared out around small glasses to prevent anyone from sipping tepid beer, I just couldn't work through a whole pint anymore.

'So are you fundraising to install those big swings for wheelchairs?'

'No, bab no, way more fun than that.' And on I went to explain all my new knowledge about loose parts and props for play.

'Fabric is great because we can mimic the visual sensations of swinging without actually leaving the ground. And loads of the equipment isn't specialist stuff; just normal things from around the house and pound shop, just used differently.'

'Like what?'

'Today we used fly swats to make clusters of bubbles. Then we made a breeze to blow the bubbles around with an airbed pump. Next week we're blacking out the hall and just wearing head torches and plugging in fairy lights.' He took a very slow sip of his Guinness staring into a space where children played. He was quiet which was rare for George.

'We try to evoke all the senses. Ya know taste, touch, smell, sight n sound. Some of the children's senses are really sensitive, others need loadsa stimulation, so our job is to find the right balance for each kid. And then give 'em a little extra playful sprinkle to expose 'em to a little bit of risk. Kids don't get much opportunity to take risks.'

That evening stood out because I felt like I was on a path, had purpose and was being taken seriously even though I was fresh-faced and youthful. I was serious about play. I didn't need to dress up smart, I could be my playful self and talk about playwork with familiarity like I'd been running sessions for years.

The reality in Birmingham was that a lot of the disabled children we worked with were from low-income families. The lack of inclusive childcare in the city meant that families were forced into single-income livelihoods because flexible working that fits around further care duties and medical appointments becomes near impossible. It just didn't seem fair; those families got a really raw deal. I was young and impressionable and I met some incredible warriors who were giving so much of their energy to improve their communities for all children; not just their own.

To say I was inspired was an understatement. One woman's gracious attitude will always stick with me as she shared her horror story of her five-year-old son being turned away from local playgroups and playschemes on the grounds that no one knew how to look after him.

'Oh my gosh, I can't believe there's actually somewhere that I can tek 'im,' she said on the brink of tears as her son delved his hands into large builders buckets filled full of buttons.

'Watch out 'e'll chuck 'em everywhere ina minute,' she shouted to my colleague who had sat himself at another bucket nearby. He didn't want to intrude on T's space but he also wanted to be available if T needed reassurance about the new setting, or if T offered a play cue: an invitation to join in. Sure enough within minutes he threw handfuls and handfuls into the air each time cocking his head to one side and exhaling a long flat 'Ehhhhhh' in a surprisingly low pitch for a five-year-old. His huge brown eyes lit up like a fruit machine; he had hit the jackpot. T and those buttons, T and tiny gravel stones, T and metallic milk-bottle tops, T and tiny polystyrene packaging balls. There was no toy on a shelf in any toy shop that was going to fulfil him the way our builders buckets did.

We were working with many children who did not have the cognitive development to follow the rules of board games, or instructions of how to make a 'whatever' in conventional listen-and-copy-me arts and craft activities. Our resources needed to evoke the senses, and our mindset needed to liberate children, empower them to take the lead and flourish in the safety of acceptance and trust.

Shockingly, many of our play punters had had doors closed to them and their unique and revolutionary ways to play. I mean how hard can it be to let a kid that likes the sensation of tiny stones in his fingers explore a tray of rice crispies, or buttons, or sequins? These young humans were brimming with creativity and were being denied their fundamental right to play because the adults put in charge of their care misunderstood their needs.

Though I was young and unattached (settling down was totally not on my radar), I did feel a maternal instinct brewing somewhere within, a stone's throw from my innate desire to fight injustices. To hear that another woman's child had been turned away from community centres and services designed for children fired me up to fight their corner. Luckily I wasn't alone; each with our own motivations, our little platoon of playworkers subtly challenged the misguided children's *professionals* bombarding them with outlandish resources for play.

Loose parts play

I quickly learned that children are the experts of children; I gained a lot from them. They taught me that honesty was the best policy. They taught me that a snack or a story (either from a book or made up while lying back and watching the clouds or a torch race across a ceiling) could solve most discrepancies. And most importantly they taught me that toys were totally overrated. About a decade before *Toy Story 4* was released I observed that homemade toys like 'Forky' quickly became children's most beloved toy. 'It's about bloody time,' I muttered to myself when I spotted a junk-modelled not-toy hanging out with Woody and Buzz. I dread to think how many 'make-your-own-Forky kits' have been packaged up and sold to parents at extortionate prices.

I wondered why parents spent so much money on toys and prescriptive craft kits when household objects, and particularly the recycling bin, sparked so much interest from the children I was working with. When these children played with what is effectively rubbish they were enriched and healthy. How does that saying go? One man's rubbish is another playworker's treasure?

I found my treasure trove the first time I visited Worcestershire Scrapstore over ten years ago. What a goldmine! There, tucked away on some unsuspecting industrial estate, I saw recycling on speed. I was hooked.

Never mind junk modelling from my kitchen bin, this was a massive wake-up to the amount of waste factories and businesses were churning out all day every day. If you want to create a more playful home and haven't yet visited a Scrapstore I urge you to very soon; there are around 90 in the UK. They are mostly charities and run by volunteers who sort and clean all sorts of beautiful and bizarre bits and pieces from local industries. They are saving tonnes and tonnes of waste from landfill for art, craft and, of course, play.

In my early days of playwork I saw how scrap allowed children to make their own toys their way, without adult direction. This wasn't new to me on a personal level because a lot of my own play was with bits and bobs from around our cluttered home. My parents were laid back and had a fairly *laissez-faire* approach to raising four children who span a twelve-year age gap. 'Unconventional', 'subtle activists', 'almost hippy' is how I've described our family over the years. My older brother used to say, 'If we were a proper family we'd...' when he compared our chaos to his peers and their more conventional family habits. My friends would always comment on how messy our house was, but also how cool it was because 'Adele's mom is so relaxed.'

In the school holidays our home sometimes felt like a youth club as our mom didn't seem to limit the number of friends that came over. She was a school teacher and helped friends who didn't have such generous annual leave. From the five-year-olds to the fifteen-year-olds everyone was left to play their own way. I don't remember much conflict, but I do remember being sent indoors by my big brother, six years my senior, because the garden was just for him and his mates. 'I shouldn't take much notice,' my mom advised. Which, as an adult, I realise is her mantra when responding to most things in the realms of authoritarianism.

I once witnessed my big brother, probably around thirteen years old, spray a can of Lynx deodorant onto an anthill at the end of our garden and then set it alight with a match. Wooosh! It momentarily went up in flames and he and his mates did it again and again. 'I'm telling on you!' I cried because I thought surely playing with fire wasn't on, even though I was thrilled by watching it. I'm sure I only 'told on' them because they wouldn't let me strike a match too. But when my mom wasn't too bothered about the fire and let them carry on playing I began to understand that as long as we weren't hurting each other, pretty much anything goes.

I'd like to stress I am definitely not endorsing attacking natural habitats of other living creatures, however big or small. With my own learning and awareness I am growing to love and respect the natural world far more than when I was a child. But the image of my brother setting fire to anthill paints a good example of how city schools in the 90s were missing some pretty crucial lessons on the intricacies of bio-diversity. And by looking at the mounds of litter around our neighbourhoods evidently those lessons still aren't as effective as they could be.

So, after those years growing up in a free play environment, when it came to caring for other people's children, I was comfortable with just letting kids be kids. As long as the children I was working with weren't intentionally causing harm to themselves or others, or the natural environment, it was actually quite instinctual for me to just let kids do what they do best: play. So play they did for hours and hours without much intervention from me or my fellow playworkers.

Even though I worked with children with high support needs, I was extremely mindful of not dominating their play. Within teams of playworkers we created stimulating spaces, where playing with the senses was our underlying aim. Play-work done well is subtle; the outcome of the play resources wasn't always obvious, we were focussed on the process. In playwork I learned to observe and appreciate what children could do and what brought them joy rather than listing all the things they were 'dis-abled' from doing.

In 1972 Simon Nicholson wrote 'The Theory of Loose Parts'[2] which stated 'in any environment, both the degree of inventiveness and creativity, and the possibility of discovery, are directly proportional to the number and kind of variables in it.'

On my playwork-ing days I roamed around my silver-grey city in my mom's silver-grey Rover 25. Accompanied by my cherished gang of playworkers, we filled the generous boot with as many 'variables for inventiveness and creativity' as we could muster, mostly random stuff we found at the Scrap-store, or sourced from Kings Heath High Street or was do-nated from Freecycle. Before I came along with my mom's car the playteam used to take the bus; what a jolly commute!

My passengers sat amongst squidgy bags bursting with metres and metres of texturised fabric, bean bags big and small, an assortment of hats, dry food and bits from our recy-cling bins. We had wheelie suitcases bursting with random bits and pieces such as torches, plant pots, beaded curtains. Onlookers would be forgiven for assuming we were collect-ing bits to sell at a Jumble Sale or a Car Boot. But playworkers know and love these resources for open-ended child-led play. We call them 'loose parts'.

Training as a playworker in a large city exemplified that play can happen anywhere; we just need playful adults to pro-tect spaces so that children can access safe places to play. And while the outdoors can offer lots of natural resources to play with, outdoor play does not need to be limited to just 'nature

2 Nicholson, S., 'How Not To Cheat Children: The Theory of Loose Parts', Landscape Architecture, v62, p30-35, 1971.

play'. There's plenty of man-made 'stuff' that creates all sorts of wonderful play. I love being outdoors in cities. Outdoor play in urban environments can be as diverse as its people. Cities give the vibrancy that only populous places can bring. I love people. I love chitchat. And I love real talk. Some tell me the whistling leaves and creaking branches of the forest tell them the best stories, but I like to hear stories from humans. All sorts of folk with all sorts of experiences. I am a city girl through and through but I always feel most calm when I indulge in Mother Nature's pockets of natural play spaces that spring out from the murky grey mix of concrete and smog. And I feel the most happy when I gather groups of playful people to reclaim our city's spaces and lively up our concrete jungles with a van load of loose parts.

Our Playteam was as diverse as our city and our child-hoods contrasted starkly. This diversity enriched our agenda. We used the sixteen Play Types (more on these later) as a checklist and to account for a varied play offering. And because play is so intrinsically motivated, playworkers will bring their own inherent style to play.

One colleague, Nazreen, has always stood out for me and I love her bubbly attitude. I don't know much about her home life except for one tiny little insight she shared at our Christmas party one year. 'Well at our house there's a room full of Pakistanis in paper crowns gathered in front of the TV for the Queen's speech every year bab,' she told me in retali-ation when I told her I'd never seen the Queen's speech on Christmas Day. So on the 25th December she might have been a bit the norm, but the rest of the year she was doing extraordinary things in her community. I know that ten or so years ago there weren't many young British Pakistani women championing for equality in the way Naz was. She'd never take any credit for the hurdles she was jumping, the paths she was laying to help other women trapped in cultural traditions that just didn't fit into modern British life. Like many activists, she never ever seemed to take a day off.

In Pakistan, as in many countries around the world, disability remains a taboo. On one project, behind each community play session we delivered, was a journey of Nazreen building trust and acceptance from some of the most marginalised women in Birmingham: Pakistani mothers of disabled children. With these women, almost totally hidden from society, she patiently built relationships, in a way that I would never have been able to. Behind the scenes, Nazreen worked twice as hard as any of us. And no matter how much paint she'd washed out of sponges, or mud she'd wiped off inflatable palm trees, she was always giggling and joking at the end of every bloody shift. She was an absolute trooper.

Sarah was the only immigrant in our urban clan. She was a proper country bumpkin flocking from the picturesque meadows of deepest, darkest Herefordshire. She brought a breath of fresh air to our urbanite haze. As a child she was wild and free to roam the fields around her hamlet in a way us city kids weren't. Her delightful dreamy way encaptured us and we'd float up with her to bright blue skies and fluffy clouds for a Countryfile look at life. Some may call her quaint, I prefer genius. She said one day, 'I just wish the kids could play in a barn of hay.' We giggled and agreed that respite from concrete and sirens would do them the world of good and reminisced about *Young Black Farmers*: a documentary that aired on Channel 4.

But the idea stuck with me. I'm an ideas person through and through; always 'scheming' as my mom calls it. I reflected on the endless play I had seen with one bin bag of shredded paper; imagine what would happen with volumes of hay.

By the next week I had found a farm on the city's outskirts that were willing to deliver to our rather undesirable postcode in Handsworth, better known for race riots and gang warfare. And so, in all their glory, children that would probably never discover the joy of spending their summer holidays in the countryside frolicked and rolled and leaped and spun in twelve bales of hay.

The otherside

I liked that my job took me to all corners of Birmingham. Neighbourhoods I didn't usually have a reason to visit. There was a tiny bit of me that was disappointed to be living at home and back on my old turf but my nomadic spirit knew I wouldn't be there for long.

We took pit stops at family-run sweet centres where samosas were cooked fresh for 25p and a generous box of delicious chana masala was only £1.75. I've never been to Southern Asia but I've certainly had many-a-tummy-full of proper good Asian food.

I loved meeting other playworkers in Birmingham. Over the years I have come to learn that playworkers up and down the country are a hardy bunch of the children's workforce that barely get a mention. Playworkers are committed to empowering children and young people. We are radical thinkers, misunderstood by many and ready to fight the corner of silenced children when the time comes.

I came to think of playworkers as the Maya Angelous of the children's workforce. We challenge common structure and advocate for risky experiences that empower the marginalised. Just like Ms Angelou we are sassy, even in wellies and raincoats. And wow, do we have the best time at work? And damn don't we just know it.

I took English Literature in my first year of sixth-form college where I had the most wonderful teacher. I know there are lots of brilliant teachers out there who, despite the constraints of the system and the unthinkable pressure of carrying the load of thirty young minds, work their socks off to bring creativity, joy and passion to the classroom. Martin Berry was one of those teachers. It was a delight to delve deep into *I Know Why the Caged Bird Sings*. He really brought Angelou's work into a life of its own, I am sure neither great teacher will mind if I take a few moments to play around with the words of 'Still I Rise':

Does my playfulness upset you?
Why are you beset with gloom?
'Cause I beam like I've got ten kids
Joking in my living room.

Does our playfulness offend you?

Don't you know we work so hard?
But we laugh while we sip rain tea
Eatin' mud pies in our yard.

You may shoot us with low pay,
You may cut our budgets dry,
You may bore us with your formalities,
But still, with play, we rise.

Walking into schools around Birmingham, our play team received a mixed reception. My inner rebel has always felt quite playful; I never rebelled with anger but always with parody. When I was in Year Eight I dyed my hair purple. It was a subtle purple as I, at the mere age of twelveteen, hadn't realised that to get the full effect of the hair dye I needed to bleach my hair first. In all honesty there was probably more purple dye rubbing on to the inner band of my school shirt collar than there was on my actual head.

Nonetheless, the Head of Lower School sent me home on the basis that it wasn't part of school uniform. I defended myself that it wasn't affecting my ability to learn and I should not be deprived of an education based on the colour of my hair. My dad always said I'd make a good lawyer; I could negotiate, articulate a valid counter argument and held justice in high regard from a young age. 'But miss, this is discrimination,' I repeated as I was sent out of her office and off down the school drive. 'What a load of bollocks,' I could imagine my mom saying later that evening.

I strolled home where I unexpectedly found my mom. She was no longer a full-time teacher, she had moved on to supply work with agencies. That morning she hadn't got a call summoning her to cover anywhere. 'Bollocks!' she exclaimed as I told her what had happened. I couldn't tell if she was genuinely cross with me for faffing about with a hair dye full of chemicals or just pissed off at the office for sending me off their perimeters with no regard for their duty of care.

'Haven't they got anything better to be doing with their time? Go back to school. Off you go.' It must have been a lesson I liked because with no fuss I strolled back into school, snuck back into class and pretended like the last ninety minutes hadn't happened.

So at twelve years old I learned to be dubious of institutions and hair dye from Superdrug. But with mild plum, not quite Wild Plum like the box said, I learned to be cautious of my teacher's decisions and wary of labels. From that day forth I decided I'd playfully challenge the norm wherever possible. I've always been diplomatic; as much as I dug into my teachers I wasn't into personal attacks; they represented the system and I had declared that the system was broken.

As a playworker I had a professional relationship to maintain but I couldn't shrug off the sourness I'd collected from the hierarchical education system over the years. In the less playful schools I used to get overcome with a playful desire to challenge the establishment. When we first entered the building, in a non-confrontational manner, I'd carry in the most zany loose parts first, or wear as many of them as possible while navigating through their automatic security doors.

I'm sure some of those school receptionists were reluctant to press that magic 'Open Sesame' button.

At a big primary school in north Brum I earned the reputation of 'the teacher who ate a worm' with a boy with a huge heart for life.

'I'm not a teacher!' I hissed each time I saw him around school in the proceeding weeks of term and holiday club.

I recall we were playing teambuilding and communication games on the large green field which involved a huge bucket of cooked spaghetti: 'the worms'. But how I convinced him I'd stomached a squirming little creature I am still not sure. The evolution of his big brown eyes from shock to amusement to admiration stuck with me. As his expression changed from one stage of bewilderment to the next, his cheeks climbed higher and higher from a scrunched-up face of disgust to the broadest, brightest smile. He had a full set of straight white teeth (lucky bugger) glowing against his deep mahogany cheeks. His eyes advanced from ordinary brown to shining like glowworms with the tale of a wiggling jiggling insect in my tummy.

As he helped carry our kit from the field back to the main entrance the receptionist just rolled her eyes when he retold every detail of the worm now being digested 'in that teacher's tummy'. 'Go back to your classroom young man,' she sighed rather than sharing his moment of joy. I'd read his referral form and knew why he'd been selected for our play programme; no doubt that member of staff knew too that life was pretty miserable at home, so why she couldn't just jump on his bandwagon and honour that child's infectious jubilation for that tiny moment of her day remains as much of a mystery as to how I ate the worm.

A year later we were back doing summer play with another group of Year Fours on the same field. From the fence adjacent to the school playground I heard 'Youuuuu aaaaattte a worrrrrrrrrrrm.'

On my non-play days when I worked in schools as an agency teaching assistant or cover supervisor I didn't ever have those playful interactions with children. There seemed to be some unspoken obligation to uphold a demeanour of seriousness, and that as educators we were looking out for any opportunity to instil moral consciousness in our students. On those agency worker days I saw a lot of questionable approaches in talking to young humans, and unless it was downright disrespectful – which only happened on one occasion – I bit my tongue and reminded myself they were only doing as their training had conditioned them to. I was also conditioned to my training – problem was my training was far more liberating and empowering than the textbooks the teaching staff had been reading. I quickly learned it is hard to take off the playwork hat if there are children around. Respecting children didn't stop being applicable because we were in a classroom.

Playworkers create worlds where options are not limited. One child's imagination is ignited by another's. Differences are unimportant as children unite through play. Elitism, hierarchy and class are meaningless to children when they engage in unadulterated play; dirt lurks behind all children's nails, mud clumps on all children's wellie boots (or better still toes!), paint lurks on all children's skin, rain soddens all children's clothes, and sticks, well sticks are valiantly grasped by all children. And adults, adults have a choice to make. I'll steal the words of another big influencer of my English Literature studies to pose the most serious of decisions to adults; to play or not to play, that is the question?

It is a question that will receive a myriad of responses from a myriad of humans. We are built to play – fact – our brains are wired for it. But unlike other mammals in the wild who Rough and Tumble Play, rolling and leaping about with their mates, we are conditioned out of playing. So, we have to make a choice: we have to opt into a life full of play. Or at least, opt in to being more playful.

Wearing my playworker hat in non-playwork settings often caused an inner conflict. I observed well-meaning adults disregard all respect for a child's choice to opt out of something that simply didn't interest them. I gently contested as persistent professionals nagged at children to join in what they deemed 'a fun activity'. Play can't be forced, bought or organised through 'an activity'. Adult-led activities are not play, they are adults imposing an agenda on children, assuming what children want and need at that particular moment of the day. Playschemes with timetables always puzzled me: are these kids here to play or have they been lured here under false pretences, and what is actually on offer is more schooling without the end of term assessments.

Yes, as adults we can choose to embrace the freedom of play, we can choose to leave gaps in our day for free play, we can choose to let the children lead. I hazard a guess that adults

66

who are comfortable letting children lead are the same people who were given some leadership or autonomy as children. To let go of the controlling nature of the adult-versus-child dynamic I'd say one should reconnect to a part of our earlier life that was, for the most part, buried in learning objectives and timetabled free time.

Children often want a playmate and they'll expect an adult to fill the role if the right child isn't about. I saw lots of adults working with children who weren't willing to play. Or thought they were playing but then couldn't take direction from the child and so the child's play became yet another adult-led agenda.

Some adults are scared to do anything that might be perceived as silly, they live in fear of the judgements of unplayful people. It might require some courage to nurture an inner child that is scared to come out of a safe hiding place. But if we choose to work with children we at least owe it to the kids to allow them to be playful, and better still have a giggle at work and be playful ourselves. Otherwise we run the risk of inciting play deprivation upon our young (and our playful colleagues) and that is no laughing matter.

To go against the grain and live more playfully may be met with a scornful response from adults who are stuck on the path less played; that's when my inner rebel gets giddy. As my lovely mother says, 'I shouldn't take much notice.'

Awesome

Working with the parents of children with complex disabilities totally shifted my perspective of parenthood. Never mind all that travelling I had done: I was awakened by some of the most committed and courageous mothers; their journey left me breathless. In Iceland (the island, not that shop that 'Mum's been to'), Mr Isgrove, the sixth-form geography teacher, impelled us as young adults to broaden our perspective, share the magic of the incredible landscapes we were witness to on that field trip and use vocabulary that evoked the emotions of the landscape. One afternoon he sent us off to sit on our own and contemplate the scenery of Vatnajökull National Park. As we dispersed he called out to the thirty or so of us, 'This! This, my friends, is truly awesome,' with his arms out wide and the biggest grin. 'Awesome' is a word that is totally overused by my generation. Something that is awesome may evoke impressive wonder and even a bit of fear.

In Birmingham those parents were truly awesome and they too evoked impressive wonder. And while I was never on the receiving end of any malice, far from it, I could sense their parenting journeys had been struck with fear, anger and despair. Kids will always be brilliant, no surprises there. But those parent-led community play organisations taught me the stark realities of another sort of parenthood. Their commitment to the cause was sheer brilliance.

No parent should have to experience the exclusion these families had faced: repeatedly turned away from under resourced children's services, suffering with can't-do attitude because their child required a little more attentive tenderness than some of their peers without a complex diagnosis. In twenty-first-century Britain, where resources are abundant but unfairly distributed, disabled children are repeatedly being deprived of meaningful play opportunities in their community.

I didn't know much about disability or paediatrics or palliative care, but I did know a lot about acceptance, equality and respect. I felt it in my gut that all children have a right to play. And I felt that no parent deserved to be left at the sidelines because some people working with children weren't prepared to widen their perspective.

I was eager to widen mine further. The travel bug had well and truly got me. I knew playwork in Birmingham was always going to be an option and I was twitching to try my luck in my graduate field of International Development. I was accepted on an EU Youth Mobility scheme (like Erasmus but with work instead of study) with a paid internship at a health charity in Lisbon. I'd also hooked up with my university chums who had just launched East African Playgrounds (now called Play Action International). I planned to brush up on my Portuguese, get some meaningful hands-on work experience while building a playground in Kenya's Kibera slum, then head back to Brazil in search of some kind of community work.

To cut a beautiful, convoluted story very short: I fell in love a few weeks after moving to Lisbon. I cut my trip to East Africa short and moved back to Portugal two days after flying in from Nairobi. Mr Lowprofile and I moved to England a year or so later.

Part 2 - No time to play

What if we are told to find a play–life balance?

I needed a noble reason to move away from Lisbon. It sounded idyllic and romantic moving abroad to live with a dreamy Portugeezer but the go-getting opportunist in me was well and truly bored. Not for want of trying, I just couldn't wangle my way into local projects or interesting work. I visited afterschool clubs, community centres, dance schools and gyms offering my services as a volunteer. But the locals in our suburb outside of Lisbon just couldn't understand why I was living there and why I was willing to work for free.

I spent most of the year being unemployed or being paid an abysmal, but legal, €3 an hour as a receptionist of a back-packers' hostel near Parque Eduardo VII (the one on the hill with the biggest flag I have ever seen on all of my travels). We were living through a recession in Portugal, probably some sort of trickle-down macroeconomic aftermath of the Credit Crunch. Youth unemployment skyrocketed. Mr Lowprofile was working nights when I met him because the pay was better and there was more chance of watching films on his laptop when the big bosses weren't around. When we moved into our new flat together he switched to a daytime rota on less pay but ended up taking a second job on weekends to cover the shortfall.

We agreed staying in Portugal wasn't an option. We shortlisted our options to Geneva (where I had cousins), Bristol (because it was cool), Dubai (because recruitment agencies were crying out for tax-free candidates) and London (where all the jobs were). I landed a place on a postgraduate nursing course at King's College London, complete with a bursary: I felt accomplished.

The day before I flew back to England I got a call from an interviewer I had met with three weeks earlier casually offering me a reasonably paid job in central Lisbon, like we had met the previous day. I had already called up the broom cupboard in Birmingham to ask for summer work before Mr Lowprofile and I moved to London. 'Oh, we knew you'd come back to us eventually, Little One! Let's see if we can't keep you here!' And they duly booked me into as many summer playscheme shifts as I could squeeze in.

So I boarded my Ryanair with mixed feelings; had I given up on Lisbon too soon? Did I just need to be more patient?

Though I was far too brazen to admit it, that summer moving from Lisbon to Birmingham to London turned out to be extremely unsettling for me. I belittled the huge shift we were making as a couple. No longer just an extended summer fling, we had lived together in a country that was not home for me, and in a neighbourhood that was not home for him, and were now migrating together as one. I disregarded the upheaval of doing two big moves in one year and I think back in the UK we both missed the familiarity of our setup in Portugal and the simpler life.

I knew I did not want to train to be a nurse but back then I needed a viable way to move two steps forward, not one step backwards to Brum. I think that year or so living unplayfully in Lisbon had brought me to the conclusion that I couldn't see a future in playwork. In Lisbon I'd seen no clues that anyone really understood or valued play the way I did. I assumed I couldn't pursue a playwork career if it was not transferable to a culture I was rapidly becoming attached to. I deemed playwork *un*international (how wrong was I?!). And I *needed* a job that I could travel with. So, because I'd changed plenty of adult-sized nappies on age-appropriate play projects for young adults in Brum, done a few PEG feeds and steered a handful of wheelchairs, I pretty prematurely decided nursing would be that convenient global career I was still trying to fix up for myself.

'You are just nervous, it is normal,' I recited internally every day in the build-up to moving day. Turns out I wasn't nervous. It was just my intuition planting a tiny acorn that would slowly sprout. Back then I ignored it like we learn to ignore our period pain. Over the years I've learned to listen to it and act in accordance to where it is guiding me. It was no doubt an agonising process for me, but I really learned to listen to myself. I think we could all do with listening to our intuition more.

Not so Great for me

Ten taxing months after moving to London, I was back home for a weekend visiting my parents and sister. We went for a walk in the picturesque fields around Henley-in-Arden, near Birmingham, which ended with an obligatory stop at the landmark Henley Ice Cream who have been dairy farmers and purveyors of mighty fine ice cream for almost a century. My sister had just moved back from three years working in Central America and I was more excited than ever to have her back home: she was six months pregnant. 'Don't you find it really sad?' she asked of my new job as we strolled across a trickling stream and out into a redundant agricultural field blooming with poppies dancing in the breeze.

There was a real buzz about Great Ormond Street Hospital (GOSH). I felt proud and accomplished to be part of a team of world-leading health professionals. After dropping out of nursing training at King's the previous year I felt I had something to prove. I was desperate to remain in a caring role and thought the NHS was a better employer than a lot of the smaller care agencies. I had made some really special friends in those first few months at King's and, even though the prospect of being a nurse had crumbled before me, their tenacity and commitment to 'the cause' rubbed off on me. So a hospital playworker felt like the next best thing, especially at the world-renowned Great Ormond Street.

'I find all the medication really difficult to deal with; there are way more chemicals than I ever imagined their tiny bodies could handle.' Till this day the potency of the chemotherapy drugs seeps in my nostrils and makes the corners of my mouth dip in grimace. 'But the mindset of everyone there is so positive,' I added.

I loved cycling up from Camberwell over Waterloo Bridge and through the quieter backstreets of Covent Garden; up Drury Lane with the fragrant hanging baskets of Sarastro restaurant and the vibrant window sills lovingly tended to by the residents of the distinctive Peabody Estate on the opposite corner. Despite the chaotic roads and the pollution, I think cycling saved my sanity in London. Sitting on the 68 bus first thing in the morning made me twitchy. But pedalling along the car-free bike lanes and along central London's quieter streets allowed sacred moments to discover and acknowledge the tiny oases of greenery. I saw signs of life beyond the rat race: thriving communities, growing families and traces of Mother Nature scattered around my urban dystopia.

Our GOSH induction instilled in me a sense of pride. I sat with doctors, nurses, cleaners, medical secretaries and we worked through the process together. It was the only time I felt equal and valued. Hats off to the Human Resources team who made that week actually very engaging. They had made a wonderful video about health and safety. All the dull guidelines were presented by patients and survivors. Note to self: always ask children to deliver health and safety training. It was so playful! Not the slightest bit cheesy but just very brilliant. But it quickly unfolded that I was not brilliant. Dropping out of nursing had really, really knocked my confidence. Another hierarchical institution was not the place to regain it.

The older and wiser me can see clearly how that Purple Ward was not somewhere I was going to last. On my first day a tour around the other departments did not give me much hope: outpatients' waiting rooms homed sorry-looking piles of colouring sheets. Back in my Brummie broom cupboard we had heckled at colouring sheets: a manipulative technique to keep children sedentary and subliminally compliant. Colour in someone else's creation, colour in between their lines, sit still and be quiet. What a waste of trees, and what a way to exclude children who did not yet, or may not ever, hold a standard-sized pencil, crayon or felt-tip pen.

On our ward there were playrooms empty of children and full of plastic toys and board games with pieces missing. None of these resources resonated with the loose parts and props for play that I had been gathering from Scrapstores for the community play projects in Birmingham.

But within weeks of that lovely summery walk with my sister and that yummy Brummie ice cream, the same feelings that had overcome me at King's started to chase me down the corridors of Purple Ward. I was well and truly lost and I didn't feel like I was going to be allowed to be the sort of playworker I had trained to be.

I was young and anxious and was too proud to admit that I was uncertain of what I was doing back in a hospital again. My heart was in the community. Even in my nursing interview I was reassured that there would be ample time for placements in the community. Upon enrolment at King's I learned this simply was not true and so I had started to tumble out of my nursing training almost as soon as I began.

I quickly learned that like fine china the Hospital Play Team was brought out and displayed for special occasions: fundraisers, Christmas and a photo shoot here and there. But day to day I felt institutionalised as I saw my colleagues photocopy reams of colouring sheets, print off 'how to make' instructions and was directed to Argos in Holborn to buy into the commercialisation of childhood which I fiercely detested. I guess there is little room for ethical consumption when a child is on their deathbed; just buy whatever makes them happy. The whole process made me incredibly unhappy.

F's Bakery

When I was told by my line managers that I couldn't build dens or recreate sensory rooms with torches and fairy lights in the patient's darkened bedroom, I tried to not be disheartened. We all have our play preferences, hers is not den building. 'Just get over it bab,' I told myself. (Yes, I also call myself bab, I don't just save it for others.)

Another day I prepared messy play with a boy who dreamed of being a chef. F loved the BBC's culinary duo the Hairy Bikers and all the board games we had played were food-themed as were the colouring sheets I had begrudgingly delivered him as I shadowed Miss Shrill in the first fortnight. He was Nil By Mouth and he often talked about what he would like to cook when he could eat again. We planned 'to bake' a big gooey strawberry cake together and his parents agreed it would be good fun for him.

Through gooey giggles of cornflour and fluorescent sprinkles we connected and I felt like I had finally turned a corner and found my happy feet. F decided 'I want to sell my cupcakes through my window,' and asked if we could make a sign. So we rebranded his fishbowl bedroom window into 'F's Bakery', nurses giggled as they pretended to be customers. I felt like my colleagues finally understood why I was there and by engaging in our play they valued my presence. I felt like the real me. F was engrossed in the cornflour and I didn't feel that I had to be an all-singing, all-dancing, hi-pitched jazz hands

78

children's entertainer. I like the analogy of playworkers being invisible until invited by a child to join their play. But believe me, it is difficult to don a cloak of invisibility in a patient's hospital bedroom, and in a 1:1 scenario it is not appropriate. Nor is dominating their play.

I respected his space but was there to play when he asked or I sensed that he was ready to add another element to evolve his play. I didn't have to replicate Miss Shrill and I could go at a pace (and a volume) that I deemed more conducive to empowering that child through his play. I had my own playful toolkit and through the giggles at F's Bakery I could feel that my colleagues on Purple Ward understood the real playful Adele. After an uncertain start at GOSH I was feeling like there was a place for me there after all.

But whatever confidence I had developed that day at F's Bakery was diminished in the following Multidisciplinary Team meeting. As I retold the joyful play with F and his bakery, the matron told me, in front of the room of twelve or so doctors, psychologists, nurses and the chaplain, that it was 'cruel' to use real food with a child who was Nil By Mouth. Cruel was a word I associated with Victorian institutions, or maybe I am thinking of gruel. Nevertheless, I remain adamant that it was a poor choice of language to throw at a new colleague in a meeting with an audience.

I shrank into my seat and zoned out for the rest of the meeting. I was bottom of the pile again; playworkers, like student nurses, were thrown in with the piranhas. I felt it. I found it ever so hard to value my work. I found it even harder to admit that I wasn't enjoying playing every day. So many playworkers would love to be paid, on full-time hours, to play every day, in a world-famous hospital like GOSH but I could not find value in my contribution to these children's lives and it was bringing me down big time.

London dread

After a few months at GOSH one patient inevitably took a substantial decline in her bone marrow transplant. I had never been so close to death. And I didn't know how to talk about it: how it saddened me, how I dreaded her death unfolding before me, how I worried about seeing a child die. I had worked with children in palliative care in Birmingham but I now realise I only ever saw them on their good days, when they were well enough to attend our community play days.

But the combination of secretly wanting to become a liberal parent, grow life in my own body while working alongside parents who were sat at their child's death bed, was a total head fuck for me. Dread is a very strong emotion. And I think I totally overlooked the power it held over me. Worry, anxiety, panic were words I associated with my mental health but dread, which I think was the foundation of my anxiety, lurked at the bottom of my backpack. At work dread followed me all around Purple Ward.

I put on a brave face and tried to see the light that my colleagues carried with them. Their light didn't seem to shine on me for long: it was blocked by a stormy cloud of dread. I was a pendulum swinging between light and dark, hope and despair, life and death, all the while trying to bring out those brilliant juicy hormones in those really poorly kids.

Those few months at GOSH I was so overwhelmed by the notion of feeling unplayful while employed to enrich children's play that I had disregarded my own need to play. I was totally overwhelmed with the fast pace of life around me outside of work, and the faster pace of imminent death when I arrived at work. No workplace training could prepare me for what I was feeling. Utter sadness. No matter how positively I tried to start my day I think I left my own supply of brilliant juicy hormones on the 68 bus. In my depressed state I had stopped cycling.

There were days when I dreaded going into work because I knew that there were children who weren't going to survive and I was terrified of my reaction to being on shift when the first one passed. In the first few weeks I spent every lunch break sitting on the edge of the flower beds at the main entrance. My packed lunch was contaminated by the smokers lined up against the wrought-iron fence a few metres away from me.

One day I begrudgingly retreated indoors, away from the tobacco pollution and into the staff canteen, and was waved over to the playworker table where a group of women sat solemn and still as they ate from tupperwares and small insulated lunch bags. I placed myself awkwardly amongst my team.

'How you finding it?' one of them asked probably out of pity and politeness. We both knew that this well-meaning conversation was not going to go anywhere.

'Different,' I replied diplomatically. 'I miss the outdoors and the freedom of play.'

I can't remember who told me about the roof garden but it became my almost hidden sanctuary. I am extremely thankful to whoever pointed me in the direction of the new building. It was almost the opposite end of the hospital from my ward, but the trek was well worth it. Whatever the weather, of each thirty-minute lunch break I spent twenty-two minutes on the almost empty rooftop. I tried to clear my mind but I was distracted by the reason the rooftop garden existed: it was a dedication to the two nurses who were killed in the Russell Square bombing on 7th July 2005. Even on my lunch break I was uneasy from the presence of death looming over me.

I wish I had listened to myself, my desperation to sleep, my weird appetite and the tension in my body. I called in sick a few times, and then signed myself off for a couple of weeks during which time I googled work-related stress. I felt comforted that I was not alone; it was actually very common. I followed the wellbeing advice from those articles and my GP, but the few brilliant juicy hormones I mustered when I swam at Camberwell Leisure Centre or bought fresh fruit and veg by the tonne at East Street Market seemed to disappear as soon as I parked my bike back at work or stepped off the bus at Holborn. I never said out loud to anyone that my stress was not related to work. I was simply petrified of witnessing death.

I was mostly working on my own; dread accompanied my strolls along the clinical corridors. I felt like a misfit and daydreamed about my favourite community play environments: bouncing a storm of buttons and glistening milk-bottle tops on a hammock of glowing ocean green fabric; wafting mountains of bubbles over children while they layered themselves in improvised cloaks, gowns and capes from vibrant offcuts of material; the magical gleaming eyes of children poking their heads out of cardboard boxes, jumping over skipping ropes wrapped with fairy lights and bellowing voices down cardboard tubes.

Each time I entered the anteroom I pulled myself together. In that tiny cupboard I psyched myself up while I hand washed, donned an apron and waited for the air pressure monitor to signal that it was safe to proceed. When the light changed I switched off negativity and switched on my smiley happy people vibe. It wasn't quite an act because I did genuinely care about giving these children the best opportunities to play. They didn't know that I was dragged down and entangled in the way I had to go about bringing them the best childhood their circumstances would allow.

Worse still I knew what the three strategies were that would have made my working week more positive and manageable but I was not brave enough to ask for them. I wanted to resource my patients' play from Scrapstores. I wanted flexitime. And I wanted to dedicate some of my working day to Reflective Practice with a group of colleagues.

The first was logistically difficult because I was working in the most stringent part of the hospital in terms of infection control; but it was not impossible. The flexible working should have been totally fine to arrange; I wanted to work ten-hour shifts so that I could accumulate an extra day off each week. As it stood, my eight-hour shifts spread out over seven days which meant I rarely had two consecutive days off. I did not mind working the weekends: the hospital was quieter and the families seemed more relaxed. But my rota did not give me the headspace I so desperately needed for rest.

The Reflective Practice was certainly possible but by the time I figured it out I was so deep in a downward cycle of low self-worth that I couldn't bear to ask for something that would benefit me, or be the driving force behind a workplace shift with open dialogues with colleagues about our (un)playful practice.

Being fiercely independent I found it difficult to ask for help; like it was a sign of weakness which is why I avoided asking for Reflective Practice. I was missing working with my team of Brummies; my like-minded humans who were open and pragmatic about working under complex circumstances. Back then I hadn't realised how important my colleagues in Birmingham had been in what was also very emotionally invested work. Sharing honest reflections about the complexities of the children we were working with and recognising our own reactions to their barriers to play were a deeply meaningful and rewarding part of building working relationships. I just didn't have that at Great Ormond Street.

I don't doubt the other playworkers on the other wards were really brilliant practitioners who would have welcomed new ideas. I couldn't see it at the time but I think I hit bad luck because all my work was one-to-one in patients' bedrooms unlike on other wards where they were more often working as a team in the playroom, where the Reflective Practice would have come more naturally.

Instead of giving up on a potentially brilliant playwork opportunity, I wish I had had the confidence to say 'I am not coping. How can we make this better?' Does anyone have that amount of confidence to declare that amongst a group of strangers? I certainly didn't. I called in sick again and again and then eventually I did not go back.

For a while I carried with me a shadow of shame. I tormented myself: who gives up on Great Ormond Street? (Urm, probably loads of people!) As I moved on to community work I felt awkward answering my new colleagues when they casually asked, 'Where did you work before here?' And if ever I mentioned working in hospitals I had the double blow of explaining that I dropped out of nursing school AND then quit playwork at GOSH. Ouch.

It took years to brush it all off my shoulders and hold my head high again, but of course the time did come. I was delighted when a university friend and fellow play enthusiast Carla told me she had met Laura Walsh, the new Head of Play at GOSH, while attending a playwork conference in Eastbourne. 'I was telling her about you. I think you'd like her,' Carla reported back to me. I was strangely relieved and excited at the prospect of new energy in the play department. I don't even know why I cared so much! It was years since I had left London, and even longer since I had waved my little white flag at Purple Ward. I had no desire to move back to London and try to pick up where I had left off at GOSH but I was hopeful that new leadership would mean more creativity and genuinely meaningful play opportunities for the children being treated there.

A few months later I was in a Zoom meeting with some playworkers and up popped Laura on my screen. I squirmed in my seat and sweated because it felt a little bit like I was meeting a celebrity. She had no idea who I was and particularly that I had nose-dived out of my playwork role (mostly) because the play practice was so heart-wrenchingly dull. So it was music to my ears when she started describing lots of messy play and lots of child-led art. She talked about junk-modelled puppet shows, playing with light and shadows, lots of sensory art exploring textures, children building impressive structures around them while bed-bound and I heard about enough use of shiny fabric and lengths of ribbon to make me burst with all that brilliant juicy good stuff.

Now of course I know that their play practice is not about MY play needs or MY play preferences. But I am so pleased to know that the patients of Great Ormond Street Hospital, arguably some of the most unwell children in the country, if not the world, are being sprinkled with the magic of empowering free play and are being given more opportunities to explore their own creativity.

Out in the community

After GOSH I had a brief stint at a community development job that just didn't make sense to me. Like at university, I found myself in another structure of privilege where mostly white graduates were contracted by London boroughs to help 'grow communities'. We were shipped in from all over the country, working for a charity, so we thought we must have been helping. What a load of bollocks.

Some days I travelled ninety minutes from my home to talk to a small group of residents living in council houses to encourage them to start resident committees and develop community gardens. Sounds idyllic, what a lovely job. I knew shit all about their community, but they soon told me.

Each group I met used the opportunity to list all the issues of living in council housing with a landlord that just didn't care. The same landlord that was subcontracting thousands of pounds to a national charity to sort out their mess. And the charity was shaving off precious public funds to social-media campaigns, favourable salaries for the top dogs and for glossy publications to share all their success stories through case studies for the annual review.

It seemed to me like none of my senior colleagues or our clients cared about tackling the muggings, the needles, the noisy alcoholics, the human excrement in the communal corridors, the fly tipping, the kids climbing the roofs. (I usually forgot to report that because I'm all for teenagers, and for the record: younger children too, engaging in a bit of risky play.)

I was the project manager with a very limited budget for each site, no face-to-face time allocated to build trust in the all very unique communities that I was meant to be 'developing' and a bank of zero-hours gardeners who didn't want to work on these estates because they already knew about the shit going down, literally.

We all knew that a few raised beds built by some well-meaning outsiders were not going to change that community in the way the contract's outcomes had outlined. The consultation didn't raise much enthusiasm for food growing, so naturally I suggested engaging with the community through play. I wanted to redirect the budget from timber, soil and seeds and pay some playworkers to ignite the community through weekly play sessions for a minimum of six months.

Although the charity had been the driving force behind some huge play projects in East London linked to the London Olympics, my proposals were not even considered viable because they didn't fit on the project management software I was supposed to update to report back to our clients. That tedious 'Computer says no' is all I heard from my manager in our weekly reviews. No one wanted to listen to the people, even though the outcomes were clearly set out to improve the lives of the people. After the initial site visits, traipsing around estates miles away from our flat (I was reluctant to call it my 'home'), my momentum soon diminished as I unravelled the shambles of that community development role from my desk in a gloomy office in Angel.

I couldn't match my brainpower to that software. And I didn't have a team of colleagues to share my frustrations with. I just had a really crap manager who was always popping out to Pret and relentlessly telling me how much she loved the work that the charity did. Evidently, I was taking it all too seriously. Again. Just like at GOSH my mental health started to suffer. One morning after an early site visit to a little pocket of council flats near Holborn I sat in the gutter in panic. My body could no longer cope with the weight of the city. I was floored. Literally.

When the street stopped spinning, the darkness had lifted and the commuters that had been stepping over me had all disappeared off the streets, sat at their hot desks sipping their flat whites, I found an incy bit of calm. I raised my head from the cradle of my arms and realised I was sat opposite Holborn Police Station. I've no idea why, I guess I was desperate, I walked in and off-loaded onto a young man sat behind a glass screen, babbling incoherently about gardeners, urinated corridors and questionnaires. He just looked at me, helplessly nodding. I don't know what I was expecting; let's be real: if I was a young Black woman in the same state, there was a good chance I would have been sectioned.

That whole morning is still a blur but I know I spoke to him for quite a while and sat in their quiet waiting area for some time. I needed stillness. He gave me a glass of water. It was the biggest gesture of love I'd ever felt from a stranger. I eventually boarded the 68 and went home to bed and slept for sixteen hours straight. I learned to never underestimate the power of rest. A few weeks later I had handed in my notice. Again. I started counselling. Again.

Learning to listen

The more honest I've been with myself, mostly thanks to a fair bit of counselling, the more I have trusted myself. I was mortified that I wasn't coping with life in my mid-twenties.

Back then I was so ashamed to be seeking professional help; that fifty-minute slot each week was my dirty little secret. But over the weeks and months and years I really got my shit together and now I often encourage my friends to speak to a counsellor too. Not because I don't want to help them through their problems, but it is just so liberating to dump all your baggage on someone else who is totally detached from your life. There's no guilt, just off-loading and unpicking in private with no 'I know what's best for you' narrative from well-meaning friends and family.

Nearly all the middle-class Brazilians I met on my travels when I was eighteen had an hour with an English teacher once a week and an hour with a psychologist once a week. The first time I heard a friend casually say to a table of colleagues over lunch 'then my psychologist said that...', I almost choked on my Pão de Queijo.

I grew a lot in myself during those three years in London and I'll be the first to admit that sometimes growing hurts. My truth hurt me because I wasn't brave enough to buck a trend. With two counsellors, one through King's and another through my GP, I just didn't feel ready to be open with them, or more likely I just wasn't ready to be honest with myself. I darted around what was really bothering me and focussed on the ills of work-related stress. I attempted to keep it strictly scientific; reciting to them what I had read about with hormone imbalances, loneliness and the burnout of sedentary hunter-gatherer humans. I was desperate for their advice on how I could find a practical balance between work and play.

It was only when, on my third round of sessions with a small charity in Peckham Rye, that I was really honest with myself and my counsellor. I kept on circling back to one thing and one thing only: a hangover in Birmingham when I realised I really wanted to be a mom.

I retold her about a morning, and, like a few others after we moved from Lisbon to Birmingham, my head metamorphosed between dense concrete and fluttering feathers. My tummy felt as delicate as candy floss, my tongue brushed across furry teeth and I pretended to enjoy the mug of extra-milky, extra-comforting PG Tips. Between sips the triangle bag bobbed cheerily at the surface while I, myself, was drowning in doubt.

It was during that awkward summer before we moved to London when I started to feel outside of my own skin. I had sat on the cold leather sofa and couldn't get comfortable. Someone was hammering spikes through the sofa and into my back. On that morning, or probably afternoon as I was entitled to being selfishly timeless back then, a shift was taking place in my body. There was a feeling brewing, not the urge to sip the hair of the dog, but quite the opposite. As pints of orange squash and milky tea diluted the alcohol that had bombarded my body from the night before, a very particular feeling overcame me. By late afternoon I had silently decided that I didn't want the life I was living.

The feeling of purposelessness as I sat in my hungover state was nauseating. Maybe I was testing out whether or not I could handle morning sickness by manifesting it and

91

sitting with it all day. It didn't seem too bad so by the time the early evening sun had turned our ungenerous living room golden I looked out of the corner of the window, the only bit unblocked by the front hedge, and saw a woman pushing a buggy into the park on the opposite side of the road.

'I want a baby,' I said out loud.

'Are you still drunk?' my boyfriend replied plainly.

I sat on that uncomfortable sofa in our living room with a cheap Ikea fleece blanket over my legs and thought about the night before, and the night a few nights ago, and the night the weekend before. 'What the fuck? Is this my life now?' I scorned at myself. Only in Birmingham did I socialise this way and treat my own body so callously. I used to find it laughable, piecing together the antics from the night before; wondering which takeaway we'd gone to because a cocktail of sheesh kebab, katlama and mango Rubicon was repeating on me. But most disturbingly: how had I arrived home safely? And what had made me so sure I was safe?

So that day it all changed because somewhere in that hangover this unthinkable desire to have a baby uncurled and right then, in that moment, I had decided to stop drinking alcohol as if it was the first step towards treating my body like the life-giving temple it had been designed to be.

'Great if you have cut down on your alcohol consumption then; that is a really great thing for anyone who is experiencing anxiety or depression,' the counsellor said trying to comfort me.

And so, since that hangover in Brum two years earlier I had been ignoring this burning desire, suppressing one of the most natural urges of many women, because I was stuck in a conventionality that told me I wasn't ready yet. I poisoned myself with a narrative that I needed a secure job before having a baby.

I conveniently ignored the fact that loads of parents I had worked with in Birmingham didn't have steady work or had given it up when their child's care had taken precedence. I told the counsellor that my peers spoke of salaries and maternity packages and I was drawn to hourly rates just above the London Living Wage and the freedom to pick and choose my hours on zero-hours contracts. 'So what?' she challenged.

She helped me realise that I was an adult, a presumably fertile woman and I had a man in my life that I trusted and who cared deeply for me. But as I tried to be more and more adult I was stuck in a limbo between being fun-loving, careless and calm and the other me that was desperate to 'make something of myself' and achieve a level of financial security that was deemed reasonable to have a baby.

Without realising it I was so fundamentally uncomfortable in being stuck in the middle-class mould of white British life: finish school, go to college, go to uni, get a job, find love along the way, get married and/or buy a house, THEN have kids. I found this existence of many of my peers and family friends' kids painfully predictable and the prospect really quite petrifying that all the adventure I'd had as I journeyed into adulthood would be forgotten and my life would become so formulaic. And there lay the trigger of my anxiety and the biggest barrier to starting a family: being conventional.

On top of that, my yearning for a baby felt wildly unambitious when I had a world of opportunity at my fingertips.

I liked to think I wasn't so conformist but was well aware that the next stage of middle-class predictability was always looming. The assumptions from certain circles of what I was going to do next were suffocating. Mr Lowprofile lurked in the background of all this. His upbringing had forgiven him for not fitting my mould. He wasn't even aware there was a mould. And in my distracted state of desperately not wanting to be so predictably part of the mould, I had overlooked the fact that he was oblivious to my mould-avoidance. We were lost in translation: not with words, but with culture. 'Suffocating in middle-place predictability' was incomprehensible to a second-generation African immigrant who had recently settled in a new country.

This weird state of affairs meant that my early twenties were plagued with a shitty phase of taking life way too seriously. I did not play enough. I did not relax enough. I did not respect my body. 'Fun' had often involved excessive alcohol consumption, and when curiosity got the better of me, a few class As. This was fake play. It was a desperation to fit in disguised as fun. Yes, that hangover had put me off drinking and I had become almost teetotal, but that choice also alienated me from a lot of my peers. Meeting up with university friends, day or night, often meant drinking and on visits to Birmingham, nights down the pub were fun for the first couple of hours. I liked seeing familiar faces, but I soon hit my threshold for slurring drunken banter and the odour of boozy breath steaming in my face.

In London I eventually found my happy place, sober on dancefloors where the music let my body and my mind travel, or deep in conversation with other almost sober souls and the worldly perspective from the melting pot of humans that opted for the smaller, backstreet nightclubs in search of global beats.

Pre-Lisbon I had found a wonderful community dance class at a contemporary African dance school in Birmingham. The group that descended upon ACE Dance and Music in deepest, darkest Digbeth were mostly second-generation Caribbean women in search of their bit of carnival all year round.

The classes were fun, lighthearted and bubbling with intrinsically motivated movement. I loved that there were always apologetic late comers followed by their flock of children who settled in the corner with books and magazines. The older kids kept the younger kids from interrupting 'mommy's one hour'. Those mothers were prioritising their play, so in London I persevered with dance classes even though I often felt uncomfortable with the calibre of dancers at my side and out of my depth with the choreography. London was full of semi-professional dancers and Birmingham was full of moms wishing they could go out and dance all night. I was stuck in limbo somewhere between the two.

Through counselling I also came to realise that I was finding that London was a very difficult place for me to be spontaneous: ticketed events sold out before the box office even opened, everywhere and everyone took at least an hour to get to and my friends that had already established their young professional rhythm in the big smoke needed one month's notice to meet up. I realised that I had been desperate for a life where we could just pop in for a cup of tea, enjoy a homely, mid-week non-show-stopping-dinner-party meal together and laze in the living rooms we were all paying extortionate rents for but hardly using.

The pace of London exhausted me – the commuting, the crowds, the pavements full of people rushing day and night. I had never been so keen to stay at home and rest! But I kept on persevering with going out and exploring because everyone else my age appeared to be having a great time ticking off all Time Out's must-see, must-do, must-try, must-embody, must-eat, must-drink lists. I can see now that my life wasn't full of freely chosen, intrinsically motivated decisions, so I can see I was suffering from play deprivation.

Like a teenager who did loads of sport through their teens then suddenly put on loads of weight when they stopped as a young adult, I had loads of free play in my youth and then got weighed down, heavy, when I stopped. When I didn't play my mind and body suffered the ills of play deprivation more than say, Mr Lowprofile, whose experience of play was very different from mine. He had had less free play, and as a consequence didn't seem to have the same yearning to play as I did in London.

The same can be said for community: I had a huge sense of place in a handful of communities in Birmingham and Leeds. Even in Montreal I felt connected to the place because each time I visited and went out with my brother or sister we would bump into someone they knew, and everyone made the time to stop and chat. In Lisbon and London I lost the familiarity: I felt like a local because I was working and commuting on a daily basis but I didn't have a tribe to call upon.

Though he loved me unconditionally through that period of wobbles in London, Mr Lowprofile absolutely could not understand what all my stress was about. Despite his presence, I felt very alone. I honestly cherished that he sat at my side each time I fretted about having steady work and a steady home, but he just didn't know what to say. He was lost in my maths of having a job and our own home to equal the correct time to have a baby. My maths did not add up. His formula was different. My conventional was different from his conventional.

Slowing down

A vice of being nomadic is the burden of finding a sense of place, belonging and becoming part of the community; I was transient and therefore unaccepted with real Londoners. But I can pinpoint now that what suited me best about that city was that there was space to be unconventional. Sure, the radical nonconformists have all had their buildings bulldozed to make way for luxury apartments. But the melting pot of people, eventually, allowed me to escape anxieties about not coping with middle-class conventionality. However, I wasn't a night owl so despite the intoxicating nightlife of afrobeat, funk n soul and hip hop the daytimes often felt lonely. But I did eventually find my peace with London, and now thoroughly enjoy being a visitor to what is, in small doses, an incredibly enchanting city.

Under the counsellor's advice I practised being kind to myself. I stopped forcing myself out to every free event, gallery or mini festival. I listened to what I really wanted to do which was sit at home and read. I borrowed books from Camberwell library and much to Mr Lowprofile's delight I stayed home with him and watched films and documentaries and whatever other gems we found to project onto our living-room wall.

One twenty-minute clip massively changed my perspective. Would I go so far as to say it changed my life? Maybe. I fell in love with TED Talks. They were fresh and thought-provoking: the best thing since sliced bread. I particularly liked the TEDx local events because I found ordinary people talking about the extraordinary things they were doing or ideas they had.

Yes, with TED Talks at the tap of my fingertips I had no need for a spiritual epiphany on some international retreat; I just booted up my chunky old laptop that used to make a whirring noise louder than our washing machine... And voila! I heard about the slow movement from a TED Talk. A twenty-minute talk by some Canadian dude that didn't want to rush bedtime stories with his kid. I was desperate to read bedtime stories to my child-that-hadn't-even-been-conceived-yet and vowed I would never rush bedtime nor any part of their precious day. Playwork had taught me the powerful lesson of embracing the pace that each child set, meeting them where they were, and that TED Talk reminded me that children deserve to live without the pressurised time limits that adults, particularly in the west, put upon themselves.

And so, to honour the unrushed pace I wanted to pursue with my future family I vowed to stop rushing myself.

Mr Lowprofile will not be rushed. Ever. There is absolutely no rushing him, so much so that soon after we met, and he was piecing together all my travels and all the work I'd been doing in Birmingham, he told me 'Woah you need to slow down or you will be burnt out by the time you are thirty.' Well, I even rushed my burnout because I managed to do that by the time I was twenty-six.

Mr Lowprofile was working a seven-minute walk from our flat on Camberwell Green. He liked living 'in London' but he barely left Camberwell. I wanted a slice of his pie so in my commitment to slowing down, and therefore living with less panic, I decided I would do *any* job that was within 2 miles from our home. And preferably shift work because I didn't like routine. Did it work? Ohhhhh yes. My new slower lifestyle meant that I would only need to walk or cycle during the week and go further afield on weekends or on very special occasions.

Well within my two-mile radius rule I found a family on Gumtree that needed a part-time nanny with preference to someone who was willing to cycle. Bingo. They were suitably unconventional; I spent most of my interview on a trampoline in their garden throwing leaves into the air which had fallen from their neighbour's tree. I was offered the job and on the Sunday before I started the dad took me on a test drive of their beloved Christiania cargo tricycle which was their preferred mode of transport for their two girls. He pedalled me to their daughter's school nearly 2 miles away, and then I pedalled him home again to prove I knew the route and could manoeuvre the moving vehicle.

I had grown a soft spot for cargo tricycles when I helped convert one into a mobile kitchen with Brixton People's Kitchen the previous year. Christianias are the Rolls Royce of trikes; I felt like I should have been wearing a chauffeur's hat and gloves when I pedalled my boss home through Kennington Park.

I was more of a private playworker than a nanny. I was delighted that the family valued open-ended child-led play and time outdoors as much as I did. It was my dream job and my happiest way to commute. One day after school I squeezed in seven kids to the box on the front of the tricycle and did laps around Myatts Field. Apparently, it was better than donkey rides at the beach.

While Mary Poppins had the other servants of the Banks' household, I was not in such company. I didn't really have any colleagues which I actually felt quite relieved about. I had free rein to organise play dates with their friends and on the way home from the school run we often swung by local parks and Lollard Street Adventure Playground which was the first adventure playground in Lambeth. It had moved from the original site which opened in 1955 on a derelict bombsite in good view of the Houses of Parliament, strategically in view of the decision makers who could look out across the Thames to watch children playing with junk. Nowadays it is unthinkable that an acre of land in Zone 1 could be left derelict for a decade after the war ended. It was most certainly the golden age where residents weren't fighting land-grabbing developers for every last inch of community space, and children played out for hours without their parents helicoptering over them.

I liked working by myself and got my fix of community as I regularly chatted to familiar faces on the playground. In the parks I sensed that parents were almost queuing up to have a bit of company with someone outside the mom bubble. The stay-at-home moms were all really honest with me; they were desperate to get back to their careers. They made me lunches from their Ocado deliveries and they each relayed why they hadn't gone back to work yet like I was judging them for being at home. For all I knew they could have been trying to piece together why this multilingual graduate with all such worldly experience was *just* a nanny.

I even met a mom who was a researcher in Labour Markets and her area of interest was the exploitation of Eastern European women employed as private nannies to wealthy families in West London. She'd never met a British nanny before and she kept on apologising for asking questions that sounded like she was interviewing me.

These little insights into parenthood over cups of tea in Camberwell fascinated me. It was weird because I actually got to know these other moms and dads better than my own employers. I cherished being part of a family, and hanging out with other young families. This little taster of motherhood reinforced that yearning that had been tugging at me for four years since that weird hangover was no longer to be ignored. Mr Lowprofile was as encouraging and relaxed about my decision as ever. I started tracking the days of my cycle and taking a daily dose of folic acid. While I had found my peace with the city that had caused me so much pain, we agreed that we weren't particularly keen on starting a family in London. And so we planned our escape...

Part 3 - Motherhood, mother good.

What if we bring new parents bountiful boxes of brunch and nutritious snacks instead of baby grows?

'Shit just got real' I texted a few friends with our first scan photo.

'Shiiiiiiiiiiiiiiiiiiiit!' more than one replied.

It was good to have a sense of humour about all this very serious stuff that was happening inside of me.

At our second scan when the sonographer asked if I wanted to purchase the printed photos I replied, 'No thanks'. I glanced towards Mr Lowprofile who was sat next to the hospital bed. 'I'll just send his mom my sister's scan photo.' He lowered his head, feeling awkward by my terribly dark humour. 'She won't know the difference. And no one else really cares about the second scan photo.'

I felt her grimace a little; she clearly didn't know if I was joking or not, and she obviously took her job very seriously. A minute or so after we had left the room, she chased us down the corridor and waved a strip of paper in front of me. 'Here you go, I just couldn't bear to think of Grandma looking at the wrong baby.'

Oh, I do like to be beside the seaside

In cities with large populations there were plenty of like-minded peers for me to choose from. But when I moved to Bournemouth this didn't appear to be the case. I had never lived anywhere so conservative and Conservative before. It was also very English, and by English I mean polite, well-to-do and conformist. Though I was swept away by the breathtaking views over to the Purbecks, and my sea swims at the end of our road, I just couldn't help finding Bournemouth rather dull.

I found it tricky to make friends when I moved to Dorset. But of course, with time I began to find small circles of people united over common interests. Little gatherings of the left of centre folk; the activists, the spiritually inclined (though not particularly religious) and the artists. A collective of rebels bobbing along in a sea of blue. My instinct told me that there weren't enough nonconformists around to be ageist so I began to socialise with a wider age range than I was used to in London or Lisbon. Back in Brum I always liked a chat with my friends' parents and my parents' friends. With none of them on my doorstep I was grateful to keep finding more and more harmonious groups of respectful people, where age just wasn't an issue.

Not too far from us lived a friend of a friend who I'd raved with a few times while up north. I hadn't seen Matt since our uni days and he was living a far more settled existence with his girlfriend Sarah and then three-year-old son Ronnie. We warmed to their gentle Sunday afternoons on the beach, popping into pubs, and late and relaxed dinners all with their three-year-old adding his life and soul. I guess back then we were the cherished and refreshing friends who subconsciously accepted that they would bring their baby whatever the occasion.

When my older brother visited us from Montreal he commented 'I don't really hang out with anyone who is not my age.' He, my nephew and my younger brother and his girl-friend were part of a fairly spontaneous bank holiday get-together on the beach where around sixty friends and friends-of-friends and their families gathered to enjoy a fine summer's eve together. That evening I silently honoured the full force of my villagers around me.

As uniformly as Britons switch on the kettle at 7 am each morning, at 6 pm all along Bournemouth's nine-mile stretch of sand, tiny flames begin to flicker from beach-goers' BBQs. It was just after six o'clock when three generations of Bour-mouthians and visitors gravitated to the shore in the late afternoon sunshine. We respectfully obeyed the 'No BBQs before 6 pm' rule even though hungry children with hearty sea air appetites had already been nagging their parents for food. Much to the kids' approval our small BBQs dotted around the sand began to glaze orange as the smell of lighter fluid and just-struck matches rose into the cloudless expanse of blue above.

I couldn't name all the people there but the youngest in attendance that evening was Matt and Sarah's daugh-ter Maya. She was only seven weeks and placid wrapped against her mother's chest. She barely made a peep all evening which gave Sarah and me the chance to enjoy some much-needed giggles together over ginless tonic water.

Matt was the biggest kid there. He is a gentle giant, a kind and friendly bloke that despite his slight stammer can start a conversation with anyone. He holds traditional values around good old-fashioned outdoor play, but is a modern dad who wanted to reduce his working hours in order to share the childcare at the end of Sarah's maternity leave. He's a proper outdoorsy type who loves building dens in the woods and digging holes in the sand.

That afternoon he and Ronnie, who was fast approaching his fifth birthday, had embarked on their biggest architectural challenge yet. With a garden shovel and his child attached to his bicycle, the two of them had popped down to the beach to prepare for our soiree. Between them they built, or more specifically, had dug a huge circular sofa around a raised platform which would now home the fire.

Amongst the flock were a few local drummers; they ceremoniously beat djembes and dun duns as the fire was lit. The tribal children mimicked the flames as they moved to the beat of the drums and the sedentary adults cheered on the older movers and the shakers of the pack. Even the teenagers let their guard down and enjoyed the freedom of expression in this non-judgemental gathering.

The children didn't keep still long enough to count them. But as daylight disappeared around them, these tireless warriors played until they could no longer see each other. When it was too dark to see their friends' faces they retreated and slouched onto the sofa by the fire, none too shy to vocalise their expectation that surely an adult had remembered to bring marshmallows.

The Canadian tourists who were visiting a Bournemouth-based great aunt for a few days announced that they called them 'S'mores' back home. And through sticky mouthfuls explained how they usually sandwiched the gooey charred marshmallow between two biscuits. 'How peculiar,' we responded; biscuits should really only be dunked in tea.

So from seven weeks to sixty- or seventy-something our flock of nomads partied until the last block of firewood scorched and then vanished into the embers. I wasn't aware of alcohol or drugs consumed that night; I was seven months pregnant and certainly didn't feel I was missing out on another-level party. My jolly, and I am pretty sure I wasn't alone, was created by gently crashing waves, the intermittent jam of drums and voices, human laughter, the crackle of the glowing fire and the scent of charcoal encroaching into our cardigans that would linger like a hangover the next day.

A major feature of Bournemouth beach life was the organisation around food. Wow, the food! Though bags of coal were circulated amongst the villagers, everyone seemed to naturally self-organise around their own little cluster of shopping bags and portable grills. The evening sun shone over feasting families; plastic picnic plates piled up with grilled goodies accompanied by spoonfuls of salads scooped out of mismatch tupperwares and reused takeaway boxes. I chuckled as all the children across the entire village were banished from each micro banquet for fear of clumsy feet contaminating the feast with sand.

In one part of the village I enjoyed a row of small faces, all with dishevelled sandy hair, and bodies panting from running so wild and free in the sand. Each one chomped on the ray of sunshine; a grilled cob of corn between their grainy mits. Molten butter dripped down each chin and skins of kernels wedged into a mix of milk teeth and gnashers. Except for one child who had no front teeth. He gallantly pushed his tongue through his gap trying to catch the drips of butter before he went cross-eyed and lost his aim.

At a safe distance from the sandy children we adults tucked into ranging levels of culinary dedication. Some had bought simple minted lamb burgers from the closest supermarket. Others had well anticipated a barbeque over the bank holiday and smugly brought three-day marinated ribs. One family trumped us all with picture-perfect whole tilapia. And then some of the villagers, to much heckling from the marinaters and the pescatarians, cheated and let the Jamaican takeaway on the high street grill their jerk chicken for them. They didn't take much notice as they triumphantly plonked themselves down and pulled from their brown paper bag an ice-cold can of Ting.

'No fuss required,' announced the villager in a deep West African accent and a broad, broad smile. I didn't know the man but enjoyed his loud chatter with anyone who cared to sit down next to him. He waved his arms, smacked his thigh occasionally and started most sentences with a loud astounding 'Eh! Chale!' and ended most with a gasping 'Ah'. He must be Ghanaian I thought and fondly remembered the banter at local drinking spots where I tucked into kebabs of grilled goat rolled in chilli powder and sipped on small glasses of Star beer most Friday and Saturday (and Tuesday and Wednesday and Thursday nights), while studying at the University of Ghana in Legon.

The festivities finally drew to a close around midnight. Even my jetlagged nephew declared he was ready for bed so we poured seawater over the hot embers; their sizzle closed our ceremony. As the last few standing we walked together slowly up the clifftop.

It was a magical evening and I was pleased to have shared it with my brothers as part of their little holiday at the British seaside. My siblings meeting my community of brothers and sisters was a silent validation of the extended family I had around me. I cherished walking alongside the mother that headed home with her three-year-old asleep in the buggy. We talked about the importance of families coming together like our parents did in the old days. She said she didn't do it much since she'd had her son but liked being around a fire, sharing stories and seeing young and old together. 'Wise words,' I thought; she and the other mothers that evening unveiled to me how important it was for mothers to be out amongst their villagers, even if it meant bringing the baby.

My prenatal courses

Just as our route out of Lisbon had been my nursing course, our exit out of London was aided by Mr Lowprofile being accepted onto a course with the School of Health & Social Care at Bournemouth University. He also bagged a place at Sheffield Hallam and I was thrilled at the thought of moving back to Yorkshire. But my spirits were dampened on one very soggy visit up north; I knew the weather would well and truly make the decision for us. One interview took us to a very gloomy Steel City and the other was on a glorious crisp winter's day. A short walk from the interview room we sat on a clifftop bench and watched the sea shine all shades of bold

green with crashing waves dancing about the feet of the Purbecks. We were sold.

A year and half later he was approaching the end of his
course. I'd spent every spare moment of my day inhaling sea
air which made a monumental shift in my mental health and
I was blooming. I felt healthy. Being pregnant felt right. A
lot had happened in the five years since that revelationary
hangover, more than two years of nil contraception and one
miscarriage. We had been patiently waiting and I felt so ready.
I enjoyed my body changing and I made sure that I enjoyed
every last bit of independence that I could. Healthy, happy,
pregnant women are left to feel a bit guilty and sometimes I
felt resented. My colleague used to ask me when I was going
to stop cycling to work?

'When I can't reach the handle bars anymore,' I cheered
back.

I was so thankful that I had my sister's recent positive
birthing stories to hold close to my heart while strangers I
encountered loved to moan and grumble, sharing their horror
story or two and how long and complicated their labour was,
how much it hurt, how painful it is to walk, sit, lift another
biscuit up to their mouth in the weeks after.

Some days I felt like screaming, 'I am growing a tiny
human inside me, and if she is a girl then my eggs are inside
her ovaries, so she is already carrying my grandchild, can we
please take a moment to recognise how bloody brilliant this
is?'

I was buzzing from all that brilliant juicy good stuff
that growing life can bring. Throughout my pregnancy I

continued to do all the things that I loved about living in Bournemouth: the cycling and the sea swims and my dance classes. Of course, I'd cycled and swum and danced in London, but it was the backdrop of the sea that was missing for me in the Big Smoke.

I think it also helped that we didn't buy into all the baby stuff either. We pleaded for records instead of baby grows as gifts. We hoped to build a music education from our community, not an introduction to fast fashion. As we prepared to move into our little family home – upgrading from a one bed flat, to two – we scoured Pinterest for 'vinyl storage in small spaces' instead of 'nursery' or 'baby's bedroom inspiration'.

With the money we'd saved on parent preparation courses and the cash we knew we wouldn't spend on brand-new baby paraphernalia I spent a long weekend in Sweden when I was five months pregnant. It was to be my last solo adventure; though I very much felt the presence of my growing travel companion. My girlfriend Maya, who serves herbal tea with endless, unrushed conversation, had moved from Stockholm to Malmö. I had met her working in a backpackers' hostel in Lisbon. I didn't tell her I was pregnant before my arrival; I enjoyed seeing and feeling her reaction when my bump and I (and my extra chin) rocked up at Malmö Central Station.

She had a spare bicycle, most Swedes do, and I spent five magical days absorbing how so many wonderfully playful Swedish parents embrace life around other adults in adult places with their kids in tow. We took several slow bike rides along smooth cycle lanes, picked up produce from Möllevångstorget and drank mocktails up the sky bar. Around every corner were more families, all shades and colour combinations, tootling around on bikes n trikes, enjoying cafes, outdoor dance classes and thoughtful, desirable, secure communal gardens bustling with life in between tower blocks. On every bike ride I spotted playgrounds and little nooks to play. Maya made sure we cycled most of the city over the five days. I took in the industrial, the natural, the history, the modern and all the humans. There were places to meet and to play and to eat everywhere around the lively, but far from chaotic, city.

Most memorable was the sunny afternoon we spent at the Ribersborg bath house where (mostly) naked women of all shapes and sizes circulated in and out of the sauna and into the cold, cold river with toddlers and baby bumps pottering about with them. There was no hoo-hah about the pregnant mamas going in the sauna and no fuss about the children being in a 'place where adults go to relax'. Do I go as far as to say that I think every British birth preparation course should include a long weekend in Malmö? Yes, I think I do.

Even the jumble sale we stumbled across in the shared gardens of a block of flats had a live DJ playing out of his window while his newborn slept tied to his chest. Tribes of barefoot kids weaved in and out of the semi-partitioned lawns. The block was a hub of grassroots community activity; I liked it. It didn't seem as if anyone's motivation was to shop. Mugs of tea and cake were being passed around amongst neighbours for community Fika, and a few musicians jammed on the lawn (the opposite end from the DJ). I could have stocked up on some really cute (and bargain) Scandy children's wear but instead I opted for a very special first edition 1967

Miriam Makeba's *Pata Pata* record for about a fiver and a bump-friendly stretchy Zara blazer for the equivalent of £2. Happy Mama.

By choosing a home birth early on I was fortunate to have all my prenatal appointments at our home with the same midwife. This was golden and I've learned since that it is extremely rare in the NHS. At the time the home birth 'team' consisted of just two wonder women. I was disappointed that after every single appointment with Karen she was on annual leave when I went into labour.

I felt so comfortable with Karen, she reminded me of my friend Carla: petite with empowering body language. Their shoulders sat effortlessly strong and poised with unassuming confidence, their smiles human, and their identical nose studs that twinkled from their button noses in harmony with their smiling eyes.

Most importantly for me neither woman had ever appeared uncomfortable in the company of Mr Lowprofile; some find his reserved demeanour unsettling, like they are intruding on his space. But Karen and Carla were never phased by his introverted way and built a natural rapport with him.

Karen was always straight-talking and smiling, even when there were minor concerns with my blood levels. She reinforced my belief that I would birth at home. On the morning after we moved into our new flat, when I was 37 weeks, she examined me on our sofa bed in a living room full of Lidl banana boxes and overflowing Ikea bags. Not only had our baby gone breech, after previously being desirably head down

114

for weeks, Karen told me quite frankly that I couldn't give birth at home if the flat continued to 'look like this'.

I thought 'give me a bloody chance bab we only moved in twelve hours ago,' but in hindsight I think she was actually trying to kick Mr Lowprofile into action.

Poor sod, a few days earlier he had fallen off his bicycle on the way to work and dislocated *and* fractured his shoulder. We were a right useless pair! Waddling and hobbling, we'd called upon everyone we could think of to clean both our old and new flat, decorate, and move all our stuff in. It was a real village effort and great preparation for calling upon our villagers once our baby arrived.

In the approach to my due date, well-meaning hand-me-down baby clobber started piling in from all directions. Our tiny flat in Boscombe suddenly had little piles of supermarket bags brimming with clothes and other gizmos. Baby clothes are a puzzling commodity. Yo fashionistas, our daughter loves being naked. And I love her being starkers because it means a lot less laundry and I can sneak a stroke of her deliciously soft skin anytime she's within reach.

Yes, babies need to be kept warm but endless tiny garments on top of the mountain of other baby gadgets were puzzling. We really questioned why a tiny precious newborn needed volumes of brand-new clothes (it seemed that even the most composed of our friends went giddy for the tiny ranges of Autumn/Winter 2016) and toys that are mostly mass produced by other people's children slaving away in sweatshops. The international obsession with buying stuff needs to change and I think we should start with the peculiar phenomenon of

115

dressing babies in clothes that replicate adults' clothing and even worse restrict their movement; what ever happened to babies wearing baby grows?

To the families that are obsessing over baby outfits and children's wear, I urge you to consider a new hobby (naked dancing?) and buy some Premium Bonds with the money you save. Believe me, the novelty of opening an envelope disguised as a credit-card bill only to find a winning twenty-five-pound cheque has never worn off.

The record collections didn't really take off except for one lovingly sourced charity shop gem from my bestest Brummie down south, an absolute wonder woman and mother of three. Rachel has her tea with 'just a bitta coconut milk in so it looks like bad fake tan. Ta bab'. She popped over in mid-December when our baby had safely arrived and was eight or nine weeks old. She brought with her a homemade saag aloo curry – 'I'll pop it in tha freezer for when you *really* need it bab!' – and a copy of UB40's *Labour of Love*.

I was beside myself. 'Our first record bab!' I shrieked. (Yes, we really do say bab at the end of most sentences.) I couldn't help but hold it close to my heart. The wide surface of the sleeve smothering my baby and crushing her between my beatin' heart and my Brummie heart. I don't even consider myself much of a UB40 fan, not that I dislike them but they weren't the soundtrack to my childhood like I imagine they were for many across our city. Turns out that the record was warped. It kinda made me love it more.

Rachel and I have grown an extremely valuable friendship bonding over brightly coloured fabric, all things Brum and a love of drum n bass. And even though they lived a good drive away in deepest darkest rural Dorset, her strong girls, who were aged 3, 5 & 7 when mine was born, quickly became her surrogate sisters. She reaffirmed my belief that women should mother together, helping each other to share the burden.

She was once a painter-decorator and so she was one of the many villagers we summoned to help us make our house a home when I was too pregnant, and Mr Lowprofile's upper body was too broken, to do it alone.

It was well and truly a race against time; 37 weeks and counting. Rachel worked like a trooper that fortnight to get the place 'lookin' propa'. We sat back to admire the fresh coat in the living room. She was chilling in the Ikea rocking chair and I was bobbing about on the birthing ball.

She sighed. 'Oh bab, you'd better let me paint 'em skirting boards tomorra. Trust me you'll be staring at 'em for the next 10 months, at all hours of the day and night just wishin they were all the same shade a brilliant white. It'll drive ya mad.' Oh, the gifts of sisterhood: saag aloo and same shade skirting boards!

A few days after the skirting boards were painted uniform, at 40 weeks minus 5 days my big sister came to visit me from Brum with her third child who was nearly three months old. It was the first time since just before her firstborn had arrived, nearly four years earlier, that we have had several consecutive hours of uninterrupted conversation. We took a very quick frolic in the flat grey sea, staying close to the shore, while my niece slept oblivious in the buggy on the sand. The sea air kept her asleep most of their visit which meant I got my sister all to myself.

We ate pizza outdoors at Boscombe Pier while her baby remained in deep slumber and then indulged in pints of decaf tea, with just a dash of milk, on the sofa. All the while her baby was sound asleep. I think babies know when their moms need a really good chat. My sister marvelled at how much better her tea tasted when she could drink it without the constant interruption from her brood. Grey skies, tea and sea, it was all very ordinary, but with my big sister it was magic. For nearly four years I'd observed her every mothering move, subliminally surveilled the systems she'd set up around her house and taken note of the things she'd always packed in the baby bag, or cursed herself for forgetting. I don't feel like we ever spent hours and hours mulling over the ins and outs of what to do with a baby, but sitting and watching her muddle through all those years and still be good company was a comforting message that I'd muddle through too.

What is more she had birthed two ten-pound babies at home; her mere presence was all the preparation I needed for a happy home birth. She drove back again along the A34 five days later so her three kids could meet their new cousin and see the sea. What a surreal week.

Dance like nobody's watching

I was incredibly fortunate to have discovered a dance teacher that I trusted with my expanding body and my growing child. She was a mother of two and a respected practitioner who encouraged me to listen to my body and enjoy the movement when I kept on dancing through each trimester.

In her classes she used the Loketo technique for breathing and grounding that she'd learned with Zab Maboungou, a Congolese and contemporary dancer and founder of the acclaimed Zab Maboungou/Compagnie Danse Nyata-Nyata based in Montreal. Natasha invested in her students to share an appreciation of breathwork like no other teacher I have learned with. The focus on the breath is probably why I was able to keep up with classes right until I was thirty-six weeks pregnant.

Just before we conceived I was at my fittest I've ever been. Through running, cycling, swimming and yoga I enjoyed the connection I had with my body. I didn't feel the need to let it all go just because I was pregnant. I, of course, had to slow down and modify my movements. It took me a little while to adjust to using my body less. I was totally gutted when my yoga teacher Ellie gave me other positions to do when I went to my first class, with child, around 9 weeks; I begrudgingly stopped going to her classes after that and found Pregnancy Yoga at the back of the huge Tesco, a horrible place to practise. So I stuck to cycling, slowed my run to walk and kept dancing. I didn't ever feel as if I overdid it. I listened to my body and I acknowledged my limits. I felt a deeper connection to my body and consequently felt empowered as my womb filled with joy and my tummy rose with love. 'This is what my body was designed to do,' I told myself as my pregnancy progressed healthily.

I loved dancing in the Seafront Studio at Pavillion Dance South West, one of Bournemouth's dance schools. In the summer months we flung the large doors open to let the sea breeze in and cool our moving torsos. When I needed to rest I'd stand against the doorway and catch glimpses of our beautiful ocean (Mr Lowprofile always teases me for calling the English Channel an 'ocean') and the Purbecks stacked beyond the horizon. One warm evening after class I gently mounted my bicycle and glided past the rainbow of beach huts and back home along the seafront to Fisherman's Walk. I arrived there fairly effortlessly but I just couldn't face pushing my bicycle and my bump up the 100ft zig zag clifftop path to home. I sat for a while and rubbed my neat bump, figuring out my next move and soaked up the sounds of the evening shoreline.

I realised I was hungry. Really hungry. I'd had a busy day and I was not prepared to work my body any more than was comfortable. The seafront kiosk selling chips and ice creams was already closed so I called Mr Lowprofile, who thankfully wasn't working a late shift, to come meet us at sea level. 'And bring a banana.'

I wasn't quite a Damsel in Distress but I knew my limits. My Knight in Shining Armour said he liked, from time to time, to feel needed by his otherwise fiercely independent wife. He was only too glad to push my bike up the steep ascent and get us home safely.

Another warm Wednesday evening that September I waddled off the bus and down to the class. I wasn't expecting to move much. I just wanted to lap up the atmosphere and forget about moving house for an hour. At the end of the class Natasha reminded me that I could use Loketo in my labour, 'you know, only if you want to... Keep it in mind, the deep breathing and the grounding movements will help.'

It never would have occurred to me to use a contemporary African dance technique in labour; but her advice stuck with me and Loketo I did!

Through labour we danced in our living room, in our corridor, I gripped and pushed against the doorways: grounding through the intensity of the contractions with Loketo breaths. 'Lo-Ke-To,' I puffed, grounding down on the 'Lo', bending my knees on the 'Ke' and groaned out the 'Tooooooo'. 'Lo-Ke-To.'

It felt all kinds of magical that my dance classes had prepared me for labour. Between contractions we swayed to popular Brazilian bossa nova songs, and lesser known upbeat rhythms of Cape Verdean funaná and coladeira.

We still weren't totally sure that Bournemouth was our home, but one thing I was certain of all the way through was that I wanted to have a home birth. I was of the mindset that women have been birthing in bushes and caves for thousands of years so why do we need medical interventions? I'm the first to agree this is indeed narrow-minded given all the health scares women face in labour. And having heard several birth stories, I feel incredibly fortunate to have experienced a pleasant and straightforward pregnancy.

I read the introduction to a hypnobirthing book which I found useful because it poo-pooed clinical tendencies such as birthing on your back and other mostly male physician-led practices. I wanted a home birth as I knew that is where

I would feel most relaxed, and couldn't see why I could complicate my birthing day by traipsing off to a birth suite when I could have a highly skilled midwife at my beck and call.

On the sixth of October 2016, I woke myself up with pangs coming from my midsection. There was a deep drum beat calling for my attention. I rolled over and ignored it, only to be disturbed again a little while later. I reached across the bed and shook Mr Lowprofile, 'Começou,' I hissed. It has begun.

We lay there for a while not sure what to do. 'Are you sure?' he enquired.

I think I was a bit annoyed that he was querying my maternal instinct. I felt suitably awakened to Mother Nature's power within me: of course, it was the start of my labour. 'Oh, amor it is 4 am and all I can think about is washing up and cleaning the kitchen. Of course, this is it.' And I rolled out of bed to make a cuppa and don the marigolds.

The pleasant arrival of a small baby girl around tea time ensured we served a high tea of buttered crumpets and Earl Grey to our superwoman midwife Shona. She respectfully honoured our space and the vibrancy we chose to create. Our home was a celebration of a long-awaited addition to our family.

Yep, just one midwife, not because we were stingy with our crumpets but because the home birth team were short-staffed that day and the community stand-in only rocked up once our little water baby had splashed out into the pool. Luckily Mr Lowprofile is a fellow NHS hero so, despite his fractured shoulder, he willingly pulled up his healthcare professional sleeves. Well, almost willingly, I had to help his fragile shoulder out of his hoody as he clumsily transformed into my midhusband. While Shona focussed on recording my vital signs, he scooped out poo from the birth pool.

I had no idea women in labour are so prone to pooing. We went to three birth preparation classes at the hospital and I really would have liked to have heard 'Blokes, you might shit your pants at the thought of being a birth partner, but don't be scared, your Mrs will probably shit herself too so you're evens stevens!'

Broken nipples

In the first forty-eight hours of being a mother I was on a crazy ecstatic high with oxytocin radiating so much we could see it bouncing off the walls I had to swerve to ensure the rays didn't hit the baby. I was smug. It didn't last. I dipped into mayhem sharpish.

If I was a first-time mom again, I'd want to spend my pregnancy meeting moms who wanted to breastfeed, struggled to breastfeed and either got through it or found a loving way to embrace bottle-feeding. Through pregnancy I didn't really consider an alternative; 'breast was best' and would be the continuum of my expected natural birth.

I associated tins of milk formula with Nestlé, a brand my mom had boycotted since the early 1980s when aggressive marketing campaigns brainwashed poor women in poverty-stricken countries to buy milk powder. Not only did these women have very limited disposable incomes, but most alarmingly to me was that access to safe drinking water was limited and so there was higher risk of the babies ingesting contaminated water mixed with formula. Nasty business. I don't remember our mom snapping at us much unless me or my little brother picked out a Nestlé product in the supermarket: 'No! Put it back,' in disgust that we had touched something so foul. Before I placed non-supermarket brand items in the trolley she showed me where on the packaging to check the manufacturer; this has become a lifelong habit of mine and I'll be doing the same with our daughter.

Breastfeeding was my normal; our mom publicly breastfed four children. I didn't see many other babies as a child so without giving it much thought I perceived that dolls had bottles and babies had boobs.

We have holiday photos of my sister and brother, maybe aged three and one, hanging off each boob each while on the beach in Greece. And another snap nearly ten years later of me and my then baby brother, again on a beach in Greece, also indulging in a breast each; history repeating itself.

My dad used to joke that 'when I grow up I am going to be a photographer', which always made me chuckle in that way that kids chuckle when adults tell jokes that aren't really all that funny. I chuckled probably more out of curiosity, or maybe this was an early attempt to decipher irony. He was evidently a grown-up and he took ages to position us, get the angle right, tell us which way to look, assume a natural pose, slowly turn to look at the camera and say 'Riiiiittttttaaaaaaa' as he pressed click on his chunky SLR to snap a photograph.

We'd then wait weeks or months to revisit that moment when we all muttered 'Riiiiittttttaaaaaaa'. Apparently, our mom's name was a more natural way to produce a smile than 'Cheeeeessssseeeeeee'. He has stacks of shoe boxes, piled up in cupboards at home. The boxes all have handwritten years on, and inside they are bursting with envelopes of photos and negatives.

The special photos were promoted out of the envelopes and into albums which sit on a bookcase on the left-hand side of my parents' bedroom. There is a crimson case of four albums with gold detail and Roman numerals I II III IV on each spine. When I was younger this boxset shone brighter than the rest like a prize Red Delicious dangling in the middle of an orchard. My chubby hands used to grab the box down from the bookcase and I'd leaf through each photo asking my mom where were we, how old was I and why do we not stay babies?

Quite a few of those photos are of my mom breastfeeding with her breasts unashamedly exposed. As a self-obsessed middle child I wasn't too fussed to look at my siblings' equivalent albums. I know they exist but to this day I can't remember the colour, shape or size. When I was pregnant I fondly returned to this bookcase and gently flicked through my first years where I was subliminally reminded that women breastfeed their offspring.

By day four my initial high plummeted into what turned out to be the most intensely demanding and often heart-wrenching few weeks of my life. At night in those early weeks I used to lie in bed, unable to sleep, my body tensely awaiting her beckoning. Her razor-sharp tongue had split my left nipple in two and left the right one tattered and weeping.

Deep, deep inside I knew that I wanted to breastfeed, but my equipment was broken. Jutting out from the most poised part of my body were two scorching hot, fine-china tea pots, each with a chipped spout. In labour each contraction had been just about bearable, I wish I could have said the same for each latch.

I wanted so desperately to nourish our daughter with my liquid gold but at the start of each feed my toes curled and my body tensed. A tormenting sting shot through each nipple where her tongue had torn the thick, rubbery skin. Hot tears rolled down my burning cheeks as my teeth gritted between my locked jaw. This went on for weeks because at the end of each feed my pain and sacrifice were rewarded by my beautiful, appreciative daughter. I was totally smitten and willing to sacrifice my wellbeing for my child because I thought that is just what mothers do.

'Don't cry over spilt milk,' I used to recite when I was expressing milk in our tiny and freezing galley kitchen. The little ancient extension to our Victorian end-terrace had no heating, but the counter top was the only surface where I could stand and express comfortably. If I sat down to express, the milk leaked and dribbled everywhere.

In week two the intensity grew when Mr Lowprofile's family visited and Grandma wanted to do the bottle feeds. I know my mother-in-law was well meaning and I evidently needed the rest, but I was resentful. It was all unwelcomed interference. I was grateful for a home-cooked meal being put on the table in front of me, but I lost my appetite when I watched my husband and his mom desperately trying to inject my expressed breast milk into our baby's mouth with a syringe. Or more so heard our daughter's shrill rejection and my excruciatingly expressed liquid gold being absorbed by muslin cloths dribbling down her cheeks and chin.

At those meal times in the company of my mother-in-law I shrunk into a thumb-sized child, sat in a huge giant's chair; I was powerless. I couldn't reach the table to eat my dinner. My tiny legs dangled unnervingly off the cliff-edge seat and my hands covered my ears to soften from my baby's piercing protest against the rubber teat on offer.

The midwives and the health visitors could see how much I wanted to breastfeed; I kept on asking for help. Each appointment was always five or so days away so, much to Papa's despair, I just kept on putting up with the pain; sobbing or screaming into pillows at each feed.

'Oh bab, so just pack it in,' my sister said gently as she consoled me again after about six weeks. With three kids of her own, even getting five minutes on the phone with her was golden. I really wanted to take her advice because I knew what she was saying was precious. But she, like my mom, had breastfed all her children comfortably. 'If it still hurts so bad it is just not worth it. This phase is tough enough bab; don't be so hard on yourself.' Even though these words echoed in my head for days, I ignored my sister. Repeatedly.

It never occurred to me at the time but I should have called my older brother. On our visit to Canada I had adored giving my eleven-month-old nephew his evening bottle; soothing him in the rocking chair and sitting peacefully with him until he slept. It had been such an honour to be part of that sacred part of his day. I respected my brother and his wife for sharing that special duty with me and so I learned bottle-feeding afforded other adults the chance to bond with babies in a way breastfed babies were less likely to. Bottle-feeding allows specially chosen friends, relatives and villagers to contribute to nurturing and bonding with a baby, taking the pressure off mom. I guess back when I was in the thick of battling the breastfeeding misery I didn't associate our dinky newborn daughter with my chunky baby nephew.

But on that same visit my brother had scared me off formula when we popped into the Pharmaprix to stock up on another tin of my nephew's magic powder. 'Thirty bucks! Blimey!' I cried, astonished at the hefty price tag.

'Yup, my son's expensive addiction to white powder,' he smirked drily. 'It's more expensive than crack, eh?' He'd taken to adding 'eh' to his more wry jokes so that his mostly Canadian audience would get his dark humour. Without their British buddy adding 'Eh?' his punchlines tended to go straight over their heads.

After eight weeks of excruciating breastfeeding I'd been in pain long enough that I just couldn't take it anymore. Mr Lowprofile's shoulder had just healed and he was allowed to drive again. It was a wet Sunday evening. One of those November days when it seems to stay dark all day. After a long, deliberating discussion, I dramatically sent him out to the Co-Op. I sobbed, apologetically cuddling our baby as we waited for him to arrive back with my tin of failure. The instructions blurred as my eyes welled with tears. I wept as she, cradled in Papa's arms, guzzled down the formula.

It was my all-time low; way lower than that gutter in Holborn.

What a fucking rigmarole! I evidently loved my daughter; wasn't that enough? I want to bellow at the 'me' then and drill into her that my love was enough; that whatever milk helped her grow healthily was enough.

The rest of those first eight weeks is a bit blurry now. I don't remember much about the friends and family who came from miles away to visit for the afternoon, except thinking she was the most wonderful gift to my loved ones. Of course I remember her early smiles and especially those milk-drunk, slurry eyes at the end of a feed; we were both happy at the end of the feed. And I do remember sobbing in the shower as the water fell and pierced the tips of my broken nipples. 'Is this it? Is this really what motherhood is all about?' I asked myself while my tears dripped down onto the soapy suds.

In my close circles, motherhood involved breastfeeding. Since birth, I have been surrounded by women whose babies nuzzled into their breasts. It was such a normal sight for me and I was desperate to be part of that picture.

Still broken and very miserable

'I've stopped breastfeeding,' I declared when a neighbour and her two-year-old popped over a few days after that stormy Sunday night, now that the formula dust had settled.

'Oh well if you don't want to do it, then that is just fine.' Even though I didn't know her well yet, I knew she wasn't judging me.

'I do want to do it. I just don't want to be miserable any-more. I want to be happy around her.' I could feel my heart pounding against my sleeping baby's chest, my armpits damp-ening as I tried to hold down the tears. I felt I had known her for years but I didn't want to be blotchy-faced and snottily sobbing in front of this woman on what was effectively our first play date.

'I'm still pumping,' I added, trying to convince myself, and her, that I was doing the right thing.

My neighbour, Clem, had been mentioned a few times as a woman I would get on well with. Her name had come up when I mentioned to friends about having a home birth. I didn't think I needed a doula and wrote it off as something middle-class women with cash to spare indulged in. But when I bumped into her outside her home on our baby's first out-ing, a walk to see the sea when she was 3 days old, I sensed that we would become friends.

I guess because she wasn't yet a friend it hadn't occurred to me to reach out to her sooner. I began to relay all the hoo-hah of the previous weeks and listed all the women who had seen the state of my nipples: two health visitors, the breastfeed-ing support worker, two midwives, two trips to the tongue tie clinic and the one hour session with a research team at the local chiropractic college where three chiropractic students, two midwifery students, a lead midwifery researcher and a chiropractor lecturer had all had a go at trying to get my positioning just right. Even our male GP, a father of three, sounded surprised that they were 'still this bad' when I went to see him a second time for mastitis, a month after the first bout.

Clem sipped her tea from my favourite bright orange mug. 'Why has no one recommended a lactation consultant?' she asked. I remember feeling very puzzled. I was so worn out by it all and had wanted to forget the last few weeks had even happened. But she was so casual about it all: 'well, if you want to breastfeed I know a woman who will get you feeding. Her name is Angela. She is a lactation consultant. I met her through work.'

I had no idea what she was talking about but I took her number and booked a £90 appointment without thinking twice. It was a lot of money to us, but it was a risk worth taking; the money saved on formula would soon pay off and the cost of my physical and mental health was priceless.

Sure enough, after a two-hour session with Angela we got the position right. She explained that the roof of our daughter's mouth was quite arched and therefore higher. This extra bit of height meant that my nipple was scratching at the tip of her tongue instead of cushioning in all nice and cosy. (For the record, 'scratching' felt like an understatement; sandpapering my nipple with an electric sander sounds more accurate.) So, the combination of the extra height and her tongue tie (which was overlooked at first and subsequently snipped not once, but again and fully two weeks later) was what was causing me all the agony. All I needed to do was place a finger on the top side of areola, with a little bit of pressure so that the tiny pull would point my nipple further up into the arch.

I was also indebted to learn from her that should we have another child in the future with tongue tie (only in some cases is it hereditary), we could choose to pay privately to have it snipped, usually within 24 hours, rather than waiting the five days or so for an NHS appointment.

Yes, if I was doing this all again I would like to have known that there exists an army of independent healthcare professionals who specialise in breastfeeding. International Board Certified Lactation Consultants (IBCLC) are equipped to help when it doesn't come naturally to a new mom. It would have been really nice to have a local IBCLC on my radar before giving birth. In the UK, the NHS love telling mothers they should breastfeed; Children's Centres, GPs surgeries, the birthing centre were plastered with posters of peacefully feeding moms. But the actual follow-up support available to unpeacefully feeding moms is disproportionate to the propaganda.

There was no way in that moment that I could envisage having another child, and going through all that again, but I thought it was information worth sharing. If I was an expectant mom again and planning my finances I would certainly opt for second hand everything and keep a few hundred quid in the bank to afford these one-off specialist services which aren't prioritised by the NHS.

I have since heard about cranial massage, lip tie surgery, myofascial release, reflexology for babies, all of which I wrote off as painfully middle-class ways to deal with the shock of motherhood. But I stand corrected: labour can be physically very stressful for newborns and just because the NHS doesn't direct budget towards holistic health, it doesn't mean there aren't excellent effective solutions to common ailments, no matter how tiny the patient. If I was having my first baby again I'd do my research and save a few numbers in my phone well before the new baby chaos fully erupts.

Well-meaning but well annoying

'Oh ya got a tummy sleeper!' enthusiastically cooed Rachel, my Brummie mother-of-three friend, as we hovered over her moses basket one morning.

'Maddie was one a them. Health visita hated it.'

My mom had also consoled me. Over the twelve years she birthed four children the guidelines chopped and changed so she couldn't offer much more than 'Oh they've got to justify their time spent visiting you and if no one can solve how to fix your nipples then they've got to write something in their endless paperwork. Shouldn't take much notice.'

As new moms we are not encouraged much to sit back and let your child be. There's an underlying message that we should always be busying our child and consequently wearing ourselves out too. In a society, like I see daily in England, that is obsessed with outcomes, goal-making and meeting targets, there isn't much space dedicated to being timeless.

And yet with a baby the weeks and months fly by even though the days drag. I've heard many a mama, myself included, refer to that twitchy clock-watching state when we are waiting for our other half's key to turn in the front door, desperate for some adult company after another endless day with the baby.

The idea of the 'health visitor' is quite idyllic really. An experienced and knowledgeable woman to pop around and check in on a generation of women that don't have people popping in on them anymore. A visit will reduce isolation, check the progress of the baby and encourage new moms out of the house and along to the children's centre. I know some of my friends built great relationships with their health visitors. But my reality was that they always came when 'baby' had just finally gone down for a nap. My biggest bugbear was that calling us by our given names was too much for their maxed-out caseloads and I was often addressed as 'mum' and our daughter was 'baby'. Similarly, 'they' really was *they* as we saw four different health visitors in as many weeks. Rather than that nurturing relationship I'd been sold, I felt an instant pang of paranoia to make a good first impression every bloody time. A good first impression for me has always been one where I exude calmness; pretty tricky in the fourth trimester!

In those early weeks, back when I was desperately seeking every ounce of professional insight as to why my breastfeeding continued to be so painful, I now regret inviting these leaflet-laden ladies into my living room. I knew that they all meant well but I felt so much unease with their role. Our daughter slept on her tummy which was a big no no. Someone made a note of it in the little red book which meant anyone else who read that little red book had a duty of care to inform me of the risk of SIDs. Some said don't sleep with 'baby' in bed with you, others said the bond between babe and breastfeed-ing mother was so primal that 'mum' would never squash her

134

newborn. Another suggested 'dad' sleep elsewhere to create more space. (And even less opportunity for him to bond with his newborn? No thanks.)

Months later another health visitor came back for another review. Despite working in one of the most diverse neighbourhoods in Dorset, she couldn't answer any of my questions about bilingualism but kept repeating that early communication was really important for 'baby's neurological function'. Maybe if I had told her I had worked with a wonderful array of neurologically diverse children she could have skipped her spiel and left me in peace. I guess I was too polite, or was optimistic that she'd enlighten me with some new knowledge. She didn't and the whole visit just turned into the most tedious cuppa I ever sipped in that kitchen.

'Just tell her what you are doing as you do it, like a narration of every day jobs and activities,' declared the well-meaning but well annoying woman who rocked up at my house. I knew she had my (and baby's) best interest at heart but I just couldn't help rehearsing 'your presence and your pamphlets are causing me neurological dysfunction,' as she role played and narrated to my daughter that 'I am putting water in the kettle by turning the tap on and holding the kettle underneath the tap, I am switching on the kettle, I am choosing my favourite mug, it's orange...'

'She's the only mug around here,' I internalised and smiled sweetly.

Fatherhood, brother good

I was amazed with all the knowledge women share about growing children. Day in day out I chatted with new moms,

135

seasoned mothers of three, grandmas and healthcare professionals. I love chit chat, always have always will, so all this learning I found incredibly valuable. But I was desperately craving the company of men. I loved talking to men about fatherhood; the tone of conversation was vastly different – a lot less guilt-ridden, total awe for the things their child was learning to do, countless poo jokes.

I realised the time I had spent with my older brother and his son, though it had been in much shorter chunks because of the seven-hour flight across the Atlantic, was just as valuable as the visits to my sister's house. With both siblings I had been absorbed in their unique parenthood journeys.

I watched as my eleven-month-old nephew's chubby hands enthusiastically grabbed small chunks of melon, strawberries, nectarine and home fries from the generous plate of brunch at my favourite cafe in Montreal. Each piece was lovingly policed by my brother as being sufficiently small and soft for my nephew to smash into his mouth with gusto.

Mr Lowprofile and I had caught a cheap and therefore unsociably timed flight from London via Paris to Montreal. We were jetlagged so all-day brunch seemed the only sensible thing to do once we'd caught the airport shuttle bus downtown to Berri where we had been greeted by my brother and his chunk of a child.

'Doesn't it annoy you that you have to share your food with him?' I asked my brother as we tucked into brunch at Fruits de Folie on St-Denis. In summer that eatery blended in perfectly along the bustling boulevard of colourful cafes, bars and mostly independent shops that rolled out onto the sidewalks. Homemade display boards, professionally hand-painted signs and bicycles lined every railing and lampost. It was an education in living locally that I've carried with me ever since.

The smell of fresh coffee and tobacco disguised the pollution of the city transport, cars, mopeds and the classic North American big yellow school buses called 'Ecoliers' in Quebec. I was always distracted from the avenue's four lanes of traffic by the cafe's signature dish: a mountainous sculpture of colourful fruit standing upright on my plate. Slices of melon, partially cut from its skin, cascaded down the edge of the sundae glass where pieces of kiwi, strawberry, pear, nectarine, peach and grapes danced a harmonious carnival dance below a spiral of pineapple. It was a tantalising piece of playful craft that accompanied a plate of otherwise predictable North American brunch staples. I wondered how the waitresses kept such a steady hand that they never let the sculptures tumble on the way from the tiny kitchen out to my favourite table on the terrasse. I was a waitress for six years but I never manoeuvred a meal with such height!

My brother reduced his work when their son was born and it amazed me how much of the parenting he took on. I had no idea my fun-loving, work-hard-party-harder sibling had it in him. He ran his own business coaching 'soccer' and always joked that he wanted eleven kids so he could train up his own football team. So being the boss, he could take his kid with him, and there was always 'a tonne of soccer moms' ready to help with the baby. This father just got on with life and carried his son along with him for the ride on a big sturdy

Dutch bicycle with a baby seat up front. I have learned a lot from my brother about parenthood; we traditionally look to the women for advice about child-rearing. I'm not disregarding all that I've learned from observing my older sister have three children in the four years prior to birthing my first. But I was genuinely surprised by how much my older brother had learned and shared with me about becoming a parent.

'Nah I don't mind sharing,' said my brother coolly. The nah was a Canadianism that made him sound not so British. 'It makes me feel kinda proud,' he said fondly.

I was impressed by how on the ball he had appeared when they brought their son to Birmingham seven months earlier. I'd hastily caught the train from London after work and got to our parents' house after my nephew's bedtime. My brother let me sneak in and we watched him sleep, whispering and weeping about how magical he was.

My brother was way off clocking his 10,000 hours for expert status. I guess some blokes just find fatherhood easier than others. My nephew was the best gift that Christmas: the first grandchild, my first nephew. I shouldn't fail to mention that my niece also arrived in early December 2012, joyfully on our grandpa's birthday, but we let her off the Christmas entertainment duty because three weeks of life just isn't sufficient time to work a crowd. Of course, my sister's tiny daughter stole my attention; I spent hours just holding her and soaking up the joy. What I lost in time down the pub with old friends, I gained in love and insight from older siblings and their life-bringing responsibilities.

The weeks after that Christmas break, instead of feeling topped up with oxytocin from baby cuddles and family comfort, I escalated into darkness as I missed my siblings and yearned to be closer to them. I was muddling through that community development job after the overwhelm of Great Ormond Street.

One of my colleagues, who sat on the opposite side of the small office, had a small child at home. We often arrived early, well before 9am to avoid as much of the chaotic commute that unfolded after 8am travelling across central London from our shared sanctuary of south east London to N1. We spent those quiet mornings sharing stories and photos of the tiny humans that enriched our lives so greatly. Chatting to that father, his name now escapes me, helped me feel closer to my brother who lived over three thousand miles away and was transforming from a Plateau Party Boy into a Plateau Papa complete with a posh poussette (buggy) and a ziplock bag of rusks always at the ready.

I didn't miss my nephew so much then, he was only four months old. Of course, I hold magical memories of several adults chuckling at his poo face, his yawns and raised eyebrows, and luring him to his first roasted carrot stick at our Christmas Dinner. Our younger brother hooked him up with the ultimate hipster-uncle gift: a novelty dummy with a bold moustache painted over the top lip which gave him an exquisite handlebar. He had six adults roaring and sobbing with laughter.

I was amazed as to how naturally my brother was tending to his child's needs. His wife was there too but she was, and

139

quite rightly so, making the most of having five additional adults around the house to fuss over their baby. She rested, caught up on jet lag and enjoyed the novelty of uninterrupted cat naps. Our family respected her need to rest. I learned from their visits to the UK and now whenever we visit my in-laws, I try to do the same: hand our baby over and discretely disappear into the quietest corner of their home.

When I'm at my in-laws I feel no duty to get involved; it's not my home. No one has fond memories of me being there as a child; it is not the nest I have flown so I have no duty to fill it in the same way my husband does. He reminisces, he digs out old belongings and questions why his parents keep his boxes of crap piled up in the corner.

'Um dia vais perceber, meu filho,' – one day you'll understand, my son.

'One day you'll get it, Delie,' my brother said wisely as he reached for the peanuts and took a swig from a small green can of Estrella. That week he and I chatted a lot. It was the year after *that hangover* and I was still, secretly, yearning to have a baby of my own. I had a hundred and one questions to ask him about his newfound parental status.

'So, you really don't miss partying?' I raised my eyebrows at my brother who pinched his bottom lip between sips of his beer. Ever since I can remember he has gripped his bottom lip or the excess skin on his neck when he is in deep thought. Mr Lowprofile touches the crown of his head. My younger brother's eyebrows sink inwards, just like my dad's. My sister's lips close tightly. My mom projects her chin as if to speak

140

but makes us wait a moment for the wisdom to be revealed. I must do something too.

'Not yet but it is early days.'

We were sat on the sofa in front of the fire in our parents' front room. The tiles around the fireplace were glowing with the reflection of the flickering flames, dancing under the draught of the old chimney. The room hasn't changed much in decor or layout my whole lifetime. 'The house feels smaller,' my brother said on one of his annual trips back home. I cherished his transatlantic trips home, I still do.

My sister, in the depths of adjusting to life with a newborn, was quite rightly mostly at home resting. She'll probably tell me that those first few weeks definitely did not feel like rest. My mom was more than likely at the other end of the house loading or unloading the dishwasher. Our little brother was young and living it large with his mates down the pub. He'd sit with us in front of the fire, guzzle a few little green cans before grabbing one more for the walk to the pub. Our dad was sat in 'Dad's armchair' prime position in front of the tiny television surrounded by horizontal shelves of CDs on top, the vinyl and their old 1980s silver stack hi-fi still going strong, followed by DVDs underneath and, much to the disapproval of their offspring, the stacks of VHS videos piled up below. Our parents' house hasn't changed much since we were younger.

'I miss just walking out of the house on my own,' he declared.

'What do you mean?'

141

'Well, there's always shitloads to remember: diaper bag, bottle, muslin, hat, rattle, change of clothes. It feels endless.'

'You forgot something,' I said smugly. 'Your baby.'

'Kevin!' he screamed, impersonating Kevin's mom from *Home Alone*. We watched that film on repeat as kids so we were quietly confident that we were not going to forget our baby. We'd also heard many times about when my dad left my sister at a jumble sale crèche in the early 80s. She got immersed in the toy pile, and my dad got asked to do an errand which involved leaving the building and driving a minibus to another nearby. Luckily no one purchased her for 5p like in *Dogger*.

Mama's Delight

I am comfortable saying I am a confident mother, but I by no means always get it right. I know I am not perfect, mostly because I don't know what perfection looks like, or believe in striving for it. I know I've messed up here and there. By the time our daughter was nearly three I ended up quitting my part-time job because I got too stressed to cope with balancing family life and work. I've ditched some of my best friends; not just last-minute cancelling on the odd coffee here and there, but actually feeling I've put our friendship on pause for a few years, and grieving how things have changed between us. I've had two miscarriages, racked up a Working Tax Credit overpayment debt (I hate the fucking system) and at times I've been really unkind to my husband.

Despite all this pretty normal, yet rarely publicly discussed, chaos that arose during the first three years of our child's life, I have remained adamant that I am a great Mama. And the truth is I've been surrounded by other great Mamas, but I just don't hear women say it about themselves. This makes me sad; it makes me feel awkward. So much so that I often downplay how much I think my husband and I have accomplished in being great parents, and I'd really like to encourage parents to feel prouder of themselves and acknowledge their accomplishments.

I have a friend called Daisy. She is a fellow enthusiast for creativity, community and collaboration. She has her tea with 'a splash of milk, one sneaky sugar and a Choux Bun thank you very much'. Time and time again Daisy has said, 'When I have a baby I am going to try and be a mom like you.' The first time she said it I thought she was being kind. Her partner describes her as 'relentlessly enthusiastic' so I took this comment with a pinch of salt. But she has repeated it. And she has acknowledged that she has repeated it because she sees that I am doing it differently and I am happy.

She was a freelancer when I became a mom so that meant she was one of the precious childless friends who could pop round during the daytime. She came to my front door ready and willing to rescue me in my desperate state. And more than once!

I was convinced I would scare her away. On one occasion I thought she must think I am outright taking the piss as I asked her to bring me a cabbage. I was told cabbage leaves cupped around my engorged breasts would relieve the pain from my second bout of mastitis. Another time I asked her to go to Poundstretcher for one of those super absorbent dish-drying mats because the baby's nappies kept leaking onto her moses basket mattress. It wasn't a fancy Mothercare gizmo, but I thought it would do the trick. It did.

And my personal favourite, friendly favour was when I asked her to bounce our sleep-averse baby to the full 14-min-ute-and-45-second version of Rapper's Delight because she required persistence and rhythm to get her to nap (and I secretly enjoyed the vision of each of my friends rockin and poppin and rapping to the beat with only my baby to gawp at them). In a quarter of an hour I could shower, moisturise, get dressed, put in a load of washing and make a brew all with playful Sugarhill Gang boogie oozing from our living room. And have a sleeping babba at the end of it. Winner.

Each time Daisy arrived I kept apologising for asking her for weird things from the high street and interrupting her work. Each time she left she thanked me for making her dance with my baby. And she went on to sort of apologis-ing for bringing Choux Buns when I'd mumbled I knew I should be eating something healthy. Seriously, sweet treats did absolutely no good for me, but I ate them anyway. We all do things we know do absolutely no good for us. Can we try to do things that absolutely do good for us instead? I think parents allowing themselves to go out and play is a good place to start...

Part 4 - Can I bring my baby?

What if societies just accepted that babies came along for the ride?

'I wish I'd been brave enough to bring the girls when they were this age,' Leila told me while she bobbed up and down holding my baby. A few moments earlier my daughter had reached out and grasped her index finger tightly, which I interpreted as 'I'd like a cuddle with this human, please', and so I duly passed the baby.

'It is so good for them, and it is so good for us,' Leila told me. Anyone who wore such fantastic colourful leggings to dance class won how-to-live-right kudos with me. She had two girls over five.

'I tried to get our children's centre to do yoga for mums and baby, even joined the parent forum to have my opinion heard but it never happened. Instead we just sat about making small talk and ignored our need to look after our bodies and de-stress a little.' I quickly warmed to her gentle yet straight-talking attitude.

'So well done you for coming to class and looking after yourself.' My daughter was about three months and at her first dance class. It was Leila's enthusiasm and encouragement, and that of others too, that helped me to keep bringing my baby.

No turning back

Back in the broom-cupboard days, someone mentioned resilience. I remember researching what resilience meant because it wasn't in my vocabulary when I was twenty-two. It was a bit of a slap in the face, a stark reminder of how loving and

146

privileged my upbringing had been. Lucky little me; I'd never needed to bounce back from misfortune or been faced with huge challenges to overcome.

I realised that I had in fact overcome plenty of hurdles, but I saw them exactly as that: hurdles. I always found ways to leap over them. Others may have perceived the same hurdles as brick walls forcing them to stop and be still for a while. So how did I find these magic ways to leap? Well I think it is because I had built lots of resilience through free play as a child. So, from then on, I used to write a lot about the resilience children build when they play when I was writing bids to raise funds for community play projects.

During my time in London it was my very own evidence-based research that helped me conclude that when I don't play I get depressed; it really was that simple. When I was pregnant the midwives with their questionnaires frequently asked about my mental health – past and present. I was honest, I said I was fine now but that I had a history of low-level depression.

Before I had my baby, I had read up on post-natal depression (PND) in the luxury of my own company. I did genuinely feel fine throughout pregnancy, better than fine most days, but knowing I was at higher risk of PND because I'd previously been depressed niggled at me. I was determined to not go back to those dark corners in London, sitting in the gutter sobbing and drowning in helplessness. I'll never forget being in Superdrug in Camberwell, when I spotted a friend, a really close friend. I couldn't face speaking to her because I was so miserable about nothing in particular. I'd never turned and fled so quickly; re-routing along another aisle and scuttling out like a cockroach. I didn't want to be that woman again so the following week in a poignant counselling session we talked about how I could shift my life and live more playfully. From that day on, I promised myself I would prioritise play.

Play for adults is a little more than 'having fun' (forget all sexual innuendos from here onwards, please). I now find it quite hard, on top of the burden of responsibility and general parent fatigue, to feel like I have to be the one that makes other people have fun too. 'Fun' seems to have a lot riding on it; to be fun carries yet another expectation when I feel I am already juggling plenty. Play for children can be very serious: it is their way of making sense of the complex world around them. I don't assume that play must be fun. Children can, and will, determine what they perceive as fun, it is not something a bunch of adults should dictate. So, I don't strive to be 'fun' anymore; not for my friends and not for the children in my company. And I don't expect children to have fun while playing; they might have fun, they might have some very serious interactions or they might heal pain – physical or emotional – while they play.

Somewhere along the line, in the past twenty years or so, 'fun' acquired a pretty hefty price tag. 'Just go out and have fun after work and we'll all be happy,' they say. I wish it was that easy. I'd like to see more people strive for 'playful' ways of being because the hope for me is that we will all realise and re-value the importance of a life full of freely chosen, personally directed and intrinsically motivated living.

Of course, as adults we do not need the early cognitive development that play produces in children, but surely, we need all the brilliant juicy good stuff that we release when we allow ourselves to be a tiny bit silly?

You know those giddy feelings from shaking our hips like Shakira Shakira, the magic of mixing up a really yummy pasta sauce without the pressure of impressing all the taste buds attending the dinner party, dressing up in fancy dress costumes, that tingly feeling when we dip our toes in cold water or the safety and solace we feel as we sneak off into a quiet place, a den void of distractions and to-do lists? I regard all of this as play.

Leisure pleasure

Leisure has replaced play. The leisure industry has become more and more whacky and the associated kit that is required for these quirky experiences has become more sophisticated and hence there's now a pretty hefty price tag on adult experiences that make us feel free and 'like a kid again'. I have often been priced out of leisure. Unsurprisingly the expense of leisure is so high that many governments recognise that they need to subsidise leisure services to incentivise the population to partake in what I like to describe as 'adults wanting the best bits of their childhood back, please'. Most adults don't talk about their own play. They may reminisce on how they used to play, but day-to-day adult play has flown out the window like a flaccid paper aeroplane. I want to bring day-to-day adult play back like a boomerang! BOOM!

Adults can have endless 'fun' experiences but often they must pay for the privilege. So, now throw a firstborn into the mix. All that leisure that adults are sold as being imperative to a healthy and happy adult existence is overnight out of reach to the majority of adults because the leisure providers have policies in place that exclude parents from participating if their child is accompanying them. Ouch. Though we weren't massive consumers of organised, mainstream leisure, Mr Lowprofile and I suddenly hit a massive barrier to accessing wellness and culture when we wanted to bring our tiny human along.

I firmly believe children need to see adults play. It is reassuring. I know that I know how to play in my own intrinsically motivated way and I am comfortable not striving to be some all-singing, all-dancing 'fun' entertainer for my child – CBeebies has that covered if that is the soundtrack you choose for your home: I am not judging. But I know of lots of adults, some parents, some not, who admit they have forgotten how to play. If you are nodding in agreement (and possibly despair?!) then I really hope the remainder of this book will rustle up some places to start. I actually just got off the phone from Justin Timberlake who agreed to re-release his 2006 hit (yup, fifteen years already) 'SexyBack' with a new message 'I am bringing playful back YEAH!'

With the exception of the minority who are born to playful adults, most children rarely see their parents having fun because children are prohibited from the places where adults revive and thrive in that brilliant juicy good stuff. Given the modern family's obsession with being busy, the only time many children get a glimpse of adults engaging in prolonged playful activity is during a family holiday for a week or two once a year, if you are lucky. The rest of our 'free' time parents are dedicated to racing between a timetable of adult-led activities targeted at either a child or adult consuming a 'fun' service.

As a pair of new parents with no family living nearby, we needed to source and potentially pay another adult to care for our child, while we went out to play without our child. We were caught in limbo: neither of us was particularly inclined to be without our child, but we did both crave adult company. We wanted to spend time together where physical activity and other adults distracted us from the seemingly endless rigmarole of chaos with a newborn. We didn't want dinner dates or trips to the theatre or cinema because we didn't have the brain capacity for much conversation or creative stimulation.

On a modest income a babysitter felt like an unnecessary luxury for an hour or so of exercise, and ridiculous because we both knew that our daughter would be no problem if she came along with us. We just wanted a taste of normal life from time to time, a distraction from turmeric poos, burping, sleep patterns and colic. Every so often we wanted to resort back to how life was and we both agreed that if a babysitter was at home with our daughter, we'd probably be so distracted and thinking about them that our focus wouldn't be on our 'fun' or 'relaxation' we were supposed to be treating ourselves to. It just made so much sense to bring our baby. So, we did. And what a joyful experience for all involved.

Saturday Night Fever

One surreal encounter that actually became the initiation of bringing my baby was a Saturday night out in January. I don't know if it was FOMO (fear of missing out) or cabin fever that spurred me out the house that Saturday evening to a bar in town. I was anxious about walking through the bar with my baby but knew the warmth from the friends in the function room would be well worth it. So, I wore her in the sling, underneath my baggiest coat and my widest scarf, and thought the bar staff wouldn't be expecting to see a baby, so I could probably just smuggle her past clinking martini glasses, rattling ice buckets and sloshing spirits straight upstairs to the private party room.

It was raining heavily but I was determined to go out. I asked Mr Lowprofile for a lift so he could drop us really close to the door. Usually I'd avoid paying for parking and walk twenty minutes so a lift was a proper luxury: one perk of having a baby! With each swish of the windscreen wipers I convinced myself it was a good idea; as he drove us into town his silence questioned why I was so desperate to go out. I knew he wouldn't ask but I recited my answers just in case.

I knew I needed vaguely interesting conversation about adult things with adults who didn't know me well enough to dare ask anything too deep about the past 3 months. I knew these people well enough to tease that 'I don't want to talk about baby stuff; it's like talking about work at the weekend'. I knew they would make me belly laugh. I knew that my colleague who was going off on his travels wasn't a big boozer so I knew the night wouldn't all of a sudden get rowdy around

9pm. I knew by 9.30pm we'd both be ready to leave and be heading for our routine armchair feed to sleep for her usual 10pm. I knew there would be enough arms patiently waiting to cuddle my baby so that I could sit a few seats away and indulge in chat. I love a good chat.

I didn't know that as I walked in conveniently through the main doors, before I got to the main bar, there was a lift! Yup, there was a shining bright light with its arms wide open calling 'Come in out from the rain, Mama.' No walk of shame across the bar. No tipsy women diving in for a peek, hooting at me for bringing my baby out on this cold rainy wet night. No shame on me for bringing my newborn to an establishment that encourages intoxication. No shame on me for not having bathed my babe and settled her to a good night's sleep an hour ago.

The following weeks and months she pursued her 10–10 pattern. 10pm was the time she would wind down after being super alert and very charming most of the evening. I was smitten; how could we send someone so cute to bed? And 10am was when she woke ready for another day. Seeing as Papa didn't arrive home from work until 9pm some days I really didn't mind. She was never unsettled in the evenings; she just wanted company.

A few weeks later Mr Lowprofile's Brazilian colleague invited us to a Feijoada party in a hotel function room. Feijoadas are a pretty routine part of Brazilian culture. They are usually held on Sunday lunchtimes when a black bean pork stew (the dish is called Feijoada) is served with all the trimmings accompanied by a samba band playing well-known family classics.

We arrived around thirty minutes after the doors opened and I was surprised to find, at the end of a pretty unassuming, almost dingy corridor, a vibrant little Brazilian enclave. I was accustomed to hearing Brazilian Portuguese being spoken about town, but I really wasn't expecting to find so many congregated beyond the brass-handled double doors of that unsuspecting function room.

I felt at home because kids were running riot around the spacious, part wooden, part carpeted floor. Toddlers and preschoolers wriggled around the institutional banquet tablecloths and a handful of babies were being passed up and down the long tables in an oblivious game of pass the parcel. Before we had even found a seat, the colleague came to greet us, scooped up our daughter from my arms and disappeared to introduce 'his niece' to half of Bournemouth. Mr Lowprofile and I were left to find a seat and talk amongst ourselves.

For no particular reason, we didn't go back to another Feijoada but being at that one so early on in our parenthood just gave us the permission to go out in the evening and take our baby. It became quite customary to arrive at events, gigs, classes and community get-togethers where we were greeted at the door by a smiling adult and had our daughter scooped from us to go and work the room. Presenting the newest human to a clan was an informal custom I'd seen happen in other cultures and I just went with it. She was never far away and I certainly enjoyed popping to the loo on my own.

Shitshow

I think I gave up on baby groups the day that I locked myself out of the house trying to quickly pop to the shops. I left the house in an unnecessary rush and closed the door before I got around to double and triple checking that my keys were on my person. It was a bright, fresh spring morning. Our daughter was about 5 months and still fitting comfortably on my chest in her sling. I also managed to leave without my phone. My phone used to have a card holder on the inside of it where I kept my bank cards. You can see where this is going... I left the house with a baby (hooray!), no change bag, no keys, no phone nor bank card or bus pass.

We eventually sought refuge at a Wriggle n Rhyme at the library in a more well-to-do end of town. I really didn't fit with the neatly ironed sailor-striped M&S mums, with their posh buggies and coordinating change bags. I was in deepest, darkest Dorset suburbia: a million miles from my beloved, diverse city streets of Birmingham.

As we settled into their circle I overheard conversations about mortgage brokers, gites in France and school catchment areas. On face value, nothing about my person was particularly outlandish, I'd forgive anyone who pigeonholed me into their category. I don't stand out from the crowd until I begin to chat and share my ideas.

I was used to being a misfit so that didn't bother me as we plonked ourselves down in a circle on the industrial carpet of the children's book corner. What really bothered me was the effort all these women had gone to to get themselves to somewhere that was centred around the children rather than prioritising their own interests. I could not find anything enriching about a circle of out-of-tune women muttering along to soulless, nonsensical nursery rhymes.

Our babies were placed in the middle of our circle. I watched them: vacant expressions, all in some state of sitting, lying or propped-up and inevitably side-flopping and asleep. Soon after the librarian handed out 'the instruments' I had my epiphany stay-away-from-musical-baby-groups moment. The objects we likened to musical instruments bore no resemblance to the percussion section of any musical ensemble I had ever seen or heard. I actually found it quite insulting to think those shoddy bits of plastic had been manufactured and sold as musical instruments; the noises they made were awful. I heard no music in the room.

Now I hold my hands up for not being the most together parent that day, far from it. Yes, I may have locked myself out of the house with absolutely no kit to care for my child, but in that moment in time what I was most concerned about was the nonsense we were collectively showing our children as 'music'. I valued real music so highly that I was adamant that no one was going to mis-sell the most sacred art forms to our daughter. I would not put her precious mind through that sort of mayhem again.

The brood were all gobbling the instruments; slimy slobber cascading between lips, hands and the plastic. None of them seemed tuned-in to the out-of-tune melodies coming from the middle-class mummies all lively in their animated facial expressions and copying the actions of the very enthusiastic librarian. I guessed they were probably highly educated, with a range of fascinating careers between them, but in that circle, they looked diminished and I questioned what on earth we were all doing there on a sunny Tuesday afternoon?

Our daughter was too young to sit up, and because she had been curled up in the sling most of the day I lay her down to stretch out. She looked up at me with a blank expression that I could only read as 'what is this shitshow, Mama? Where have you brought us and why do you look so bloody uncomfortable?'

So that was it. From that day on I vouched to only go where I was intrinsically motivated to go. I would not be navigated by the conditioned way-to-raise-your-baby I was being spoon-fed from children's *professionals*. I had to remind myself I too was a children's professional and I too had a brilliant set of tools to raise happy, healthy children.

Bodyrock

Culture and creativity were big parts of my life that I just wasn't willing to put on hold because in Britain the cultural norm was for women to be home putting dinner on the table at 5pm and tucking their children to bed by 7pm. For as far back as I can remember, community arts was part of my life, so it was only natural to make my history repeat itself.

When I was twelve years old I decided I wanted to perform. I liked drama at school but I deemed my one hour a week at school insufficient nurturing of my emerging thespian. It was the very, very early days of the internet; it was not yet the place to look for cultural listings. Can you imagine finding a baby group without the internet? It is a weird thought. As part of his work, my dad regularly visited arts venues around Brum. He dutifully scoured notice boards and picked up flyers to give me my options. I can't imagine a teenager today patiently waiting a couple of weeks for some information to magically appear in front of them on a piece of paper. It sounds so romantic!

One Saturday my mom and I visited a little local dance studio in Moseley, a neighbourhood in Birmingham that often gets described as 'bohemian'. This attic dance studio was located above a shop, and we discovered a flat sandwiched in between. To the right of the shop door, we climbed the narrow staircase where burning incense attempted to mask the stagnant damp on the unventilated corridor. 'Mom I hate joss sticks,' I announced in my almost teenage manner.

Our feet thudded against the uncarpeted wooden stairs and I thought about who might live behind the door on the first floor. Who would tolerate living underneath a room where twenty or so dancers plonk about every evening? Surely only the dance teacher.

I was put off that studio by the weird entrance. The cautious young me who wouldn't climb trees questioned the safety of dancing on the top floor of an old, creaky building. I pretended that the thought of giving up my whole Saturday as the 'youth' classes ran 1–3pm was too much. Going to town was the centre of my Saturdays; the freedom to ride unlimited buses on a day-saver ticket, charge around the city centre with purpose and pretend we had money to spend. We ate

Vegetable Bakes from Greggs or a Happy Meal and a Caramel Sundae if we wanted to sit down for a bit. If our pocket money allowed we bought overpriced stationery or accessories from TopShop and Miss Selfridge. We all pretended we had outgrown Tammy Girl by this stage but secretly we still shopped there with our moms.

I wanted to fill my weekends with an alternative to romping around town, except I wasn't yet ready to give up every single Saturday. Thankfully the novelty of all those trips to town soon wore off, as did the friendships that fuelled them.

I didn't go to the dance school, but I did settle for a youth theatre that rehearsed on Sundays. If going to town was going to remain the centre of my Saturdays, the centre of my entire youth was patiently waiting for me 24 hours later and about half a mile south of Birmingham city centre, in Digbeth. Of course, I didn't know it then but those Sundays and that venue were going to be my sanctuary from secondary school and my first independent step out into the real world.

I thought The Custard Factory was so cool.

I saw an arts space dedicated to work and play and in a strange way I felt part of it. Offices and workshops towered over a central courtyard with two bars on opposite sides of the lake. It was a space where grownups went to work and play. And it was a space that welcomed young adults and greeted us as professional performers.

As a teenager I was often looking for acceptance; I was mature, wanted to be like my big sister and felt comfortable amongst adults. I didn't care much that I wasn't accepted by a lot of the girls in my school; I didn't like them much either

159

and I knew that there was more to life than school. Despite being wise beyond my years I still sought out opportunities to be playful. To my school mates I was outed for being weirdly confident, but on those Sundays, I was just another eccentric who was uplifted and accepted by the other misfits who flocked from all walks of life across Birmingham to share the thrill of the spotlight.

We united in our acceptance of each other and put on self-devised plays about all sorts of random shit. We didn't want jazz hands nor genteel drama school productions of better-known West End productions. We wanted a platform for unconventional and amusing plots and we were proud that we were professionally produced but also unpolished and far from prim; we were Raw Talent Youth Theatre.

The 'theatre' was a bit of an overstatement; it was a large windowless concrete rectangle that doubled up as an overflow dancefloor for the bar next door, and sometimes a cinema and probably even a conference hall when skint arts groups were really desperate. But the quality of our performances in that concrete box was never second best.

The receptionist of the Custard Factory was a lanky 6ft-something semi-punk who had a very subtle air of camp about him. His gaunt cheeks sagged from a diet of tobacco, caffeine and cans of Nurishment. I never saw him eat food. You would be forgiven for crossing over the road to avoid getting too close to him on a dark pavement. My friend Jessica and I sparked an unlikely friendship with him. Well, not really a friendship, but our visits to him on the reception desk became a routine part of the week. Just like after Friday prayer

Ahmed might pay his respects to Mr Bashir, his elderly neighbour, we'd pass by the reception desk after Sunday rehearsals to offer our pleasantries. It was platonic and peculiar and it would probably only happen in Brum. I can't imagine he'd even be given a front of house job anywhere in Dorset, but in diverse multicultural cities all humans are more accepted; that is what I love about cities.

Though his mood was unpredictable, he received our 'honest teenagerish observations' as compliments. I remember once we told him he resembled Moby, 'but an unhealthy version'. He was probably a recovering addict, though that wouldn't have occurred to me at the time. But hats off to him, he was a reliable employee: always present and correct, if a little haggard. When the phone rang while we were visiting his desk he always performed the conversation; our own bit of micro street theatre.

Weirdly, it turned out he lived around the corner from us (like literally twenty doors away) and even when I'd grown out of frequenting the Custard Factory I would occasionally bump into him. Once at dawn I was teetotal walking home from a rave, I'd just left my friends who lived down the hill from us and I had turned the corner to walk the last 20 metres alone. There was Moby with rolled shoulders, 6ft-something, hiding under a hood like The BFG. I didn't have the time to greet him before his long strides took him past me and he plainly declared, 'Just out walking. You look like a smurf.' I was wearing blue tights.

Many years earlier, and in daylight, after a Sunday rehearsal, Jessica and I were lurking around the Custard

Factory lake. Teenagers always lurk, don't they? We were probably deciding where to go; Birmingham town centre was eerily quiet and dull at 3pm on a Sunday but we didn't want to go straight home. The glass walls of the lakeside dance studio were draped with a gentle opaque linen which gave only a little privacy to the occupants inside. Through the swathes our curious eyes peered through to a group of sculpted, sweating sort-of dancers; uniformed in white yet varied in each unique Benetton tone of human.

United in joyous chanting and repetitive melodies, they clapped entranced in a circle around a duo moving in a melange of unchoreographed acrobatic dance. They were elegant yet powerful. They were dancers dressed as martial artists in combat; quickly kicking and ducking to avoid their opponent's attack while all in flow with the acoustic music performed by the spectators in the circle. I was taken back; I had never seen anything quite like it. My Brummie friend once described Capoeira as 'a dance off on Copacabana Beach between Fatboy Slim's "Praise You" dancers, RUN DMC's B-Boys and B-Girls and some ancient Kung Fu ninjas – who had their swords detained at Customs – all with a melodic acoustic soundtrack of Afro-Latin percussion.'

'Girls! Stop dribbling at the men,' hissed a voice between our shoulders. We screamed the way teenage girls do and turned to see our beloved Moby. In a flash he sauntered away in one of his camper moments.

'What they doing?' Jessica called after him; she had blushed so probably I had too. He flung himself into a grind down the industrial scaffold pole door handle and before disappearing back to his reception desk he shrieked, 'It's Capoeira. From Brazil. All very sexy!'

Since then groups of Capoeiristas popped up at all sorts of events I went to in Birmingham and London. The unique mix of dance, acrobatics, singing and percussion permits the art form fit in with diverse cultural programmes. As a spectator I found Capoeira captivating as it was unpredictable; it is impossible to know how and where each game is going. It is inclusive; all are welcome to clap and sing to heighten the energy in the circle. The most fascinating part of the circle for me was the narrative of, or lack of, the actual competition. In London one afternoon at Gabriel's Wharf on the South Bank I finally plucked up the courage to ask a smiley woman, also spectating but singing along, her palms clapping in unison with others', creating a rhythmic seal to keep the energy inside the circle, the *roda*. I caught her eye and asked, 'Who is the winner?'

'Pardon?'

'I am trying to understand the game. How do you know who the winner is?'

She smiled a wider smile 'When you play, you know it.'

'When you play, you know it,' I repeated to myself as I wandered off, still not sure what she meant.

I never thought my body was anywhere close to being able to 'play Capoeira' so I guessed I would never know. But I wanted to know! I wanted to be part of that circle of shiny happy people.

When you play, you know it

At intervals over the seven years of our relationship I had suggested to Mr Lowprofile that we try a class together but he was never interested. His thing was Brazilian Jiu Jitsu (BJJ) but when he plummeted off his bike along the cycle path to work one morning and damaged his shoulder, BJJ was off the list.

When our daughter was four months, a BJJ buddy invited him to train Capoeira. Seven years of me suggesting it: nothing. One text message from his mate when he was a new dad and desperate to be part of the adult world again: sold.

I was mesmerised by what I'd seen Capoeristas do with their bodies; the twists, the flips, the turns, the kicks, the graceful movements, the elegant transitions from a spinning kick to a floor roll, the pushes up into a mid-air through one-handed cartwheels with a teasing little heel tap to really stir a playful retaliation from the opponent. I really had no idea where I was going to begin but fuck it, I'd just seen my body grow and birth another human so I guess I was of the mindset that my body was capable of anything.

'I'm coming too,' I announced as he got ready to go and I started fishing around the bottom of my wardrobe for a suitable bra and leggings. I was four months postpartum and unstoppable since I'd won my breastfeeding battle.

The first evening as a Capoeira student was refreshing. I was welcomed as an individual; not as the mother of a baby. We were a small group; ten or twelve at most. Many of the adults in the room were responsible for caring for their growing families but in those ninety minutes we were all focussed on our own growth as Capoeiristas.

I was respected as a beginner. Mr Lowprofile was also a beginner and after dislocating his shoulder had to take it slow in his own way. I was a woman who had recently had a baby and took due care when necessary. I felt wobbly and was aware that my core was MIA. But I didn't wet myself (not even a tiny bit), or fart, or sob, or leak breast milk which was my biggest fear in a class of mostly men.

Our baby was welcomed but not fussed over. We united with a group of adults none of whom asked me about her sleep. And she sat in her car seat and watched adults move and make unfamiliar shapes glinting in the mirror above her. She was wide-eyed and fascinated. When I glanced over to her from time to time I could see her legs kicking and her arms pumping; she was ready to join in.

The acceptance of me and my baby in the Capoeira and African dance communities set me up with the confidence to bring my baby along to wherever I thought would nourish my soul, recharge and revive the woman I was prior to my waters breaking. Seeing my daughter grow around a village of loving, healthy and respectful families helped us feel at home in a town where we otherwise felt quite unsettled.

Our Capoeira teacher was a humble fighter and his students followed suit. I'd had brief stints of training in Boxing and Muay Thai gyms but the vibe in this Capoeira community was different: no bravado. I've never been interested in contact fighting; never been inclined to hit or kick another human. So as much as I enjoyed the power of combat movement and the challenge of my mental awareness in response to another person's pursuit, my training was limited in those other gyms. I was never dainty as a kid; I was always drawn to power and physicality with rhythm like Southern African gumboot dancing, STOMP – the musical, and, of course, raving to drum n bass.

On a social level Capoeira provided us with a crucial village of like-minded families. After a few weeks of evening lessons, I helped our teacher to organise and promote a family class on Sunday mornings; a class designed for adults, where children (even my tiny baby!) were welcome and encouraged to join us as much as possible. Much like my Sundays with the youth theatre back in Brum, our Sundays were filled with another group of eccentrics; mothers, aunties, daughters (and occasionally grandmothers), fathers, uncles, sons (and just once a grandfather) dedicated to connection with their mind, their body and their family members through enriching playful combat.

On the surface level I find Capoeira very playful; it is a fast-paced game of trickery. There is seldom contact. The game is an intriguing play fight. I often found myself chuckling at the situation: one moment I was breastfeeding, the next I was in the roda swinging high kicks into mid-air and attempting to cartwheel against my mom-friend whose sister was holding our babies, one on each hip.

Next in the circle was a dad embracing the opportunity to give the most technical play fight against his eight-year-old son; both of them beaming an identical smile. All the while we are led by an extremely humble immigrant and his four loving and dedicated children; singing and playing the handmade musical instruments to keep us energised and motivated.

A significant part of Capoeira with our teacher has been about education and history of Capoeira; not just attempting badass flips n all. On a deeper level the brutal history and the foundations of Capoeira created by Africans enslaved in Brazil are certainly not something to joke about. Capoeira was criminalised because it was associated with Black culture in the sixteenth century but nowadays it is Brazil's national sport. Though Capoeira has been given recognition and a certain level of cultural prestige I can't help but notice that there are very few Black people in the higher ranks of the international Capoeira organisations. And so, despite all the loving friendships formed, the empowerment as a woman with a baby, there have been times when I have questioned the cultural appropriation of me, and thousands of other white people all around the world, re-enacting the path of African slaves and their rebellion, just for a bit of exercise.

But I remind myself that with our teacher it is not just a bit of exercise. I can't speak for other teachers but Professor Assis exudes respect. To me his classes have always been a balance between education and exercise. He shares the philosophies of Capoeira with us as a way of life; we pay our respects to a monumental struggle. We pay homage to a lesser-spoken part of history and open up these conversations to our children, who I doubt are hearing these kinds of teachings in school. Capoeira teaches respect; respect on many levels. Capoeira, if you let it, quickly becomes a way of life.

Cuba Libre

From the age of sixteen, when I discovered I could buy cheap flights on the internet, I travelled. Every purchase I considered was compared to the cost of a flight. Hmmm £60 on a pair of trainers (I love trainers) or a return flight to Barcelona? Shall I go to that day festival or buy a flight to Prague? I had no clue about the environmental impact of my budget adventures of my late teens but wow I had a lot of fun. I used to count my waitressing tips at the end of a shift and tally up how many more shifts until my next trip.

While scrawling notes and ideas for this book, over our favourite Vietnamese takeaway, Mr Lowprofile asked me casually, 'Are you going to write about Cuba?' I froze. 'Urmmm, I don't know.' And for days I thought about Cuba. And I somehow felt smug, like it was too nice a thing for potentially fragile new parents to be reading about with their newborns in arms. I didn't want my readers to hate me because we went to Cuba. But Cuba was such a brilliant lesson in parenting that I'd be stupid to leave out what we learned while we were there.

So, it all began when a fellow nomadic friend shared a link on Facebook. Stupid Facebook, planting these ideas in my head. It wasn't one of those generic top 10 tips for Cuba with a baby, just a clever observation that with all the Easter and May bank holidays in 2017 it was the opportunity to take a three-week trip for half the annual leave. Sold; a slightly adventurous long-haul trip before we started weaning.

The obvious was a long-haul flight to Canada to finally meet my big bro and show off our baby to a handful of second cousins who were good fun and real grownups with big houses that would feel like we were staying in boutique hotels. I envisaged big family get-togethers where we weren't responsible for hosting. I knew we would be fussed over in a laid-back kind of way. Best of all, they all had kids so they knew where we were at in life; no pretending to be more fun or energetic than we really were.

I duly found reasonable flights with British Airways and sensible flight times for travelling with a 4-month-old baby and we waited for the computerised annual-leave request to switch from a blue question mark to a bright green tick.

Well, thank goodness for the line manager who didn't get around to approving my husband's holiday request. By the time we got the green light I'd upgraded our relatively pre-dictable retreat with relatives to a catapult into Caribbean communism in Cuba. Mr Lowprofile was keen for a beach holiday rather than Canadian winter. Who can blame him? And my brother didn't take much convincing. I messaged him on What's App one grey January afternoon:

'Bro. Easter. Cuba. 7 days. Si?' I knew with the time dif-ference he wouldn't be awake yet so I googled a few Mon-treal–Cuba flight options while waiting for his response. A few hours later around his morning time he replied: 'Cuba. Siiiiiiiii.' Yessssss! And our childless younger brother duti-fully obliged to join us, he didn't take much persuading. We felt bad for leaving out our sister but we've promised her we'll go back.

It was good having an adult who didn't need to think about their child's hunger, body temperature, thirst or culture shock, along for the ride. He provided my older brother and me with endless carefree charm. We marvelled as our little baby brother, all grown up now, disappeared down back-streets with black-market cigar dealers... 'I'm telling mom!' we shouted after him.

Outside of the all-inclusive hotels of the resorts, and the high-end hotels of the cities, the most common form of accommodation in Cuba is to stay in the spare room of a family home. Casas Particulares were like Airbnb waaaaaaaay before those Californians made staying with strangers un-weird. Staying in locals' homes doesn't sound like a holiday but, believe me, it was. There was always a kid, a second cousin or a neighbour of the host queuing up to hold our baby.

Each morning our hosts would lay out the breakfast and then scoop her and her Bumbo seat off to the family kitchen at the back where the guests don't usually get invited. I don't think you could guarantee that kind of service in a 5* all-inclusive hotel. I'm not one for promoting baby stuff and I've since heard the Bumbo gets mixed reviews by occupational therapists, but it was very useful bit of kit for the long-haul flights, sitting in warm sea and on sand, and it fits in hand luggage – best fiver I have spent on Gumtree.

Cubans have good access to healthcare and are very pro breastfeeding. Anytime I sat down to feed our daugh-ter someone would appear with a glass of water for me and smile for the baby. There was no awkwardness about my flesh being on show; just a respectful and nurturing response to a human necessity. Milk was rationed during our visit because there hadn't been enough rainfall to grow the grass to feed the cows. Lactating women and young children were priority for the regional milk rations; the ever-popular ice cream parlour in Cienfuegos was closed for a few days, there was no butter at breakfast. Life went on.

Our hostess in La Boca near Trinidad, Marlene, was a retired paediatric nurse with two healthy grown-up sons. Like any well-meaning Grandma or Aunty, our Cuban Tia broke all the rules around sweet treats; so much for our pre-weaning adventure. It was hard to argue with her as I discovered she'd been giving our 5-month baby freshly baked bread, and even juicy mango, in the morning while we were eating breakfast with our sea view... 'Oh well, what is done is done,' I thought. 'Prepare yourself for disappointment as we wean you good and proper on a British diet of imported bananas and bread-sticks. The mangoes will never taste so sweet back home bab.'

And because I was on holiday I decided I could relax on my shoulds and should-nots. So, I drank a Cuba Libre here and there without feeling like I shouldn't. I usually only managed half; 'more rum less coke' is the Cuban mixology.

Cubans do Easter well. Everyone seems to take a week off to visit the seaside and simply sit in shallow water with a handful of plastic cups and a bottle of state-brewed Cubano. Anyone in the sea, even a Gringa and her baby, are passed a cup and a slosh of white rum to sip. Easter Sunday had never been so merry. Back home we'd all had tummy ache by mid-day from scoffing too many creme eggs. But in Cuba it was a jolly affair with the mellow hum of slowly sipped rum and gentle waves cooling our sweetened, warmed bodies.

Holidaying with my two brothers was really nourishing for me. It refreshed a lot of my memories of our happy childhoods and helped set the tone of how I wanted to live in the future. I think it helped that we were on holiday the same time Cubans were on holiday so we saw big groups of families with kids of all ages at their most playful. I loved watching all these families out together. And because we didn't stay in resorts we also met locals going about their everyday lives. Many were delighted to encounter a non-nuclear family travelling together; they invited us to be part of theirs. It was never so easy to bring my baby.

Cubans love children. And they warm to adults who act like children so me and my brothers were right in there. My older brother got chatting to an older guy with a horse and cart. My nephew loves horses and they arranged to go horse riding. 'Can we come?' I pondered. My brother looked at his niece sleeping on my chest.

'Uhuh, I'm sure we can squeeze her in somewhere.'

Can I bring my baby horse riding? Hmmm; it wasn't really something I had ever considered doing. Of all the mom predicaments, and all the places I had daydreamed about taking her, horse riding certainly was not one of them. I have never been into horses. I mean they are beautiful but getting close to animals is never really on my agenda; I am a people person.

A couple of times in London I had accompanied youth groups on horse-riding trips. One trip was totally bizarre: I discovered there was a stable and riding school literally underneath the West Way, about a mile from the Westfield Shopping Centre. I had driven in and out of London on the

A40 (to and from Brum) pretty much my whole life and I was bemused to discover this community initiative beneath our London runway that was home to around 20 horses.

Upon arrival at the stables I was not convinced, and even wondered about the ethics of keeping wild animals in such an unnatural and noisy environment. But I stand corrected; I was amazed at how peaceful the whole visit was despite the thundering traffic above. Those horses were undeniably therapeutic for the young people I was supporting. They absolutely loved the experience so much so that they inspired me to try horse riding sometime. I came home from work that evening and convinced Mr Lowprofile that we'd ditch our routine holiday bike rides and upgrade to some horses next time we were somewhere picturesque and rural. ¡Hola Cuba!

I loved that Christopher, the fifteen-year-old son of our horse-riding guide, took a particular liking to my nephew; they became buddies even despite the language barrier and the age gap. And he was always the first to scoop up our baby too. My nephew was five and not interested in babies, not even his cousin. He couldn't even bring himself to call her by her given name. She remained 'the baby' in his gentle Canadian twang for the whole holiday. But with her in Christopher's skinny but strong arms, the three of them strolled around the block bringing back handfuls of the purest-white Mariposa flowers. Chris also showed us how to gently remove the pincers from the crabs who took residence in our beach-front garden, so that the children could hold them without getting pinched.

I think more young men should be reminded that working with children is not women's work. Young children love male carers. They shouldn't be a novelty but they are.

So, one of my (GCSE-Spanish) conversations with him went like this: 'What job do you want to do when you grow up, Chris?'

'Jugador de futbol!' he replied with a triumphant smile. Of course, what fifteen-year-old Latino boy doesn't want to be a footballer?

'¡Claro! Pero... Of course, but you have to work with children. You are very kind. Children like you. You can be a teacher or a nurse.' I didn't know how to translate playworker?!

'A nurse?' he spat and scrunched up his face as if to say 'ugh' and poised his chest to demonstrate he was a man. A real man, obviously.

'Si, mi hombre es enfermero en el bloque operatorio,' I said nodding towards my husband who is a theatre nurse. I didn't know how to translate operating department practitioner!

'Oh!' he exclaimed and frowned in deep thought while watching my husband for a while. Maybe he was trying to picture him dressed in scrubs.

Amongst all the gringo families we spoke to who were travelling with kids, mostly Canadians and a handful of rebellious Americans, we spoke about how genuinely welcoming the Cubans were, especially towards our children. In our first walk around Trinidad I was disappointed when we were stopped at the door to a Casa de la Musica by a smartly uniformed security guard. There were kids everywhere in Cuba so, surely, I could bring my baby for an afternoon concert? Nope!

A compassionate wide smile at my daughter turned into a serious expression to my husband. He stated that we weren't allowed into the indoor music venues because 'the music was too loud for the children'. I respected their attention but it was initially a bit annoying that we were forbidden from entering several indoor venues. Why couldn't I, as the child's parent, decide if the music was too loud for my daughter? They meant no harm and were always incredibly gracious; it was hard to be angry at them. Especially when one guy left his station and walked us around the corner, through a large wooden door to a hidden courtyard restaurant with a live band.

'Aqui esta bien amigo.' Here is good my friend, he declared shaking my husband's hand while nodding and looking upwards while raising his other, ungrasped, hand up to the open sky.

Four adults to two kids was a good ratio for travelling; we took it in turns to go to indoor bars and found plenty of music outdoors too. Maybe it was socialism, or maybe it was my motherhood, gratefully lapping up every last ounce of Cuban cariño; everyone in Cuba seemed to have a duty of care like nowhere else I have been. Either way our little triangle around Santa Clara, Trinidad and Cienfuegos was a brilliant way to introduce our (oblivious) daughter to another part of the world with her faraway uncle and cousin.

My big brother had a harder time with his five-year-old: all those ice creams his son associated with holidays were not readily available. Convenience food was not so easy to come by. A friend had taken her two-year-old to Senegal to visit her husband's family and she said she wished she'd packed a suitcase of familiar food. 'Their spaghetti and tomato sauce tasted different so he barely ate anything for days.' I relayed this advice to my brother and, much to my distaste (they are Nestlé), he brought Cheerios!

I have loved travelling with our daughter but it occurred to me that young travellers will not anticipate a totally different world at the end of a long journey – they only know what they know. So, I figured, a taste of normality would always go a long way. I even packed a familiar fork, spoon and bowl the first time we went to Portugal after weaning. That seems ridiculous now but it made sense to me that those little familiarities might be so important and comforting to my young traveller. Of course, I'll never shy from including our daughter in sampling local cuisine, but I'll also be prepared to cook their favourite familiar food as a back-up.

I've heard a lot about identity loss over the past three years. I think our trip to Cuba helped me to hang onto mine. I loved pottering about museums and cultural centres. We embraced the slower pace of life and often sat and let time pass, soaking up the local way. Seeking out a seat in the shade unravelled as an open invitation for anyone and everyone to stop and coo at the baby. Some days I embraced the company, delving into as much my Portuñol I could muster, and other days I respectfully let our baby do the communicating.

Although we stayed out at a street party 'til 11pm – early by Cuban standards even with a baby – one night in

Cienfuegos, I was a tiny bit disappointed to not go out party-ing all night and we didn't visit Havana, so I felt the limitations of being a parent too. But that trip taught me the importance of sharing the burden, and that the responsibilities of parent-hood can be shared beyond the family unit. We felt comfort-able with our hosts (we stayed in three Casas Particulares in total) and felt trusting of these generous-hearted humans to cuddle and chat with our baby. Even in the restaurants there seemed to be more than enough adults milling about; the waitresses would put down our plates of food and reach out to take our baby and hand her about the endless supply of honorary Aunties and Uncles while we ate. I could bring my baby, and I could let her be in the company of strangers. It was a very powerful experience because it taught me the impor-tance of entrusting villagers with pockets of responsibility so the weight was off my shoulders, our shoulders in fact: Papa agrees we both enjoyed the break.

We gave ourselves a unique opportunity to be playful amongst an incredibly playful nation. Don't get me wrong, Cubans do everything by the book and respect the law and administrative procedures like no other country I have vis-ited. But beyond all the nation's regulation we discovered a playful charm. I think Cubans compensate their regimented life by embracing play wherever they can fit it in. There's a timelessness about their day that I enjoyed (except when the Regatton was blasted by the neighbours at 5am!) and an intrinsic motivation to wholeheartedly care for one another almost in the innocent way that children do. It was exactly what we two, as worn-out new parents, needed.

It takes two to tango

Parenthood between two people is a peculiar, beautiful and challenging transition. Some people talk about 'coping strategies'; I think 'muddling through' is more accurate terminology. There were days when we were so close and connected and in love oozing all that brilliant juicy good stuff over our little creation and other days when we couldn't bear to be in the same room as each other. I don't feel embarrassed or ashamed about the latter but I am extremely proud that we've found ways to avoid those days.

Before we became parents, Mr Lowprofile and I respectfully spent a lot of time doing our own thing. We gave each other the freedom to live how each other wanted. He didn't mind that I was always out partying, lapping up the company of my culture vulture friends and being a part of our community. He was more comfortable in his own company being entertained by films and never-ending Netflix series. I enjoyed my freedom to go where my tide took me and revelled in coming home to a humble, loving man who relished the sanctuary of his own space.

Then our baby came along and suddenly I was very dependent on him and our flat was no longer a peaceful home cinema. Actually, the first day of her life it was. The three of us snuggled on the sofa and watched a film projected onto our living-room wall. We snoozed and cooed at our baby through most of it so unsurprisingly neither of us remembers which film it was!

I don't mind being alone, doing things for myself, working alone, but I recharge by being with people. I thrive when

I am topped-up by the right company. So, the early days of being broken-nippled and incoherent from exhaustion meant I was desperate to be around people but I didn't want to socialise with anyone.

After intense days of working indoors in a team of several colleagues, surrounded by people in need of medical interventions, he needed down time. After intense days of being at home with our newborn baby, surrounded by unstimulating baby-centric existence, I needed my play time. I needed conversation, stories from the outside world, human connection. And he needed time alone.

I craved adult company to feel normal. I was demanding socialisation from my husband who was feeling equally unnormal and having to go to work every day where he was surrounded by people. I'm reluctant to use labels on people but once I started understanding the characteristics of 'an introvert', it has really helped me to learn, respect and admire the boundaries he sets so he can recharge.

I was demanding of him what I had never demanded of him before. I resented how much I relied on him for my recharge when I knew he wasn't able to give it. I had to learn what being an introvert means and I have only really recently started to appreciate that his way of caring for himself is to be alone. He needs to care for himself before he can care for me.

With my new mothering dynamic I became more dependent on him. As we embarked on sharing the responsibility for caring for a baby with each other I *needed* him to come out with us on weekends so we could be a family together. I needed to be out of the flat for my own sanity but he did not. It 'wasn't fair' that he didn't want to spend time with me and my friends. It 'wasn't fair' that our daughter would associate socialising, arts, culture, the playground, adventures all with me while he chose to stay home. It 'wasn't fair' that it was always me bringing the baby.

I can see now that it was totally unfair of me and I hope that some may learn from my mistakes and respect the boundaries their partner sets to love themselves. We both valued time together as a family but disagreed on where to spend the all-important quality time: at home or out and about. This dilemma divided us at a stage of our lives when actually we needed to find strength in companionship and support each other.

I hated going out without Papa because I didn't want people to judge him as being an absent father, or judge me for letting him get out of his Dad Duties. I knew he was rising to his newly found challenges of fatherhood but I had an unspoken shame when we weren't spending our weekends parading our family status.

'I have nothing to prove,' he told me when I asked him to do more 'family stuff' together because I wanted people to see what a great dad he is. I believe dads have a huge part to play in raising our children. And partners, boyfriends, husbands, regardless of the official level of commitment you have reached by bringing a child into the world, also have a duty of care to the woman that bears the child. The best gift we can give our children is the best version of ourselves. A relationship between two loving adults should bring out the best in all of us.

It could have broken us; like chalk n cheese we are, but opposites evidently attract (and we'd made an incredible human so we must have been doing something right). With time we grow. We got better at articulating what we want to do with our time, both as individuals and as a family. We both have more quality time to ourselves; we all need 'me time' and we are demonstrating to our daughter that rest is vital.

He acknowledged he needed to step up and support me more as a new mom, and if that meant going out of the house then so be it. He hadn't recognised how much I needed him; he wasn't used to being needed by me. As a new mom I was just as needy as our baby and it was a major shock to the system when I realised just how much I felt that I needed Papa to be at my side.

I can openly admit that I sometimes find his me-time choices a bit boring but he is my living, breathing reminder to slow down. He openly admits that he sometimes finds me 'chata' (annoying), but I am his living, breathing reminder that we all need to play.

We respect each other's right to play, and our contrasting play preferences.

Hell on earth

I started looking for work when our daughter was nine months. At first, I thought I'd try to find another playful family like the one I cherished in Camberwell and be a private playworker where I could bring my baby. I had advertised myself as a nanny with a baby on the premise that I would bring my baby to work. I had a hunch that not all families would thoroughly read my description and when they contacted me I reiterated that I intended to bring my baby; it was fascinating how many parents said no. I interviewed at one nursery where I could bring my baby but they were inflexible to my request to work part-time.

I didn't find the right family but I did find a part-time admin job with a small creative youth project for about the same pay. I started that job when she was 12 months old, and I promised myself I would no longer bother with baby-centric activities. My adult time was even more precious than ever. She engaged with other children at the childminder's and Mr Lowprofile was up for taking her to gymnastics at the leisure centre that I declared a no-go zone.

I still had shudders from a few months earlier when I took a short job as a cover nanny for a week while their real nanny was on holiday. In torrential rain I had to chauffeur a 3-year-old to a ballet class and then her 5-year-old sister to her swimming lesson with my 9-month-old baby just coming along for the jolly.

The ballet class started sour as the snooty teacher complained that she didn't have the correct tights. I pointed out, in my boldest jolliest Brummie accent because people in Dorset have to listen harder if I say it in Brummie, that 'she's brought her legs n her feet n the will to dance so that should be alright for a 3-yur-old'. Note to self: avoid being the parent of a child who goes to ballet classes.

After 30 minutes too many in a gloomy church-hall corridor with parents taming smaller children while comparing costumes for the summer show, or at the totally other end of the spectrum: zoning out with endless swiping on smartphones, we headed to the 'no-go' leisure centre, and the swimming pool there.

I was tired. Not even a quick blast of Miriam Makeba sing-a-long on the journey from ballet to swimming could pump me up for the chaos that was awaiting us in the swimming pool changing room. We were all drenched. As we walked into the busy leisure-centre reception I was tempted just to turn around and go back, stand out in the rain a little longer and lie to their mom we had all been swimming.

Of course, all the Parent & Child parking spaces were taken, as were nearly all the parking spaces in the rest of the car park. We were late. As we entered hell on earth, otherwise known as the family changing area at 4.30pm on a Wednesday, I muttered to myself: 'I am not being paid enough to be here. I am not being paid enough to be here.'

The echo of yelling children, begrudgingly getting undressed, was competing with the ear-splitting creaks from the individual changing cubicle doors. On top of that was the slamming of metal on metal (because who can resist whacking those locker doors?) and little ones were screaming for being under the shower and big ones were shouting about not being under there long enough. Some were too hot, others were too cold, hair was being grabbed and tugged in the name of detangling, babies and toddlers were trying to break out from behind bars as twisted bra straps cupped around boobs of mommies with sensible knickers wedged above their thighs and towels wrapped as turbans on their heads.

The combined acoustics and temperature of the poolside weren't much better.

As I entertained my baby and the three-year-old, I looked around at all the worn-out parents who were there out of choice. Swimming is a life skill but bloody hell there must be a kinder way to learn.

Of course, I survived that week of taxi-ing, I mean nannying, but concluded that families that required a nanny rather than an afterschool club probably had a week of extra-curricular lessons that called upon a chauffeur to get them from A to B. For children as young as 3 and 5 years I decided it was not my style. I valued unstructured time for open-ended play and did not want to be the adult who was responsible for timekeeping and ferrying when it did not sit within my values.

In my second week of covering for that family's nanny when our daughter was 11 months I discovered another hell on earth. They lived about 50 metres from the sea and it was the summer holidays so I thought I was agreeing to a cushty week of beach days. No such luck. It was the wettest August on record (isn't it always?) and Managing Director Mum had rather too efficiently booked the girls in at a soft play. As we joined the queue to our local Happy Hellraisers (soft-play centres always have such catchy names), I had cold sweats and flashbacks to the swimming pool changing room. I'd heard horror stories about soft play; I decided it was not my kinda place.

'One in one out,' chimed the immaculately presented sixteen-year-old at the desk. Her face was laden with precise but gentle makeup, her hair so straight and glossy I wondered how she'd avoided the rain. She stood under the strip lighting of the reception desk; an untouched cherub in an oversized soft-play fleece, misplaced against a cage of brightly cushioned inferno.

We stood patiently in line and I watched carnage unfold on the other side of the picket fence. My stomach turned with dread as we waited for a family to leave. I hadn't been to soft play since my younger brother's sixth birthday party. Even before we got through the magic gate it was evident that it was not my idea of an afternoon well spent. Far, far from it.

I shouldn't really complain because I was getting paid to be there; paid to sit and drink tea while the two children I was responsible for were mostly out of sight in a cesspit of other children's snot, saliva and sweat (and even other bodily fluids if you believe everything you read on Mumsnet). So, there were a few perks to the purgatory but none the less I promised myself I would avoid soft play forever thereafter and be honest and open about why.

My ever-observant daughter was mesmerised by the frolicking bigger children from the safety of my lap. Even though I knew her immune system was strong from licking mud and sand – my kinda microbes – there was no way I was letting her loose on any of that germ-riddled 'play equipment'. The only saving grace was we went towards the end of the day so we had to leave when the angel on the desk told the children it was time to go home. The girls emerged with rosy cheeks and lopsided, static hair. Thankfully they both avoided those ghastly burns from sliding against rope and plastic, the kid that bites and the soft-play bully. And none of us caught cholera.

Meantime, I got chatting to a down-to-earth mom from London who hated the place as much as I did. She admitted that she had forgotten to pack any waterproof clothing for their trip to the seaside and would have much rather had a rainy day out in the New Forest. I nodded in agreement and told her about our motto in my first playwork setting: 'Children do not dissolve in the rain.'

That woman from London reminded me of the Camberwell moms and left me puzzled as to why I had found it so hard to make mom friends; it had been easy enough once we had discovered our common distaste for soft play. New moms are thrown in together with total disregard for common interest. We gave birth at the same time but would we be friends if we had met under non-mothering circumstances?

Obviously as I was making new mom friends I had to take risks and dedicate time to strangers in hope they would become friends. Some did, some didn't. It is kinda like speed dating, isn't it? Here's how I see it: the baby group is the initial speed-dating meeting. We work the room, making small talk with strangers. It is kind of easy because there is common ground between us all; but is there really any common interest?

– I want you to entertain my child so I can zone out for a minute, you want me to entertain your child so you can zone out for a minute.

– I want my child to be stimulated in hope that she has a good nap later. You want your child to be stimulated in hope that he (all babies get called 'he' at baby groups if not wearing pink) has a good nap later. Both of us know that a good nap is never long enough.

– I want you to perceive me as a good mom who is coping. You want me to perceive you as a good mom who is coping. Neither of us really knows what 'coping' means.

Our time is limited to the time it takes for our children to move away in opposite directions; 90 seconds is my absolutely non-scientific estimate. Once in a blue moon these chance, rushed exchanges between two adults looking for compassion and companionship evolve into a proposed first date as the more eager of the pair suggests we should meet up and the less eager feels relieved: she didn't want to risk sounding desperate.

Otherwise it is back to mingling and waiting for your child to lead you to the next candidate. Maybe we should equip baby groups like a traffic-light sticker system. Green stickers for the moms that want to chat and open up about all the shit bits and are looking for first dates. Amber stickers for the moms that just want small talk. And Red stickers for the moms that want to bask in silence while their baby is engrossed in a sensory tray.

Oh, how I tease those groups, but coincidentally I did actually meet one of my best mom friends at a baby group. We got talking at the doors as we both escaped early. My daughter was around the one-year mark and all I can remember was a swarm of other bigger, let's say 14-month, warriors storming about at full speed each with some form of wheels ahead of them. There wasn't enough space for each one of them and their gigantic egos. It was bumper cars with the unfortunate addition of some 6-to-12-month obstacles-cum-casualties dotted about the place. Even I was worried that someone was going to get very hurt.

It was horrible to watch and, worse still, the acoustics were intrusive so the parents couldn't even joke and laugh it off. The vicar's wife took great honour in making each individual a fresh brew. No serve-yourself urn there. She hadn't got to me yet and a custard cream just wasn't appetising without the opportunity of dunking. It was a sign not to stay. I had already prised my daughter off her set of wheels and on to something tamer when one child started crying, which triggered another and then another and another. Cue departure.

I scooped up my child in one arm and our mountain of clobber in the other and pelted across the room to the exit. I sighed a rather loud sigh of relief (and quite possibly muttered something I shouldn't say in front of other people's children) and was then surprised to find another fugitive in earshot of my foul language. A like-minded woman with a 4-month-old and a 2-year-old. We laughed at our desperation to leave and consequent relief from fleeing the hellish happenings on the other side of that door, glancing back to a world we were glad to escape. 'You got out fast! It is not easy to move on a two-year-old against their will,' I congratulated her.

'Oh, believe me, we were all willing to leave.' We vowed to each other never to return to playgroups in small spaces, even if the vicar's wife does apparently make a lovely cup of tea.

We walked at her two-year-old's pace in the same direction and soon sussed out we lived really close to each other (like 50 metres away) and agreed to meet the following day in a huge church hall that had just started up a Stay & Play. A woman in our local pub had told me the week before that there was lots of space, home-baked cakes and hardly any families because word hadn't yet spread far and wide. It was a date. I was excited because she seemed like the sort of human I would be friends with even if we didn't both have children.

I woke up the next morning to a vomiting child. Shit, so cliché. It didn't seem necessary to get her number as we had agreed to see each other again within 24 hours. I had to think fast; she seemed like a good catch. I texted another two friends who I had also told about the new widely undiscovered playgroup with home-baked cakes and explained the situation. They accepted the mission and intercepted my date at the door. They reported back that she was great. So, from speed-dating hell to me standing her up, she forgave me and the following week we had our casual first date over scrummy cake that neither of us baked. Unsurprisingly our relationship bloomed and her family are now a huge part of our lives; they have become friends to whom we bring – and share – our babies.

Part 5 - When parents play

What if we pay attention to ourselves as much as we pay attention to our children?

I had these strange floaty days when I felt my whole life had become one big role play. There was this surreal ambiance as if I was playing Let's Pretend or Grown Ups. I felt it most when friends came around to play at our house and it was like I was 8 years old and opening the door to my parents' house. Some days I felt I had embodied my sister and was watching her raising her brood rather than recognising myself as a mother raising my own. I felt forthright in my actions but the whole scenario felt comfortable but also giddy, blurry, dreamlike.

I daydreamed about how my life used to be and imagined what it would be like if I had my old life back when I could just get up and walk out of the house without tending to the needs of a tiny human. Some days I felt quite overwhelmed by my love for her. Other days I felt quite underwhelmed by the repetition and predictability of the day. I was consistently providing our newborn with food, shelter, warmth and love. Job done. She'd find her own ways to play in due course. And what about my play? I subconsciously reminded myself that I had found ways to tend to my own needs when I was at my most vulnerable back in London, and now more than ever I needed to keep tending to those needs.

All the things I was doing for our daughter: I needed to do the equivalent for me.

Parents need to play

Children need to see adults play. Parents can set a good example by allowing themselves time to play either around the home or out in the community. Playful parents are reassuring for their children.

In a lively TED Talk Dr Stuart Brown, founder of the (American) National Institute for Play, says 'The opposite of play is not work, it is depression.'[3] I have a worrying feeling that children all too often see more signs of stress in their significant adults than they see the signs of play. The world is a crazy place which is why children use play to make sense of the chaos they are living in: to untangle the intricate webs of life as we know it, and all the incredible beliefs about what lies beyond... Stressed out parents forget to play.

I think the more parents are encouraged to listen to themselves and hold onto every bit of passion they sparked in their pre-parent life, the more chance they will have to create a truly happier next generation. I loved bringing my baby to feed my passions: dance classes, wild swims, gigs, wanderings with my passport. I needed to be playful in my own way and for me I had to be out and about buzzing around creative communities and in the company of higgledy-piggledy people.

Parents need to play. Play is freely chosen, intrinsically motivated and free-flowing. As adults we generally choose how we want to spend our leisure time without giving it too much thought; we all have a way to find our kicks. When bambino numero uno (forgive me, I know I am excluding parents

3 He was quoting Brian Sutton-Smith a play theorist who was recently described to me as 'simply wonderful'.

of multiples; I salute you and be doubly or triply kind to your-selves) come along, play is still important. There's that pretty famous quote by George Bernard Shaw doing the rounds, it was even printed on the wall of a yoga studio I used to go to in Clapham (another fancy gym deal on Groupon) so it must be worth a thought. It goes: 'We don't stop playing because we grow old, we grow old because we stop playing.' I'm sure dear Georgie won't mind if I jiggle it up for the parents of today; 'We don't stop playing because we have children; we struggle with children because we stop playing!'

Society is set up to serve adults who work a conventional 9–5 job. We strive to work in the daytime because evenings are for leisure and culture and relaxation. All the fun stuff starts around 7pm which is the golden hour of bedtime for so many British babies. No wonder so many parents get miser-able and isolated in the first few years of parenthood; there's no space in the day for fun adult stuff if you are committed to putting a baby to bed by 7pm. I just couldn't fathom the idea of not doing the fun stuff anymore just because most children were asleep by then. I would have gone stir crazy if I had stayed at home every evening, waiting for my wide-awake baby to round off her day at 10pm. I think even if we hadn't had a late-night baby we'd have wheeled her around asleep.

There were certainly weeks when we stayed at home. I am a totally unroutine person; no two weeks are the same for me and that is how I cope best; juggling. But when I started getting twitchy, that intuition kicked in and nudged me into going out to play.

I didn't always have to wait until the evening to go out to play; far from it. As I found my little gang of like-minded Mamas (it takes time; don't give up after the first awkward baby group, and if you spot anyone reading this book, keep them close!) we ventured into pubs. I discovered I much preferred daytime pubs to most of my local cafes for a yummy mummy meet-up, a mothers' meeting, a playdate, a sneaky swift half, getting away from it all; whatever you want to call it. It was not about getting sloshed, it was about floor space and acoustics. Pubs in the daytime are fairly quiet and have ample space; cafes are often busy and if they are busy with other women and babies they are often unpleasantly noisy.

On the flip side, pub floors aren't usually very clean; nowhere is perfect. But the long, padded benches solidly mounted on each wall and the heavy furniture to push around outdo soft play for me any day. I can excuse the grubby floor. The large plastic menus were great to play peek a boo and waft a hops-scented breeze in her direction when she was in the sitting still phase (short lived). And the shiny brass foot rests were great for my crawling babba to bat her eyelashes and drool at herself. The length of the bar to gallop along in our local was the perfect space when she hit that charging about phase at around one and a half.

On her first birthday we decided to celebrate with adult friends in London. We needed a place near Kings Cross Station to accommodate a couple joining us for our special day from up north. All the restaurants around the station needed booking, and the fun independent cafes were too small. I'm pretty sure that this babyless duo wouldn't have travelled a 6-hour round trip if we had invited them to a '1st birthday party' in a cafe but an afternoon with a group of old friends in a pub, celebrating that we survived the first year, couldn't go amiss. We toasted ourselves; Mr Lowprofile and I were proud we were still talking to each other. I thought that was worth a get-together. In my eyes the first birthday was absolutely not about our baby; it was about us, the parents.

Our child had no idea that she had turned one. No idea! So we made it about us. We were with old friends in our new life and we could bring our one-year-old baby. Yep, I urge more couples to celebrate that they are still talking to each other after the most manic 365 days in existence. If you are doing it solo, or have recently been doing it solo, gather your friends and celebrate your villagers.

We were so pleased we had celebrated ourselves. Our one-year-old did not miss out on her little buddies but we certainly cherished seeing ours. In the weeks after she turned one, people would ask 'what did you do for her birthday?' We went to the pub. We also managed to sneak out for a few hours in the low-cost Spa Experience in Bethnal Green because a very kind friend agreed to have our baby (thanks again Shilpz!). As I said, that first year (and really the first few birthdays because they are really none the wiser) should be about celebrating the parents.

Another London friend without kids told me about how she doesn't like kids in pubs. I get it. She recounted how she and a girlfriend had chosen a fancy gastropub to have a long-overdue Saturday lunch over some really special food. 'You know, it was a proper treat but the toddler from the next table kept interrupting. Like wouldn't leave us alone. And her parents didn't do shit.' I feel their pain; I'd rather leave the pub than try to police my daughter's desperation to work the room. My friend is really good with kids: a dedicated Aunty and massively in love with her bloke but they decided not to have children. She's fab with my daughter and I totally respect that she doesn't want her posh lunch pounced on by the burn-out couple from the next table's enthusiastic socialite. I fought my corner by telling my dear friend that I will continue going to pubs because we didn't go to posh pubs.

It just so happened that the Star of Kings in Kings Cross was our not-posh pub. We ate burgers and chips and drank very ordinary beverages in ordinary pub receptacles. It was just a real pub; no gimmicks on the menu. It was once the venue of Outspoken, my favourite raw Spoken Word night that drew a young-but-wise crowd of forward thinkers, appreciative of the wordsmiths that took to the mic. It felt kind of poignant that we should take our daughter to a place where the walls could recite prose from some of my favourite thinkers: Sabrina Mahfouz, Polarbear and Hollie McNish. The latter two dispensed refreshing perspectives on parenthood which paved the way for me to find a freedom in my own.

Going back to that venue was a happy accident. I found it comforting to go to familiar places even when my life felt a bit unfamiliar. By the time she turned one I was no longer desperate to relive my old life in any way; I was comfortable with my new one because I had found little tiny ways to bring my baby and keep little treasured snippets of my old life. Nevertheless, the whole gathering felt surreal; we were there because of the not-so-tiny human being passed around the table for squidgy squeals and stories. I had even rung the pub to double check that under 18s were allowed in; it would have been shit if she got turned away from her own party. 'Yeah but everyone is ID-ed at the bar...' in an attempt to sound assertive, a voice told me at the end of the phone as if I was a police officer doing spot-checks. 'It's ok, she won't be drinking,' I assured the voice who was utterly clueless of my mission.

Our pub of choice clearly didn't have many baby visitors. An unguarded staircase lurking in the corner and no baby change are enough to put some parents off. The bar staff loved having a baby at the bar. Utter novelty. Our one-year-old got free range of the dancefloor, she pottered off behind the bar, helped pull pints and we got to eat a meal while it was still warm, both of us had a tummy of hot cooked food that we didn't prepare or have to wash up for and we were surrounded by baby-free adults. I wish all kids' birthdays could be like that!

Birthday parties... Hmmmm. I've become very cautious about birthday parties. Before we had our child we hung out with a couple who had a very cool three-year-old, who then turned into an even cooler four-year-old, then he started school and was not only cool, he was popular. Bad-move parents. Every weekend he was invited to a birthday party and they lost their social life. It felt like every time we tried to arrange to see them, one or both parents were involved in attending or taxi-ing to a birthday party. Or rushing out to Tesco after bedtime to buy a gift or wrapping paper.

Another friend, with three kids, warned me that their parties cost around £200 per child (and I imagine theirs are the lower end of the party budget). What the fuck? Call me tight, call me scrooge, call me a bigot but there is no way I am spending £200 each year and not genuinely having a really good time.

Let's be frank, £200 spent on a birthday party before a child is four is just added stress for moms. I'd rather tot up all those £200 into a bank account and send her off on a city break of her choice with her best mate when she is eighteen. I've vowed I wouldn't hold a birthday party until she is old enough to ask for one and contribute something towards organising it. For her third birthday she asked for it. Dammit! So we called it a 'dinner party', had bangers and mash with five friends and their parents (our friends) from 5 to 7pm. We conveniently have an epic baker amongst our kids' parents so he made a cake. The kids brought their PJs, they all snuggled on the sofa for a few stories and went home ready for bed around 8pm. If only all parties could be that easy....

Article 31a: An adult's right to play

It's funny what we teach our children; they are a product of us and their environment. Gwen, who always seems to forget to drink her tea, but never forgets to drink her beer, is a scuba diver. By two years old their son knew all the diver hand signals. Similarly, we have footage of our daughter in our Capoeira classes at 7.30pm on a Wednesday night doing a pretty convincing jinga and meia lua kick before she was two years of age. Having not been part of Capoeira before she was born, I never even considered that my daughter would mimic us and our moves.

Sure, kids nod and bounce about when music is playing in the kitchen, but our daughter mirrored us adults learning basic movements, and we were all real beginners when we started. This learning set an example, particularly to the older kids, that we do all have to start somewhere. Learning new things is hard, particularly hard for adults, but what a great message to give our children as they grow older: we are all learning.

At our Capoeira classes I learned the important lessons that children need to see their parents play. And seeing other children's parents playing alongside theirs helped normalise the sight of adults at play. This is not to say parents can fill the gaps of young playmates; children will always need children. But when parents honour an interest outside of employment, housework and chores, and when children see their parents dedicated to something they are genuinely interested in, alongside other adults with the same interest, I think it sets a tone of respect that protects everyone's play. Just as parents respect their children's interests in toys, afterschool clubs and child-centric experiences, children need to respect their parents' right to play. When children of all ages are welcome to join in, they learn, absorb and are reminded of this important message from babe in arms right through to their teens.

I don't believe in forcing or really even encouraging children to join in. In all my play settings I have respected the right of children and young people to opt out. Mini Capoeira was a class dedicated to preschoolers but it didn't have the same magic as our Adult and Family classes. It was great to see the other little ones immersed in acoustic sounds, real instruments and playful movement; it absolutely didn't remind me of other baby-centric sessions that filled me with dread. But our daughter was not interested; she associated Capoeira with big kids and adults, lapping up our atmosphere and dipping in and out if and when she pleased. A Capoeira with fellow toddlers and tots was not Capoeira as she knew it; she preferred mixed-age play. I don't blame her!

When I clocked on that Mini Capoeira wasn't for her it just hammered into me two things: 1) I always respected the choice to opt out when I was working in playwork settings, so I should be transferring that respect to my own child, and 2) the importance of our young being welcomed to join adults fully immersed in adult-centric play. I've said it before and I will say it again; I firmly believe children need to see adults play. It is reassuring, so why do so many new parents steer clear of places where adults play? As a new parent I could have relegated myself to places where parents take children. But I chose to carry on being an adult with a playful thirst for living because I knew I would have a better time than at soft play or Stay & Play.

Each time I went somewhere deemed as a place where adults go, with my baby in tow, the villagers brought me out of my relegation zone with their welcome and acceptance. We united in our brilliant juicy good stuff bouncing off each other. And if ever there were to be adults who weren't pleased to see my baby, I would have simply repeated my dear mother's advice: 'I shouldn't take much notice' and focussed on thanking my intuition for getting me out to a place where I could listen to my needs and play.

Adults who play are happier, thriving in that brilliant juicy good stuff. Happy adults raise happy children. Sometimes we have to bustle together and make our happiness happen for ourselves – we can't always rely on others to do it for us. For example, in the depths of British winter when our Tuesday morning meet-in-the-playground-with-thermos-flasks was too cold, soggy and miserable for our group of four moms and seven children, we decided we needed an indoor place to play. We tried a local spacious cafe and caused havoc. Our pre-nap window for the youngest child was too early for the pub. So I called the owner of our local independent dance studio and asked if we could book a room for an hour each week.

'You gonna give a dance class, Adele?' Stella asked me, half teasing.

'Noooooo. We just want to play.' But actually, we danced! Really, really danced. With a DJ mix, downloaded from the old t'internet onto my phone, on the soundsystem, we flicked off the house lights and switched on the disco ball and flashing lights and had ourselves a jolly little rave. The kids jumped about on the gymnastics mats in the corner. We invited a few other families, the grownups partied like it was 1999 and it only cost us three quid per family to cover the studio hire.

One week we were given the studio's set of hula hoops – one of my favourite loose parts. Happy days!

Thalassophile vs Christmas

Swimming in the sea makes me really happy. It still amazes me that my neighbours don't swim in the sea. Not just the couple downstairs, I mean like lots of my friends and acquaintances I've made since moving to the coast.

Me: 'I went for a swim this morning.'

Neighbour who lives 400m from Blue Flag beach: 'What, are you crazy? It's so cold.'

Me: 'No, it is September, the warmest time of the year to swim. Try it!'

September is such a great month to swim in British seas. On sunny October days I feel quite smug. By November the novelty of swimming in winter kicks in, and the swims become frolicking dips of dazzling joy. And by December, well, I've got Christmas to avoid so a bit of wild swimming seems like a suitable shock tactic to deter from talking about Christmas shopping.

'What are your plans for Christmas?' well-wishers may beam.

'A sea swim.' Excellent conversation changer; all mindless repetition of relatives' comings and goings are put on hold. I can talk for hours about the sea and wild waters.

I didn't make any effort with our daughter's second Christmas. Mr Lowprofile was working nights and I could not be arsed with the hype. All the fuss – the excessive consumption, so much plastic packaging, the traditions that make some of us queasy, the unnecessary gift giving – just doesn't sit right with me. I am not religious and I don't need one day of the year to give gifts of appreciation to my loved ones. For the record there's absolutely no pressure from my parents or my in-laws to 'do' Christmas, something I am very thankful for, but the extended run-up of consumption and enforced merriment for just one day in the depths of winter just doesn't make sense to me. It simply is not joyful if I don't feel intrinsically motivated to celebrate.

She was a mere ten weeks old for her first Christmas and the only grandchild in England so we dutifully went to Birmingham where the 25th December has this uncanny time-warp of repetition that was programmed in the 1980s. We still are given stockings, and Father Christmas still leaves his boot wedged in the fireplace chimney of our front room, and our parents, now grandparents, still stay in bed till almost midday (their gift to themselves), and we still open one present every hour to make them last all day; a ridiculous yet judicious tradition.

I really wasn't fussed about her first Christmas but I had just managed to breastfeed comfortably and it was my thirtieth birthday that week so I wanted to celebrate both milestones with cake and Caipirinhas. (I got through about three measly sips of my favourite Brazilian cocktail before responsibility got the better of me! I'm totally lying; I gladly guzzled every last drop with babe in arms.) But by her second Christmas I was back at work and well and truly over the hype.

'You've got your own family now, you can make your own traditions,' somebody told me, probably when I was grumbling about Christmas.

'Too bloody right!' I thought and schemed my exit plan.

A mama friend with a similar lack of enthusiasm, a cherished comrade, decided to sign up for the Christmas Day dip at our local pier in aid of a local hospice. Perfect. And so, on Christmas morning, around 10am, in a herd of 800 gaudy loonies we galloped into the sea. As my bare feet paced over the wet sand towards the murky white, I took my gaze from the grey horizon and clocked one couple dressed as a bride and groom; what a brilliant alternative wedding day!

That frolic in the sea, complete with red tutu and Santa hat (I'm not a complete Grinch), gave me the momentum to swim every month for the following year. It was a manageable act of self-care, it was free, I didn't need to book it in, I didn't need to buy any kit (I already owned a £4 swimming costume from the high street, a towel and a heap of warm clothes to put on after), I could go with friends or on my own, it got me into nature, we explored new swimming spots so I had a mini adventure to look forward to, all in all, it was really good for my health.

Some months it made me not take my baby which, after a considerable time of bringing her, was a really healthy way to create some space. It was always on my terms, in a place I wanted to swim on an occasion that I had created by my own intrinsic motivation. It was my way of playing. Every single time I dipped, frolicked, splashed about or properly swam I felt all tingly and full of the brilliant juicy good stuff thereafter.

Papa Power

There is so much focus on the mothers and their transition to motherhood, and rightly so. But wow it is tough for dads too. Especially this generation of new-wave fathers who really want to be involved; it is more common to see shared paternity leave, dads cutting or condensing their working week to allow a day or so for caregiving. It is fantastic, and we should totally encourage it more and more.

We should also give these guys some credit for stepping up and getting involved when their fathers didn't. I think it is safe to say that we are the generation of normalising stay-at-home dads. I am by no means wanting to discredit our generation's fathers, the new grandfathers, that did stay at home. You were radical, you were exceptional and we salute you.

As mothers find their place in the working world, I am happy to see dads gaining a new importance. While we still have a long way to go, modern dads are sharing the workload of family life. Mr Lowprofile and his peers are doing it *without* a whole previous generation of fathers to guide them. And this lack of guidance is tough.

The world as we know it is isolating. The media suggests that motherhood is more pressured than ever but from speaking to the older generation, to me it just sounds different. Previous generations were isolated too because the women's place was in the home, and in particular the kitchen. Sure, we've somewhat moved on from those times and we now have more freedom, more baby-centric groups (if they are your cup of tea – I pass no judgement, promise!) and platforms to voice our struggles whereas previously mothers just had to grin and bear it. Isolation seems to haunt parents all around the world despite having an international community of parents who can get online and start, join or follow a discussion.

But all this virtual connection just doesn't cut it for me: I need humans. Anyway, I'm meant to be giving the spotlight to the papas and there I go shining the light on mothers again. How matriarchal of me.

Many women are juggling work like crazy. There are the practical and physical tasks of bringing up children, plus the mental load that comes with caring for each unique personality. House work, caring for relatives, being a supportive friend, project-managing multiple humans at home, and that is all before we've arrived at work where we are striving to keep up a meaningful career. The unrecognised, and therefore unpaid, workload of mothers means that we are demanding more of the fathers than ever before.

My respect for all that my husband contributes to our family has skyrocketed since it occurred to me he is doing this blind. With no disrespect to my father-in-law, who worked long hours and didn't really get involved in raising his children, my husband is embarking on this journey without guidance. There is so little support out there for men. I am sure many other dads feel the same.

Our male partners are the first generation to be so involved in the family, particularly in the very early years. But modern dads are doing it without role models. It has taken me nearly three years to realise and now appreciate how much harder it is to be the loving, affectionate, involved dad we want our partners to be when they haven't had that type of father to show them how it is done. It is going to take generations to change and it will probably never be an equal fifty-fifty but there is certainly a positive and welcomed shift taking place before us.

I talk to a lot of women. We come together to collectively raise our children and 'share the burden' of childcare. Many of us recognise that our partners are over-worked and are isolated as fathers. Dads don't hang out the way moms do. Being with other moms over the past three years has helped normalise the chaos and learn the tricks of the trade.

In an ideal world I'd love to see more dads comfortably parenting with other dads so that our sons see that it is normal for men to support each other the way that women do. Social norms are indeed changing and there are some great grassroots movements that are bringing men together, not always specifically around parenting, but embedding a new sense of togetherness for men: Talk Club, Dope Black Dads, Mens Sheds, Outta Puff Daddys, The Dad Course are just a few on my radar. But it is still unnatural for many men to parent the way their female counterparts do. I strongly believe that we need to encourage and nurture our male partners because in most cases their dads won't be nurturing them in the way women do to new moms.

But what about the dads? Where do they fit into this accrued busyness created for our families? When do the dads just sit amongst other dads and offload or decipher dadhood? Generally, they don't. Do dads ever just sit together and talk about what it means to be a dad?

Most dads are working full-time and just don't have many opportunities to be with other dads. Their weekends are their only real quality time with their child or children. Evenings are short and for many are made even shorter by our children's evening clubs and activities. Weekends as a family disappear as we prioritise our children's peers over ourselves; birthday parties, sports clubs and competitions, extra-curricular classes for our over-schooled and under-played children (and by the next chapter you'll be signing up to Shag Rota duty too).

The good news is that when our children come around to having children (weird thought, right?) our sons will be a little more hands-on and a little more involved, and arguably a better support for their partners than ours are to us right now. Our children are observing how we raise a family, how we connect with other humans, and most children are seeing their dad do more than their grandads did for us.

The rise of fatherless families over the past thirty years or so has demonstrated to the next generation of fathers that it is normal to be an inconsistent part of his child's life and walk away from relationships with their child's mother. I know lots of men who said they don't want that for their own kids; they want to be involved. Similarly, as women's empowerment is growing at full force many women are deciding they are better raising their child without the dad in the picture. I am not for one moment suggesting couples should stay together for the sake of the kids; I just hope we can keep nurturing and celebrating the active fathers because, like it or not, the fathers are influencing our sons.

I firmly believe that boys need to see men fathering together so it is normalised behaviour for when they eventually become parents. But us women can't force all the dads together; they have got to do it for themselves.

That library book

We experienced the unspoken suffering of a relationship between a man and a woman adapting to the sudden and constant interference of their new baby's arrival. Having a child is a complete overhaul on a relationship; sometimes for better, sometimes for worse. We always knew we'd have children one day, but seven years of it being just us was a long, long time to be comfortable in each other's company.

We were triangulating between coping and loving and scowling. We had average days, really good days and really bloody hard days. The hard were easy to hide from oblivious onlookers but they built up and built up until we had a wall between us.

Alongside that wall was a second layer of bricks: breastfeeding. That foundation I had struggled so hard to lay was beginning to crumble. Getting the hang of breastfeeding was the most painful feat I have accomplished in my whole life, so letting it go was a dilemma I struggled with for weeks and weeks which turned into months. I didn't want to sound like a stuck record so I didn't talk about it much but I sure did feel it.

I wanted my body back.

I wanted the freedom to choose to not take my baby.

I wanted to be sexy.

I wanted to stand strong and full bodied instead of lugging around my depleted torso.

I knew I needed significant rest but I didn't know how to let myself have it.

I also wanted my fiercely independent daughter to need me. It was a peculiar predicament. I continued to sacrifice my body because deep down somewhere behind all the other feelings breastfeeding was fulfilling my own sense of worth. I needed her to need me.

I was fragile and stretched between the demanding relationships between me and my body, me and my daughter, and me and my husband.

My relationship with my body and my relationship with my husband had both suffered. Neither had been my physical priority. My priority was always our daughter. Despite dancing, the quick sea dips and Capoeira classes it was difficult to create space from my daughter because she was dependent on my breastmilk. I wanted freedom but I didn't want to rock the calm and sociable child when I wanted to bring her with me, so I stuck it out.

Reconnecting with my husband took time. And at the back of my mind I had my mom saying, 'Well, I don't think anyone really has much time for their other half when your child is two.' She said it well before I was a mom when we were talking about my friend's relationship breakdown. Married for over forty years to her partner in crime; guilty of parenting playfully. I've never seen a photo of my mom and dad on the day they got married but I have seen photos of them in fancy dress as the Blues Brothers and as fish fingers.

211

My mom rarely talks about intimacy, emotions and relationship dynamics but the things she has let slip over the years have always been of great help. I've found myself repeating her nugget of golden advice over and over: 'Well, I don't think anyone really has much time for their other half when your child is two.' Each time a girlfriend confided in me that something wasn't right between her and her bloke, I'd nobly parrot my Ma, 'Well, I don't think anyone really has much time for their other half when your child is two.'

And about sixteen months into our chaos I lost my cool with Mr Lowprofile and typically I forgot that golden nugget. I was convinced we weren't compatible as parents. One week, it all got so intense and disjointed between us that I got as far as calling my friend's therapist to see when she could book us in. She was booked up for couples' appointments (a sure sign that what we were experiencing was very common) so we had to wait a fortnight. Just having that appointment looming on our shared Google calendar was enough to get us talking. We agreed on two things: we'd made a really cool, calm and collected kid so we were obviously doing something right. And we had forgotten how to talk to each other. We quickly concluded that we needed help because we didn't know what wasn't right for us. Or better, we didn't know *how* to make it right.

I carry an air of calm about me, and have the patience of a saint for others. But deep down I am unsoundly impatient with myself. I'm the sort of woman who gets shit done. My patience is reserved for others, and less so for myself because I know my own potential. I'm growing to be kinder to myself and take life more slowly. I've got to unlearn the old habits to make room for the new.

Even so, the thought of waiting a fortnight to see the therapist was like torture for me. So, a bit of googling and dipping into relationship blogs led me to a title of a book that resonated: *I love you but you always put me last: how to childproof your marriage*. I was far too ashamed to buy a copy and own it but our local library had one in stock. Well, not our local, but one a bus ride away so that I could disguise this crucial errand as a thoughtfully planned quality time outing with my adventure buddy. I duly checked that there was no hellish Wriggle and Rhyme timetabled for that library the following morning (thank you universe!). And off I went on a 'save our marriage' treasure hunt with our oblivious toddler.

A three-week loan gave us a deadline to act on its contents and an incentive to not need it anymore. From memory it was a twelve-step save-your-marriage-type guide by who I presumed was an American psychologist because suddenly everything felt very, very dramatic. I felt like we were about to be called up to be guest speakers on an Oprah-wannabe talk show to be aired on an unknown Cable TV channel, mid-morning when only desperate housewives would be watching. We were civil and there was no infidelity so Jerry Springer wouldn't have been interested.

We acknowledged we needed help, except we didn't know what that help looked like as we were still amicable. I just felt indescribably unloved. And he said I didn't appreciate him. Just reading the introduction of that library book made me feel loads better. Knowing that it was so common made me feel less panicky about where we were at.

We didn't make it through the book. One or two chapters was enough to get us back to our normal. I think I mostly needed reassurance that what we were experiencing was common; once I knew that it was pretty normal I just accepted it. I cancelled the therapy session and we spent the £60 on candle-lit takeaways over silly card games to lighten our mood. We just needed to be more playful and less resentful about our lack of quality time together.

We were never ones for extravagant date nights but as a result of that library book we're better at giving each other attention; little things like greeting and embracing each other first instead of going straight to our daughter. I've got better at reminding him I *need* a daily 17-second hug. We've got better at asking friends and family for a few hours babysitting here and there so we can go out on a date. Or better still, stay home and send our daughter out on a playdate so we can enjoy the tranquillity of our home and daytime sex.

And now, at the time of writing, this phase doesn't even feel like a particularly significant part of our parenthood; other stuff happens. A new stage of our child's development wows us, other distractions surface and our journey takes other twists and turns. That library book, as the title suggested, focuses on priorities. I quickly realised I was evidently putting myself last and that had to change. From that relationship wobble came one solid life lesson: I come first, then my husband, then our daughter.

Shag rota

Another book that came our way was Naomi Stadlen's *What Mothers Do: Especially when it Looks Like Nothing*. For the record, back in that fourth trimester I really did *not* feel as if I was doing nothing; the pain I felt feeding my child was certainly *not* nothing. Unsure if the book was for me, I glanced over the chapter list and one topic really stood out for me and it was called 'Snapping at my Partner'.

A lot of the chapter is familiar territory: relationship breakdown, resentment towards men that their life appears unchanged for them, fatigue, financial pressures, etc., etc. A lot of which can be avoided if we allow ourselves to live a more playful life. But one of Stadlen's interviewees, a mother of a three-month-old, reveals the 'shag rota' where she 'find[s] a friend with a baby that you can be honest with, and they take your baby for an hour and a half one Sunday afternoon, and you have theirs on the alternate one.' Absolute genius.

At three months postpartum, I was not ready to get jiggy or particularly inclined to organise a window in our week to even open up to the possibility but I was tempted to offer this remarkable piece of advice as my own.

But that would be dishonest and I couldn't handle the heckles from my bestest friends that know only too well that a) I've not had much sex since giving birth, b) I haven't called upon them for their shag rota duty and c) I haven't offered any shag rota childcare to them either.

Mr Lowprofile and I know we absolutely need more date nights; but honestly, they create an added pressure to go out and part with money in mediocre cafes and bars when all we really want to do is stay home and have sex.

It's absolutely undeniable that the shift in the dynamic from being a couple to becoming a family is really bloody hard to navigate. I have definitely found being a mom easier than being a wife. I have learned that it is ok to ask for help even when life is good: we don't need to wait to be in crisis to call upon our villagers.

Friends with older kids have been there and agree that those first few years were really tough on their relationship. Friends with older kids seem to love having a baby or toddler around for a few hours. I let them enjoy the novelty. Mixed-age play dates are really important, so is a shag rota.

'Early intervention', 'preventative measures' – whatever you want to call it. Call upon your community; surely a shag rota is a far more enticing reason to babysit for each other than date night?

Couples need time to be couples. Maybe calling upon grandparents for shag rota duty is a bit too explicit. My parents have a key when they come to visit so sod's law they would pop in for a forgotten something as soon as Mr Low-profile and I got down to business... And his parents rarely go out unaccompanied because of the language barrier which leaves us only to call upon our most trusted villagers.

If you embark on only one bit of play as parents, let it be whatever you get up to when your child is out with your villagers on shag rota duty. After all, we all deserve more orgasms, with or without a partner's participation!

Part 6 - Wearing my playwork hat at home

What if we stop trying to control our children?

I know our three-year-old is really playing when I have no idea what she is doing. Her voice lowers and she talks in a different tone as she enters her own world. It takes time, it takes persistence to keep encouraging her to play independently. And I have to remind myself to have timeless days at home without an agenda. And during those days I need to just let her be and gently encourage her to combat her own boredom. On these days I prioritise rest.

This journey of encouragement is not always harmonious! Far from it. Amongst many of our chalk-and-cheese tendencies, my husband Mr Lowprofile and I indeed differ on play. He is a screen-time kinda guy and I am not. Papa loves, loves, loves films and computers. His parents bought him his first Spectrum when he was twelve and when I met him back in 2010 he had recently been made redundant from his projectionist job in the soon-to-be-digitalised cinema in Lisbon. It was his happiest job: setting up film reels, watching multiple movies per shift while surrounded by popcorn fumes. After eating too much free popcorn in the first few weeks on the job he can no longer stomach the snack, but he has remained fond of the scent; who doesn't love the smell of freshly popped corn?

So, our home swings between screens yay and screens nay. Needless to say, our daughter loves television. I have lived without a television for most of my adult life; I can happily go without. Papa thinks a day without a screen is unthinkable; how else would he relax? I know I overthink what the screen time could be doing to her fantastic evolving brain, and I notice it comes up in parent chats from time to time so I know I am not alone. Screens are part of twenty-first century life, but for adults (myself included) and children I discern that screens are filling a space of time where our brains would usually resort to playing.

Each time our daughter asks for TV I respond gently with 'I haven't seen you playing yet'. 'Play first, TV later.' I am looking for that deep, fully immersed state of being. I often remind her that one of my favourite ways to play is 'throwing the TV out of the window'; it really winds her up.

Boredom leads to play; but screens have removed the excuse to be bored. Screens fill all those moments where our minds might wander off into a place that is full of play. When did you, as an adult, go a few days without using a screen? It is a rarity. We absolutely need to let ourselves switch off and get bored more often, then our children will follow suit.

I know our three-year-old daughter can entertain herself for hours with play; she just needs gentle encouragement to start playing and time to be fully immersed in her play. The more unfamiliar a child is with child-led play the harder it can be for her to find her own playful disposition. But just like animals, humans are made to play. Sad as it is, we have just been conditioned out of it because play, when it is genuinely intrinsically motivated, is mostly low-cost and therefore not so popular with the capitalists who commercialised childhood.

I recently came across a great little video from a Scandinavian kindergarten teacher giving a TED-style talk who said, 'The children do not need the toys, the factories need the children.' I am going to repeat it because this is important, 'The children do not need the toys, the factories need the children.' I am kicking myself for not noting down her name but I was too busy shouting 'YES BAB! Exactly!' and imagining a picket line of placard-clad preschoolers chiming, 'We don't need the toys! We don't need the toys!'

Nerd alert

To understand the benefits of early play we have to look at the brain. In my ode to the 90s movie star with great hair: 'Here comes the science bit. Concentrate.'

I'll keep it very, very simple. We have three parts to the human brain: the reptilian, the lower brain and the higher brain. The reptilian brain functions for instinctual necessity: eat, sleep, excrete, reproduce, repeat. The more sophisticated lower brain connects us to socialisation, our animalistic instincts to play and to bond. And it is the higher brain that is our powerhouse for reasoning. We all have a lower brain so all mammals play, but play in humans is often conscious of some social context, and as our brains evolve, this consciousness forms our reasoning.

At birth our babies' higher brains are unfinished. In fact, at birth a baby's brain is only a quarter the size of an adult brain. No pressure, but it is the carer's role to help stimulate brain growth. I was astounded to learn that a baby's brain will double in size in the first year! Double! And will reach 80% of its adult size by the time they are three years old.

No wonder these years are crucial and such bloody hard work.

But it doesn't start at birth. Brain cells are formed during pregnancy and that is why in the UK we are encouraged to take a folic acid supplement as soon as we start trying for a baby. I asked our midwife why we take it before we have conceived and she made the very good point that if a woman doesn't realise for 4–6 weeks that she is pregnant then that's 4–6 weeks of potentially insufficient nutrition for early brain cell development. I asked her what they do about unplanned pregnancies and she glanced a reassuring smile in my direction and affirmed 'the sooner the better'.

Grown-up humans with neurotypical brains have sophisticated fibres which connect the different regions of the brain to each other. In terms of the brain and play, the part of early brain growth I am most interested in is the neurons (a fancy word for brain cells). These neurons send signals to communicate across different areas of the brain. Broadly speaking, different parts of the brain are responsible for different functions: language, motor skills, logic, emotional and behavioural responses, memory and thought processes. These functions are all interconnected through these intricate brain connections called circuits. So how do we grow these essential circuits? Through play.

It's a no brainer! Terrible pun. Sorry.

There's plenty of neuroscientific research that proves that repeating (and repetition is crucial, even if it is dull for the parents), yes, repeating positive, nurturing interactions helps babies to grow the vital circuits they need for healthy brain function. Two studies in particular, one by Sergio Pellis and another by Jakk Panskepp, looked into the effects of free play on the brain.

Free play, just to remind you, is where children are left to their own agenda; where they can choose to stop one thing and start another, then go back to the first thing again. Free play has no set list of outcomes and adults should only intervene when safety (physical or the emotional safety of another child) is of concern. In the world of playwork we advocate for an adult to engage in a child's free play only, and really only, when the adult has been invited in by a child, and the chosen adult must be willing to take direction from the child or children who are playing.

Both researchers confirmed that experience of free play changed the circuits at the front end of the brain. These changes were of particular interest because they enhanced the brain's executive control system which in turn helps regulate emotions, make plans and solve problems. So, it is not a case of more, more, more circuits but most crucial is the change in the circuits which are unique to free play.

I knew I was a playworker who became a parent when I realised that I often went more than thirty minutes without talking to our two-year-old. She was full of language and words but I just did not feel I needed to speak to her all the time. One of the eight Playwork Principles[4] is 'playwork-ers choose an intervention style that enables children and young people to extend their play.' If I was intervening with

4 Playwork Principles Scrutiny Group (2004) Playwork Principles. Cardiff: Play Wales. www.playwales.org.uk.

222

unnecessary dialogue then I felt I was indeed distracting her from her play.

I think from working with lots of children, and particularly those with cognitive disabilities, I grew a sensitivity to how my presence can disrupt the flow and focus of children playing. Adults can be really distracting for children. Our generation of parents are indulging in our children like never before; we want to know where they are and what they are doing at all times of day and night. Cameras on cots, apps with live updates from childcare providers and pre-teens with mobile phones; it is all surveillance that previous generations did not have and I think it is pressuring parents into guilt trips if we don't know what our child is doing. I think my child's sense of self in her play is more precious than anything I have to say.

Over the years it has been challenging working in non-play-based settings with colleagues who overlook the value of play and have accused me of 'not doing anything'. I've fought my corner with 'Letting them play is the best thing an adult can do for a child.' But I've always felt quite misunderstood, particularly when working in schools.

As a playworker parent I can see that when my daughter and her friends can negotiate their own play it is good for their brains. Now that they are past the hazardous choking phase I don't keep an eye on them, but rather leave them to it until one is about to drag the eyes out of another. So far, all eyes are intact.

Observing her play

I remember when our daughter was a little bit bigger than a newborn, I could sit and watch her for hours. The tiniest of movement felt precious and incredible, the new facial expressions fascinated me and captured my attention for what felt like hours on end. The slightest of vocalisations rang in my ears like the strongest soul choir. I was infatuated. I am sure these observations are true of many new parents. For me, the best bit about being a playworker and a parent is how much I value observing our child at play. The more our daughter plays, the more I observe in awe.

The magic of seeing a rainbow stops me in my tracks and slows me down for a minute. That is how I feel about our daughter's creativity. Not so much her paintings, or her drawings, or her rhythmic movement, but what really captures me is her play. Just like when a rainbow emerges from the darkest, thickest clouds, or glimmers over a deep blue sky, I stop and marvel at her infinite spectrum of possibility. Her requests to help her build a crane from a cardboard tube, dig a swimming pool on the kitchen floor, make a flying dragon or a mermaid's wig. Her stamina for role play with her sophisticated facial expressions, and the soulful ballads she improvises narrating each day's triumphs and woes. The heights she climbs in autumnal orchards (or on our banisters) and the way her body scrambles across rocks at the seaside.

I love how deeply she is teaching me as she explores through her own play. And every few weeks it is evolving and organically changing direction.

Every child can show us new ways to play if we just sit back and let the play unfold before us. In my early days of playwork in Birmingham I felt it was a real privilege to watch mostly disabled children's play evolve; the creativity of some of my city's most excluded children was mind-blowing. As a parent I glow with joy because I know that all the unstructured hours for freely chosen play are the only true gift we can give her. And I know that, unlike any shop-bought toy, our gift is helping her innovation, her character and her judgement to grow in all sorts of fortuitous directions.

We have found ourselves saying to our daughter 'slow down'. She is incredibly confident and her strength of character and self-belief are up there, way out of my reach. She is wise beyond her years and sometimes I wish she'd just decelerate a little. I am treasuring these early years where play is her only agenda. Soon she is going to want to learn structured stuff which will probably involve more routine and more input from me. When she was only just three years old she asked for swimming lessons and enquired when exactly she will be going to school. I am not keen on her going to school anytime soon. There's just not enough time dedicated to free play, creativity or freedom of thought.

I love watching children at play and I have learned how to do it discreetly and appreciate the nuances of play when adults don't intervene. A playwork trainer recommended to me a 2016 publication called *Interacting or Interfering?* by Julie Fisher, a professor of Early Childhood Education.

'See if you can get your hands on this, Adele,' she said showing me the cover of the book. 'I liked it because she describes what is all familiar territory to us as playworkers – adults butting in too much – and what she concludes from her research is what we do as playworkers really, but in teachers' language.'

To supplement my playworker income I have sometimes worked for agencies filling the gaps of absent teaching assistants in special schools and with alternative provision providers. In schools, as much as possible I 'taught' children by letting them learn for themselves because with my playwork training I felt confident to trust a child with time and space for them to explore the world for themselves. I quickly discovered that schools, even with specialist provision, don't have much time or space for child-led learning, self-directed learning or play. On more than one occasion my play goggles weren't appreciated by my educationalist colleagues who sometimes accused me of 'not doing much', 'or you're very quiet with him' to which I responded along the lines of 'why would I do something for a child, if I have observed they aren't far off doing it for themselves?' And the same goes for unnecessary questions, narrative and distractions from a child's wonderful thoughts.

No, I am really not keen on our daughter going to school anytime soon. I have a friend whose four-year-old was the greatest kid. Then he started school and they shattered his confidence. When he was six his teacher described his reading as 'behind' because he didn't grasp reading as quickly as other children his age. When he was five he was playful, imaginative and physically very able. His mind wasn't ready to read back when he was learning how to ride his BMX over dirt tracks, how to coordinate his limbs to swim front crawl and how to climb branches so he was out of reach of his 6ft 6" dad.

'Oh bab, boys are still developing their proprioception at this age. He's just not ready to read books,' I tried to comfort his mom. She's a physiotherapist, so deep down she knew the importance of fully formed neurological pathways for gross motor function but the pressure from school just overrode her own knowledge. It wasn't nice to see. Of course, when he turned eight he was ready to read. He'd struggled for two years of his precious childhood being marked down against learning targets, missing vital play time outdoors with his peers, sitting inside with the teaching assistant dedicating time to 'catch up' on literacy. I think professionals that are obliged by their employment status to follow certain institutionalised structures can become so overwhelmed with the targets set upon them that there is no room for children to be the unique humans who learn different skills at different speeds.

We are rushing our kids to do things so quickly. There are endless extra-curricular clubs to broaden their horizons but I am repeatedly wondering where is the time to play? Has anyone else noticed that as the hours children spend playing have steadily decreased over the past twenty years, so has there been an increase in child mental health illnesses and childhood obesity?

Even though play can be very physical, involve lots of movement and can be great exercise, it does not require umpires, referees, scoring systems or any measure of competition so it is not sport. Play is creative but it is not art; play is the journey of the creative process, not the masterpiece to be displayed at the end of it. Although there are spaces dedicated to children's play, play can really happen anywhere, anytime. We just have to have adults that are comfortable in allowing it to happen and children who are not being rushed through the schedule of their day.

Children grow confident as they explore and establish their play preferences. Back in the 90s, Bob Hughes, a scientist who became a play theorist and activist, classified play into sixteen Play Types.[5] Here they are:

Recapitulative Play: 'play that allows the child to explore ancestry, history, rituals, stories, rhymes, fire and darkness. Enables children to access play of earlier human evolutionary stages.'

Symbolic Play: 'play which allows control, gradual exploration and increased understanding without the risk of being out of one's depth.'

Object Play: 'play which uses infinite and interesting sequences of hand-eye manipulations and movements.'

Locomotor Play: 'movement in any or every direction for its own sake.'

Role Play: 'play exploring ways of being, although not normally of an intense personal, social, domestic or interpersonal nature.'

Imaginative Play: 'where the conventional rules, which govern the physical world, do not apply.'

Fantasy Play: 'rearranges the world in the child's way, a way which is unlikely to occur.'

5 HUGHES, B *A Playworker's Taxonomy of Play Types*, PLAYLINK, London, 1996

Dramatic Play: 'dramatises events in which the child is not a direct participator.'

Communication Play: 'using words, nuances or gestures for example, mime, jokes, play acting, mickey taking, singing, debate, poetry.'

Mastery Play: 'control of the physical and affective ingredients of the environments.'

Rough and Tumble Play: 'close encounter play which is less to do with fighting and more to do with touching, tickling, gauging relative strength. Discovering physical flexibility and the exhilaration of display.'

Exploratory Play: 'to access factual information consisting of manipulative behaviours such as handling, throwing, banging or mouthing objects.'

Deep Play: 'allows the child to encounter risky or even potentially life threatening experiences, to develop survival skills and conquer fear.'

Social Play: 'during which the rules and criteria for social engagement and interaction can be revealed, explored and amended.'

Creative Play: 'which allows a new response, the transformation of information, awareness of new connections, with an element of surprise.'

Socio-dramatic Play: 'the enactment of real and potential experiences of an intense personal, social, domestic or interpersonal nature.'

As a playworker visiting schools in Birmingham I used to plan and design Play Curricula to ensure children were getting opportunities to engage in all 16 types of play. We didn't get too hung up on Play Types as a framework, or a tick-box exercise: 'yes, he did Role Play today', tick. But we did have to talk the school's language so we used the 16 Play Types to challenge us to provide resources that diversified their play and gave children the opportunity to engage with all the different types of play. If we were doing an indoor session in a school hall, what natural resources could we bring indoors to provide meaningful opportunities for Mastery Play?

Learning this bit of theory, all those years ago, has really reinforced that our daughter is playing all the time. Right from when she was a few months old I felt comforted to see that when I left her to her own devices, she found ways to explore through play. Without me doing very much at all, I could see that when I gave her the time and the space and the quiet she would occupy herself in her own wonderful little world.

As her Mama I can see the importance of all the little ways she is playing. Way before our daughter discovered my job is 'a playworker', I knew I needed to use language that shows I value and encourage play. Any time I am fixing, making, writing, and even cooking or lying down for a rest, and my daughter asks 'Mama what are you doing?', as often as I remember I respond with 'I am playing'.

I often crave movement so I prioritise Locomotor Play through dance classes and occupying dance floors till the wee hours. That soothing feeling of sand filling my hands and spilling through my fingers? Yes, that too is play; in Mastery Play I can control the ingredients of the environment. I see my thirst for understanding human relationships, building playful communities and my fascination with living as tribes as Recapitulative Play. Learning languages, widening my vocabulary and rearranging words on a page for me are all forms of Communication Play.

I struggle with Fantasy Play and Role Play. I like real life too much. I didn't go for fantasy books or much make believe when I was young. My mind doesn't explode with enticing stories for children, twists and turns and magical kingdoms. I didn't get on with Narnia and haven't read Harry Potter. I much preferred to read a real-life diary than an adventure like in the *Neverending Story*. I will read Harry Potter one day, I just decided I'd wait until I can curl up with my daughter and read it together.

I love it when our daughter thinks like a playworker, or better still thinks as a child with unbounded creativity ready to manipulate objects for limitless play. When she was three I cut her tube of toothpaste open to scrape out the dregs. She said, 'when it is finished can I use it in the bath? Because water can go through like this,' weaving her index finger towards the cap and then out of the hole the other side. I love it when she innovates her own toys and I know she has learned that from me.

I also love it when she climbs trees. Her fearless, nimble body navigates trunks and branches in a way I have never experienced. Unlike the toothpaste tube, I can't say she has learned that from me. But I can say she has learned to measure risk because I have allowed her to explore it. I have trusted her judgement. I have trusted her strength; both in her muscles and in her determination. I accept that I won't always be there

there to catch her if she falls, but I will always comfort her and encourage her when it is time to climb again.

Risk taking through Deep Play is absolutely crucial. I think all too often adults belittle children's capabilities because we are caught up in our own fears. I was not a confident tree climber but our daughter does not deserve to carry the burden of my fears. I firmly believe that no child deserves to be deprived of play opportunities because the adults around them are tangled in the worries of 'what if...'

I hope that no one reading this wants to hurt their child. I have worked with children who have been intentionally hurt by their parents; their stories haunt me but their play liberates them from the dark beginnings documented in local authority filing cabinets. My professional role was to empower these children, help them through play to feel comfortable in their own abused skin. I have used play therapeutically, but I am not a play therapist. The psychological trauma should be unpicked by trauma-informed practitioners only when an individual is ready to explore their trauma. I don't know about trauma, but I do know that children exude resilience when they are playing freely.

Respecting their privacy

There's still the hum of the expressway beyond the bird song. As a city girl born and bred I've always noticed cars and their effects on my play but I've become immune to their din. I think it is safe to say, I'll never stray far from the whirr of the city. On this particular day the chorus way up beyond the top of the tallest shoulders provided a cheery soundtrack to our semi-urban play area. In this corner of a local park there were no slides, no seesaws, just lots of fallen branches, a rope swing and the floor awash with thousands of pine cones: our props for endless play. The winter she turned three, she could never gather enough pine cones.

We had planned to seek shelter from the unfavourable seasonable wind at the base of our local pier. Since moving to a home where outstanding natural beauty surrounds us, I tended to avoid concrete play places but of late I had started to welcome that tiny cement sanctuary: protection from the winter winds and a huge blank canvas for chalk drawing. I also really enjoyed having a backrest while I sat and sipped milky turmeric chai from my thermos flask, with cardamon punching my nostrils as I unscrewed the lid. That wall is screaming for some art; I'm always keen to lively up dull concrete walls. I think that is why I found Montreal and Malmö so enchanting: there was so much street art.

As we mounted our bicycle I double checked Madame's required destination. I had an inkling that in the time it takes to go downstairs, don two shoes, a coat, a helmet and attach her bike seat, her objective for the day may have shifted. Sure, as such, she declared that she wanted to climb trees in the woods. And so we cycled north towards Queens Park, instead of south towards the sea. I really don't mind not having a plan for the day. I'm well aware that this is a luxury of only having one child. Going with the flow is way easier with only one child; and I genuinely enjoy the freedom of just mooching about our parks and open spaces without an agenda for the day.

So the chalk we packed for the wall beneath the pier could have been redundant but instead she made the fallen down branches look a little more lively. A kind soul had built a round den from fallen branches and logs. It made the perfect 'tent' to eat our sandwiches. While I rambled in my 'otebook' she chalked the interior of her holiday home.

I try to give our daughter privacy when she plays. My presence, sitting close to her, might be the reassurance she has asked of me when we arrive in a new place. In more familiar places she may run far and free. Either way I can give her privacy by busying myself in my play, while I let her crack on with hers. Over the years I have noticed a lot of playgrounds that forgot to include hiding places. This is one reason I prefer Mother Nature's playgrounds. I love a good nook! A lot of brightly painted metal-framed play structures in exposed open spaces do not provide nooks.

I have worked with a lot of children who find busy playgrounds very overwhelming. They need private places to make sense of the world they experience from a place of relative safety; most playgrounds do not meet their play needs, but forests, or beaches, or more secluded community gardens give them the privacy they need to play. And even the most sociable of children need a place to unwind and play at a slower pace.

I love creating play environments, setting up a load of loose parts and anticipating what the children might do with each one. I am always wrong! Their creativity far exceeds my ideas. Or sometimes I overcomplicate what a broom could be used for and actually sweeping is the most satisfying way to spend a day. Who am I to say what is between those bristles and the floor?

I probably spend several hours each week inside my own head designing large elaborate play spaces and intriguing little nooks. When I was a child I used to say I wanted to be an artist and an architect; I think as a playworker I am fulfilling both roles beautifully.

A really core skill I have taken from playwork into motherhood is the ability to set up (or cycle to) a play environment and let her be. I do not need to involve myself in her world of play, unless she invites me in. I take something that says, 'This is my playtime too.' For me it is a notebook and a pen, anything that can be readily put down when I am needed and then picked up again as I am dismissed from duty.

When it is just me and her we rarely go to playgrounds or parks where there will be many other children. If I am having a notebook day I don't want to make small talk with other parents so I choose a secluded spot where I know we can both get on and enjoy our own headspace. She observes that I am relaxing into my preferred type of 'play' and that is her cue to find hers. Every so often I check in, does she need my care? Not my intervention into her world of play, just practical things like water, a wild wee or a reminder when our departure is imminent. But other than that, it is down to her and the company she imagines herself with to go with her flow.

I know when she is playing deeply because her voice lowers to just above a whisper and she chats away, mostly in a language that is spoken very quickly and doesn't make sense to me. But that is the point of play; it is how children make sense of the world, so quite naturally they must make their play make sense for themselves. And that is why it is so empowering for them; they make sense of their own world in their own way. I don't fret that I don't know the ins and outs of her world. I don't fret I don't understand the language she speaks in her world. I just try to make our days safe and secure while she leads on the rest.

Urban wonder

When we uprooted from central London life of childfree frolics to a quieter life in sunny Bournemouth it initially felt like a downgrade. It was definitely a downgrade on culture and our citified social lives but an upgrade on fresh air and woodland. The first few months were a total cultureless shock but some six years later I've grown to love and value our upgrades and how much more time we spend outdoors in spectacular forests. Woods, forests, small collections of trees offer children and adults endless opportunities for nature-based play. Very few of us live close to forests but collections of mini woodlands and protected nature reserves are dotted all about British cities.

Nature has a calming effect on humans so once the first bit of steam has been let off, I tend to notice children's play evolving into slower Socio-dramatic Play or pottering about in the earth through Mastery Play. I have seen children charging at full pelt on man-made, tarmacked playgrounds and then the same children take life a little slower in Mother Nature's ground for play. Most nature reserves in built-up areas have wheel-friendly nature trails and often host friendly volunteer-run cafes selling home-baked treats to satisfy fresh-air appetites.

But as I cycle around our neighbourhood, it is urban. I can't help but imagine closing little corners here and there for a little bit of sneaky community play. Pocket parks and street play are two low-cost solutions to raising active children in playful communities. As I tootle around on two wheels I daydream about road closures to make our doorsteps inviting places to play. I'm not reminiscing about 1940s post-war Britain when kids played out all day on bomb sites and only came home for tea. Nowadays play streets are happening all over the world. Here in England, on 13th June 2019 to be precise, the Department for Transport wrote to all local Highways Authorities encouraging them to occasionally close roads to facilitate children's play. Playing Out CIC helps residents get started; they've already supported 1000+ streets in 88 local authorities to play out in England.

I used to cycle through a subway every day to work, and again a few years later when I cycled to another job in the same direction. I didn't like staying on my bike so I used to hop off and walk through the semi-lit tunnel, pushing my bike down the slope to its approach and up again the other side. I didn't much like the first job so my morning commutes were an unhealthy narrative of negativity. I wish someone had told me then to try to notice five tiny gifts from Mother Nature each morning as I travelled to work; it would have been a much healthier start to the day.

Small children are really good for noticing the tiny wonders in life; they are so good for the soul in this sense.

When we let them go at their own pace their eyes see all sorts of wonderful (and weird) things, reminding us that there is beauty (and intrigue) in so much that we often overlook. My friend had her second child soon after her first turned two. She didn't get on with the double buggy so she ditched it pretty quickly and just accepted she was going to travel at the pace of a two-year-old for the foreseeable. Those guys see so much! They have so much appreciation for the tiny details of nature, of architecture and even of the quirky humans in our neighbourhood. Their scrutiny of our locale reminds me to cycle slower. Children, when given time and listened to, can be so sincere about what they perceive as ugly, but they have a hunger for investigation and pass little judgement on the things we think of as undesirable as we grow older.

Recently, as I approached the same subway, but now with my daughter in the rear passenger seat of my bicycle, we took it a bit slower (the bike is heavier these days) and she noticed all the patterns on the bricks throughout the subway. I marvelled at what I had never noticed before. I suddenly wanted to engrain each groove with fluorescent chalk.

Around Bournemouth Pier, at the end of the Lower Gardens, there's a huge bit of terrible 1960s town planning in the form of a concrete overpass just by all the fancy Victorian mansions. For years I've been imagining different ways of making the space below the flyover more beautiful for the millions of tourists (and us locals of course) that walk under it day in day out: glass mosaic tiles so it glistens as the sun moves from east to west, an intergenerational yarn bomb using bits of wool and fibre optic cables to celebrate our 'retirement town' vs 'digital hub', or even covering each pillar in netting so passers-by can attach their own little mementos. I love it when citizens detour the planners, the strategists and the directors to innovate gentle little playful rebellions leaving the message: playful people live here too.

Designing cities as places to play occupies a happy little corner of my mind. Making our cities more playful places requires residents to unite and challenge the status quo of Planning and Highways departments. Not an easy task, but also not impossible.

Play fighting

I think Capoeira gave me the confidence to play fight with my own child, even when she was small. Sure, as a playworker I've engaged in many a battle scene, an arm wrestle and 'pow pow pshhhhht pshhhhht wom wom' superhero fight club. I guess Rough and Tumble Play came naturally in our home because Mr Lowprofile and I have both learned martial arts as adults. But a recent conversation with two mom friends revealed that they never had play fights with their sons who were fast approaching five and six years of age. Rough and Tumble Play helps children to develop self-control, physical awareness, boundaries and compassion for others.

Children will always charge at young men initiating Rough and Tumble Play. Uncles, big brothers, male child-care practitioners and male playworkers; oh, the novelty of a young man working in a sector dominated by women! They all bear the brunt of children's physicality. But the females of

239

the species tend to steer well clear. So, I just want to sow the seed for a few more tough-mothers. Rough and Tumble play releases all those brilliant juicy hormones in moms. And it only needs to be five or ten minutes on the sofa or the floor or the bed. No prep required. Just a willingness to be a little bit silly and get out of breath. Sure, your kids will be surprised and once you start they will not want to stop, but the more you do it, the easier it will be to round it off when you have had enough and leave them anticipating the next session.

'It'll end in tears,' my parents used to drone. They weren't ones to stop much but they would point out the potential damage we could do to each other. I think fighting reaffirms a sense of protection and love. There is that split second when my daughter anticipates that she is about to get hurt; then phew! It is just a humungous bear hug!

Of course, accidents happen, but I think that is all part of the process. Let's be clear, I by no means set out to hurt my daughter and she quickly communicates (mostly with her words but also with her facial expressions) when it is too much, too scary or too surprising. I trust myself and know I will always err on the side of caution. But the risk is out-weighed by the reward. Each time we fight we always end up giggling, our hearts racing and my daughter feels strong. We also manage to have a few minutes laid on our backs at the end of it to let the dust settle which inevitably instigates round 2. I've set my limits and will never let it go past round 3.

If you are really struggling to visualise what you might look like as a tough-mother roughly tumbling about, I urge you to google EVE Riot Grrrls of Wrestling. EVE is a fantastic example of what happens when grown-up women allow themselves to fully embody Rough and Tumble Play. I didn't watch The Rock or Hulk Hogan in the WWF – Worldwide Wrestling Federation – as a child, though I saw glimpses of it when my brothers did. I thought it was ridiculous and weird. I am still not inclined to dedicate any of my precious time to watching it now, but what I can take from it is the playfulness. WWF was way too scripted and over the top to be play; it is totally adulterated. But the nuances of EVE, and even a Burlesque cabaret I saw in Birmingham last year, exude playfulness. They both champion women's right to freedom of expression regardless of their body shape, their sexual identity, their skin colour or their age. Yes, both are theatrical and choreographed but what I really see is a distinct lack of script and sequence, and a whole lot of intrinsic motivation which of course I link to play.

Our play kitchen

In the flat we lived in until our daughter was two and a half, the lowest of the kitchen drawers was strategically full of tupperware and other child-friendly kitchen items: tea towels, kitchen foil, plastic cutlery. The toddler-height cupboard was similarly packed with lightweight child-safe food containers, small tins (and bigger ones as her fingers and toes became less fragile) and cartons that wouldn't break so she could take some autonomy while Papa and I were cooking and unpacking the shopping.

She played in that drawer and the accompanying cupboard for hours and hours; packing boxes with cutlery, matching boxes and lids, hiding the boxes under tea towels, stacking the boxes one on top of the other, chewing on the lids, wearing the boxes as hats... I wondered why we bothered having any toys at all.

When I was working I loved coming home to find out how they had spent their day together. He used to show me what 'not toys' she had played with because he knew that is what I was most interested in. Those little stories they'd tell me and all the little ways she'd make him marvel.

I was delighted that he'd risen to the challenge of being a play-at-home dad albeit for one day a week. It was one day more than his father had done for him; he's breaking a mould. 'Daddy day' has been diluted a bit since I'm home more and our childminder days have changed; they don't have that uninterrupted day together at the moment so I miss hearing the little stories, but this is one that I treasure:

Mr Lowprofile chuckled as he fulfilled his 7.20am ritual of packing his daily peanut butter sandwich into a reused takeaway tupperware.

'What's so funny at this time in the morning, amor?'

Mr Lowprofile isn't from a snacking culture and he hates matching tupperware lids to the box. So, raising a child whose metabolism relies heavily on snacks with a woman that hates disposable plastic bags for snacks is a triple headache. He relayed his story of when I was out at work; in the sanctuary of his beloved snack-loving, waste-hating wife being out of the house he told our then two-year-old, 'Sorry, we can't take a snack, I can't find a lid for the box.'

Being her mother's daughter, 'What nonsense,' she thought, and without saying a word went straight to the kitchen cupboard where the tupperwares were kept. She methodically worked through the pile until she found a lid to fit the box and secure her snack.

Come on, Papa, you gotta do better than that.

Sharing is caring

Is sharing really caring? I'm still undecided. I agree it is tedious to watch two- and three-year-olds squabble over the same toy; it is another reason I don't buy many toys. The squabble is always short lived. I allow our daughter to choose up to three 'special toys' that when her friends come over she can declare are her 'special toys': no one is to play with them and she doesn't have to share them. They go on top of the fridge, out of reach, until everyone has gone home. After those three, it is a free for all. It seems to work.

If she is fussing and being possessive, I don my playworker hat. Playworkers like every day ordinary objects used in extraordinary ways; we call these objects 'loose parts'. Generally speaking, playworkers don't advocate for predefined, single-purpose 'toys'. Children fight over toys but varied loose parts catch the eye of varied children. So I pick out and big up something rather mundane and unprecious, knowing that I have multiples to hand, like a tupperware box, a kitchen utensil (but not my finest chef's knife; sure, playworkers like risk but we sure know our limits) or (my personal favourite) a roll of colourful sticky tape from 'my desk drawer' and offer that to our small guests as a consolation for my daughter's disastrous hospitality skills and the three special toys that are out of reach but not yet forgotten. The introduction of something 'adult' and 'not a toy' usually distracts from whatever they both wanted in the first place; sodding toys.

Toys are evil.

Surely all parents have seen the picture on the internet? My cooler younger brother politely informed me over text message that it is not a 'picture on the internet. It is a meme.' So this 'meme' depicts the combatant Lego plotting attack on the sole of a foot. I'm not sure how that picture on the internet has made the Lego look so evil. Bloody genius.

A few weeks later, in a real-life face-to-face conversation with my best friend Sara who politely and gently eased me into 2020 (for the record, I know memes were not invented in 2020, but I've had my head buried in toddlerland), I learned it is not pronounced 'me-me', but 'meeeme', which made me feel massively uncool. Just when I thought I was getting back into embracing the modern me I coiled back into my luddite, clueless, mommsy persona.

I'm from a generation of now adults who as children were forced to share, to help and to think about others. I think this self-sacrificing has resulted in far too many adults of my generation suffering from this unnerving obligation to people-please which inevitably has led to the demise of self-care and the rise of burnout. We need to be kinder to ourselves and we need to let our children be kinder to themselves too. And my first step towards that is not insisting that she has to share every single toy.

I do remind her that she enjoys playing with her friends' toys, and that sharing is kind, but I never assert that she must share. 'Sharing is caring,' I hear people sort-of-sing around children, as if sort-of-singing magically makes a child comply. I love music but I am less keen on musicals and I dislike sort-of-singing. If we are having a conversation, a dialogue between one or more people, please for the love of chitchat let us talk. If we are singing, we want to fill a space with the sweet sound of harmonious human voices, please let us sing. But this deliberate sort-of-singing to give a message to children is not for me. I am sure there will be a paediatric brain study that concludes that sort-of-singing to your child is beneficial for the development of what some think is sophistication in the system of the somewhere lobe of the lower something in some place.

I also don't force her to play or to socialise. She'd of course love to have the TV on alllll day but I prefer to let her be bored. She sits in front of the TV hopeful I might keel and press the red button; I don't. I just let her be bored. Eventually she empties her book basket and flings it over her head, or moves the sofa cushions around, or hides down in the child-size gap I purposely left between the sofa and the wall. Within minutes of me not turning on the TV and creating space for nothing, she is playing. Sometimes I have to stop what I am doing too; so I lie down, back flat on the floor in stillness for a few minutes to show her it is ok to do nothing. She seems to always find a way to combat her own boredom, or she has a nap. Rest is certainly ok with me.

Why should I tidy my room when the world is in such a mess?

I hate housework. I never used to hate it. But nowadays I regularly find myself thinking how much I hate it. And it is never ending. And I promised myself I'd never be one of those women who sat and talked about housework, so I honestly hope this section gets edited out, but all new moms seem to need to offload about it at some point in the early months of motherhood so... here I go.

Some days I feel momentarily shitty that my husband has been at work all day and comes home to the shit-tip created from our play day. The sewing machine occupies our dining table along with a heap of half-cut segments of three different sewing projects (I heard crafters always start a new project before completing another), a children's book or two, a glass half full of water, a forgotten cup of tea, another half drank, a deposited half-bitten slice of cucumber.

Then there is the floor; littered with an ecosystem of evolutionary play, just like the forest. Our child lives, breathes, nurtures and evolves through all the processes of life that unfold throughout our home; on carpet, on laminate, on tiles, on mats and even a little faux grass out on the balcony. The uninterrupted unfolding of her soul trails through our home. She handles and controls all sorts of objects and unintentionally creates an obstacle course for my unsuspecting soles. Mr Lowprofile, after a ten-hour shift and bike ride each day, is not quite so nimble on his feet and thus not so appreciative of our litter. Sorry bab.

Some days my feminist, my artist and my don't-give-a-shit ego follow him in through the front door and I don't think any more of it. Other days the fairly timeless me clocks that his arrival is imminent and I conduct a twenty-minute frenzy of tidy-up time to ease the guilt. Guilt is such a strong word that is thrown about the mothering world. Housework, or lack of, is way way way down my list of things to be guilty about. But some days I would just really like a clean tidy home. Some people have a knack for tidying as they go. I do not.

As a playworker I vouched that I would never tidy up after children until I was totally sure that they had finished playing with whatever 'mess' was on the floor/table/wall/tree, etc. And as a mother I've honoured that with my daughter. But it means our home is often messy. Mess doesn't bother me, most of the time. Mess means creativity is flowing; I feel liberated and free to play. But I seem to have built up in my head that a messy house is unwelcoming and I love welcoming people into our home.

Although extremely perfect homes look great on Instagram, they are, in my opinion, completely unwelcoming as a guest never knows where to put themselves, or anything they may be carrying in, like a tornado, I mean a toddler. And then play dates in immaculate homes end up being this apologetic awkward union where guest-mom apologises to host-mom for making her home a mess. This is utterly unfair; playdates are for children to play. If I feel I need to put on a spectacle for the family coming to play then chances are I am not at ease with the parents and I question why I am dedicating my precious time to them in the first place? I need them to enjoy my home in whatever sort of playful mess they find it.

I'd just like new parents to give themselves a break, and twenty minutes rest on the sofa is often way more precious use of time than tidying away behind your child. I think most new parents are so grateful for someone else making them a cup of tea, or someone else's sofa to sit on, that they really don't care what state your home is in.

A very kind nine-year-old came over with her mom when I was having a particularly bad day. I texted various women asking for their company and superstar Rachel turned up at my door with her three girls. It was raining and half term and I apologised for dragging them out as I opened the front door. 'Dun't be silly bab, a visit to see the babby will be the high-light of their half term.'

'Your flat is really messy,' declared her eldest once she'd been to inspect all the rooms.

I was on the brink of tears for other reasons but hid it with laughter and said, 'Oh, I know bab, I just need a brew and then I'm gonna sort it all out.' About twenty min-utes later Rachel and I went to sit in the front room with a cuppa each and her eldest had blitzed the whole room, neatly organising everything into little piles in each corner. What a superstar. Who knew our villagers could step up to duty from so young?!

Part 7 - Persistently playful

249

What if we stop trying to control ourselves?

Just a few weeks of little or no creative stimulation has turbulent effects on me. Hormone imbalances, months and months of disrupted sleep and probably a diet that could do with more fresh veg – that's when it is guaranteed that shit will hit the fan.

When did a parent stop being a person and start being an activity? An obsession? A bloody life sentence for the most heinous crime? I definitely tried to avoid the modern parenting trap, ditch the parenting vibe and hold close that I was still an adult, a human who just happened to have an extraordinary little person in tow. Don't get me wrong, I was just as besotted with her as the next mom in the room, I just refused to add the burden of parenting to my list of responsibilities when being a playful parent made so much more sense to me.

Don't believe the hype

One thing that surprised me about parenthood is how much fellow parents were obsessing about doing it by the book. I'd never heard so many of my peers parrot other people's practices, methodologies and guidebooks. We've been spoon-fed information, given directions and orders all our lives and now we rarely have to look beyond the end of our palm for answers to any of our questions. Parenthood was a stark reminder of how my generation is addicted to being told what to do, and buying things (even if we can't afford them). We buy books, visit forums and even enrol in online courses that impose rules, theories, skills, techniques and care plans on us, new parents.

We live within an economic system where, just like childhood, parenthood has been commercialised. As with the leisure industry, and child-sized everything costing twice as much as a normal-sized, we readily part with our hard-earned money and line other people's pockets to create an appearance that we are 'doing it right'. Problem is that when we buy into these goods and services we disregard our ability to listen to our intuition and trust ourselves.

The free baby groups that I did go to – I think I averaged one per month for the first year – were full of chitchat about which techniques or methods were being used for sleeping, weaning, communicating and introducing quantum physics to our newborns. I felt terribly under-read, but not terribly ill-prepared. I was confident even though what I was doing would probably be described as 'winging it'.

Why weren't more parents just winging it? What's the big deal about all these expensive babysign, music-making and sensory courses and online communities of parents wanting to be coached? I couldn't predict that I'd be available for the same 45-minute slot for six consecutive weekly classes so there was absolutely no way I was going to part with any of our modest family budget to find out what all the fuss was about. Would those 45 minutes each week really make this transition to parenthood easier? My biggest bugbear was that those groups were always centred around the baby. Never mind the baby, I wanted the attention on me. Me, me, me!

'Meeting other moms' always popped into moms' advice but the humans I wanted to spend my time with didn't all miraculously give birth in the same month I did. I just wanted to hang out with my friends; surely my baby could join us for a cuppa or a swift half after work? Why was all this parenting malarkey so prescriptive and so structured? Why did every session need an underlying baby-centric theme or objective? And most importantly why didn't the mothers get a group that was just for them to sit and talk and offload the constant chaos and utter joy of raising tiny children?

I never heard anyone say it at the time, with babe in arms, but so many women have revealed to me, now that their kids are older, that in the early days they felt depleted by the shock of the transition to motherhood; the new requirements of nurturing newborns felt totally overwhelming. I felt it too, but I do think I got off very lightly because I found so many ways to prioritise my own play while caring for a newborn. It has become obvious to me that if new parents are not nurtured and supported, then we, as a community around the child – and I really believe that the onus is not only on the parents to carry some responsibility – we, as villagers, collectively run the risk of not giving that child the best start in life. It goes without saying that if we want villagers to form part of our lives, we also have to be villagers for others.

I'd like to think about how we can give new parents, as well as their babies, repeated positive, nurturing interactions. How can we nurture new parents to a place where they feel confident and able to trust their intuition? I think we could start with re-branding Children's Centres as 'Places for Nurturing Parents'.

I feel so fortunate that in these first three years overall I felt nurtured and consistently supported by the villagers we built into our life. In the early days, loneliness had a tendency to pang at my window; that higher risk of PND was faintly tapping like pebbles thrown at the pane of glass between stability and stumbling. Somehow, I had the tools to not open the window and let it in; training as a playworker enabled me to prioritise play in my daily life which has been a great tool to cope with the chaos of motherhood.

My solution is to encourage parents out of overwhelm and into play. To invite and include potentially struggling adults and their potentially screaming baby to join other adults for normal everyday life rather than banishing them to a place of baby-centric solace. And longer term, invite parents and their potentially screaming disabled child to join other families for normal everyday life rather than excluding them to a place of disability-only solace. I have worked with a lot of families whose disabled children have been excluded from children's services that fail children with diverse abilities. I am fully supportive of the families that choose to exclusively socialise with other disabled children; I am merely highlighting that no child should be excluded.

Like any playworker I am still human so there were days when I did stumble and loneliness seeped through like the unwelcome odour of my neighbour's cigarettes. But on those days, I opened another window by going out to play; jotting my thoughts in a notebook while being outdoors, sitting on a bench in my park and chatting to a stranger (I particularly found chit chat with older people good for my soul) or phoning one of my best faraway friends, those who know me best, when I needed real talk. By engaging in something that was freely chosen, personally directed and intrinsically motivated I felt those unhelpful, but very valid, feelings diffuse.

Time and time again a little bit of listening to myself and a whole lot of play really did go a long way. I've learned that I can choose to dissipate the hard stuff, the difficult times and the shitty days, or I can allow it to overcome me. Anytime I'm in an unfavourable situation, if I stop and listen to myself and do something playful, life gets a little lighter.

Kitchen raving was my favourite go-to to get the brilliant juicy good stuff going: I put on an oversized hoodie, hood up, blast drum n bass and videocall a fellow raver who I suspected would be at work, sat in an office. I always got the best reaction when they were at work; awkward apologetic 'not now' expressions, subtle desk dancing or sometimes a full-on groove with an office full of colleagues who all thought it was hilarious I could so blatantly gatecrash their working day with a video call.

Elaborate middle of the day baths with candles, Epsom salts and singing along to Queen was another playful place I could bring my baby; either in a bouncer seat next to me in the bath or splashing about with me. Both brought me intrinsic joy and plenty of the brilliant juicy good stuff that we need more of.

Working towards expert status

I came across the '10,000 to be an expert' rule in Malcom Gladwell's *Outliers*. I haven't even read the whole book, I just opened it up on the 10,000 theory when our daughter was three, and liked the sound of it. In a nutshell Gladwell writes about how 10,000 hours of practice in something leads to expertise in the given field. Draw for 10,000 hours and you'll be an expert illustrator. It got me thinking about motherhood and how in the early days I hung around with a lot of women who had older children and they seemed to do everything pretty effortlessly. It absolutely does get easier as they get older but in that sleep-deprived, wobbly state I just wanted to know when exactly?

When indeed? I didn't have this 10,000-hours theory to play with when I had a baby in my arms, but I think it is quite fun to share and might give new parents something a bit comforting to work towards.

There are on average 730 hours in a month so we hit the 10,000 mark roughly around 14 months. But some of that month we are sleeping, right? Or at least attempting to. So, hitting that 'expert' mark is delayed a little. I guessed in those first 14 months I slept for maybe 2000 hours (it sounds a lot, but it certainly didn't feel like it) so I guess I hit 'expert' around 18 months. I think that is quite encouraging. Surely, 'I am working towards expert status' is a far more encouraging mantra than 'I am failing my child' or 'I am a rubbish mom'.

Take this a step further and I think it would also help the primary caregiver be less expectant of the breadwinner. If one parent is spending significantly more time with their child than the other parent then it is paramount that there is leeway and encouragement for the less experienced parent to catch up. One of the duo will become an 'expert' before the other. I found myself getting frustrated when Mr Lowprofile didn't know stuff about our child but seriously I ask myself now, how was he meant to know all those details when he hadn't yet clocked his 10,000 hours with her? How could he know the stuff I knew when he spent half the amount of time with her that I did?

Of course, this isn't hard-proven science: I just like to find playful ways to embrace the chaos. We are two laid-back adults, we can be organised for work but we live our personal lives with as little routine as possible; we go with the flow. It is much harder to calculate when Mr Lowprofile clocked his 10,000 hours but he most certainly had by the time she was two. They've always had an undeniable bond, he has risen to the challenges of parenthood and I have loved watching his confidence bloom.

With every developmental stage came a new hurdle so that brilliant juicy expert status feeling ebbed and flowed. In her first year, just as I thought I was getting the hang of things, the season changed and with each new season came a new set of hurdles.

That night in the armchair

Parenthood for me wasn't just about seeing to the needs of my child. It was, still is, about adjusting and understanding my place in her life and my place in the world around her WHILE maintaining a meaningful relationship with the human I chose to procreate with. It is an exhausting process to say the least and one that drained me from time to time. Family life for us didn't work when I put myself last. If I wasn't on good form (or even average form!) our family dynamics crumbled.

The peak of my depletion, and the peak of putting myself last, surfaced one night when our daughter was 18 months and I was close to approaching my 10,000 hours. In some expert status epiphany, I became wise to my own needs too.

In the quiet darkness of another lonely night-time feed I felt another sensational low: that night I shrivelled as I felt the cotton armchair beneath my buttocks dampen. I was paralysed by her needs and I sobbed as I finally acknowledged that I was sacrificing my own needs. I needed to gently pop my little finger in her mouth to release the latch and stop breastfeeding. I knew I needed to allow myself three minutes to wash myself, change my undies and put on a fresh pad, but I knew my needs would cause her to stir and make a racket. I didn't want to wake up Mr Lowprofile who had a ten-hour shift ahead of him.

So, I just sat there utterly uncomfortable in the armchair as all my life-building fluids, milk, blood and tears, were seeping out of me interrupting my much-needed rest. I wasn't yet ready to accept that our dynamic had to change. I couldn't then see that I was too stretched and not resting. I needed rest. A lot of rest. It seems so obvious now!

But we Mamas just keep serving everyone else first.

The discomfort of sitting in that armchair lingered for days. It was the wake-up call of all wake-up calls: I was forgetting to play. I came to realise that a big part of my exhaustion, mental and physical, was down to my lack of play.

I know when I haven't played enough because I feel miserable. I get stuck in a rut. Most of the time I am upbeat, forward-thinking and good company. But every so often I dip. I forget to do the things that feed my soul and my mind goes a bit toxic for a few weeks at a time. My body is void of all that brilliant juicy good stuff. I have to remind myself to play. I have to stop and listen and do whatever I feel intrinsically motivated to engage in. My play usually involves making something with my hands, physical work, mixing up delicious, fresh ingredients to nourish my body. In my twenties in London those 'few weeks' extended into months and months with regular trips to counsellors while working desk jobs and the desperate downloading of wellbeing apps from which I conveniently ignored all notifications because I am not a techie person. Apps don't do it for me. The hunter-gatherer in me needs to get up from the desk and work: I need to use my hands, move my body and talk to real people. I am a people person but when I was twenty-something I didn't know how to admit to everyday humans that I wasn't ok.

With practice, and every day I'm getting a little older and therefore wiser, I have learned to articulate when I am not OK. I have no shame in admitting that I am feeling a range of emotions; it is OK to not be OK. I am allowing myself to be more and more honest. I think my varied emotions as reactions to different circumstances are valid. The more I am honest with myself and my loved ones about what I am feeling, the more sense I can make of it all.

That night in the armchair the message came loud and clear for a second time; I come first, then my husband, then our daughter. That is the hierarchy of need that makes sense to us in our little family.

Baby raver

Around the same time, the same sodden armchair (now clean of course) was host to another pivotal night: the night we went to bed and left her awake by herself. Our needs came first. Well, not really first; we had spent the evening trying to get her to bed as usual but this night was different. She was wired, bright-eyed and switched on, even at 10pm. In her softly lit bedroom her wide pupils glowed with an intensity I associated with the grimmest drum n bass clubs in Birmingham. Nightclubs that have probably closed down and places I probably wouldn't have the 'balls' to go to nowadays. The thought of them now makes me shudder. More hugs, less drugs please, people.

In the first round of teething, we listened to a lot of drum n bass: skanking with her in the sling was the only way I could think of to distract her from that first tooth splitting through those horribly raw gums. But as her mouth filled up, getting through her scalding gums of emergent molars, top and bottom, was certainly a team effort. On the darkest days of teething I resorted to Under 2s sessions at the children's centre to distract us from her emergent molars. My jokes about 'my gurning baby' didn't go down well.

A year or so after that first tooth poked through our little raver was back in business. Her fervent pupils were almost disturbing. I say almost because her demeanour was calm. And I believe when a baby's demeanour is calm, I have no place to intrude.

In the depths of those intriguing pupils, pages from my GCSE Biology revision guide flickered. Brain activity was illustrated simplistically as a series of lights and lines; one tiny glow, with a wiry stem jutting out connecting to another tiny glow, with another wiry stem jutting out in another direction towards another tiny glow, and so on and so on.

But there was nothing simplistic going on. Each gleaming iris was colourful and pirouetting around each pupil. Her eyes were host to a night-time game of 'Tig! You're it', children wearing amber, emerald and chestnut head torches. I could see the intricacies of the game as the brain cells connected; one light whizzing towards another, each light's own wire diligently trailing behind and being pursued by another light. In her eyes was a bokeh playground where children bounced and spun and looped around each other; their headlights bobbing as they ran.

'She's wired. I guess her brain is growing or something,' I said to Mr Lowprofile as I sat on our bed approaching a state of exhausted despair.

A few deep breaths and a silent 17-second hug helped calm my rationale; the all-important five minutes away to recharge and re-think the game plan. I'd left her playing in her room. She was peaceful and determined as she purposefully chose, positioned and repositioned wooden blocks and plastic tupperware boxes. She placed them along the armrests and seat of the armchair where I'd cuddled, read, boobed and soothed her for the previous two and a half hours.

'Ok, I'll just tell her we are going to sleep, when she's ready she'll do the same.' No sugar-coating, no negotiating, no consequences, no meaningless promises of treats for compliance, no authoritarian rule. We were just trying to keep it real:

'We are tired. It is bedtime,' I declared.

So, I returned to her room where she still stood silently against the armchair in her beige hand-me-down sleepsack. Rectangular takeaway boxes lay next to standing plastic cylinders interspersed with square cubes and green and blue milk-bottle lids. The particular composition was unremarkable to my blurry, sleep-hungry eyes but it clearly meant the world to her.

I peacefully told her that 'me and Papa are tired, it is bedtime, we both have work tomorrow, it is late, we are going to bed now. Boa noite.' Good night. She nodded in acceptance and continued to scheme and strategise. I paused at her bedroom door, fascinated by her intrigue and her stamina and her dedication to her play.

I grinned at the shadows created by her stretched out baby grow with sagging sleeves. Her dramatic silhouette reminded me of Jingu, the ancient Japanese warrior. Indeed, she was our little Onna-buegeisha in training, peacefully plotting to protect and honour her household.

I'm aware that some parents may be horrified about leaving our daughter alone and awake that night. The baby scenes from *Trainspotting* scared me as much as it did the next mom.

261

So, before you panic and call social services please hear me out.

I'd like to say I remember vigilantly closing every other door along the corridor in our flat that night in order to limit her danger; I don't. But I do recall lovingly kissing my daughter. I do remember thinking, 'I trust you to do what you need to do right now.' I do recall thinking how much I admire our way of judging her needs and not resorting to panic and a state of feeling inept when she has a different agenda. I felt like between me and Papa we'd done everything our daughter needed of us, and we'd even tried lavender oil.

There was no conflict, no bitterness, just trust and acceptance that we all need rest and we all need to play. And sometimes the specific time slots for rest and play don't harmonise between three unique humans living together.

I lay down and rested. I don't know how long she took to come to our bed, I don't know if I fell asleep. But I do know I sensed her there, stood at my side. Her tiny hand, heavy with her worldly wisdom, tapped me until I scooped her into bed with me. She lay on my chest for a while, her head cupped in the curve of my chin. Her face turned inwards across the bed where she mirrored her Papa; peaceful warrior facing peaceful warrior.

I sluggishly summoned the momentum to deliver her back to her own bed, sliding my legs out of bed and down to the coarse, wooden floorboards with enough umph to heave up my upper body laden with the weight of our sleeping warrior.

I crept down the left edge of the corridor, the side where the floorboard creaked less, and laid her down on her back in her own bed. And of course, in a stealth ninja flip she returned to her tummy and nuzzled into the pillow to recreate the nook of my chin.

Drop n Go

Soon after our third Christmas I spoke to a Mama friend who was pissed off about spending all her annual leave at her in-laws' house in the home counties. 'And I got into London one evening to see my friends and that made it all worth it.'

'One evening? Is that all? Were you just sitting around their house the rest of the time?'

'Yep,' she sighed, 'for a whole fucking week!'

'Oh bab you gotta just hand them over to the grandparents and disappear for the day. Honestly, it's better for everyone. Drop 'em off and bugger off.'

I have frequently felt sorry for my daughter caught in between two very different styles of love during visits with her paternal grandparents. On occasions it has been heartbreaking to watch her emotionally torn between her mother's love and her grandma's love. I show my love for my daughter merely through my physical presence; I am unconditionally there for her. Granted, her well-meaning overseas paternal grandma, of course, deserves all her grandchild's love, but she has the heart-wrenching task of earning it in record timing on each short visit. All the while my tiny human is piecing together clues as to who this almost stranger is and what the tension in the room is all about.

If my baby could have spoken I think she would have said, 'I know I should love her but I am connected to my mama who

263

I can sense is not entirely comfortable with her being around.' Now that she is that tiny bit older, and I have matured, I can encourage our daughter and my mother-in-law to cherish every moment they have together. In fact, my maturity on this matter came in at around Grandma's 16-month visit; remember that expert status I mentioned!

I think the kids have a better time because the grandparents can indulge in their grandchildren, spoil them with love (and often plastic crap that makes noises) and sweet treats; 'Just a little won't do any harm.' Infuriated smoke puffed from my flaring nostrils the first time I caught Grandma giving her a biscuit despite my explicit opinion that babies really don't need to taste processed sugar. So, my tactic with my in-laws is to drop and go. We are all much happier if I am out of the picture for a few hours, a day or even a week. Our daughter feels loved, is perfectly well looked after and isn't torn between the conflicting styles of love being launched towards her.

In the earlier days, of course, I fretted. I worried about her not sleeping enough, watching too much television. I wanted her to need me; my leaking breasts needed her after a few hours of us being apart. But as she has grown older I just accept that we are all different in how we raise our children, but so long as love, respect, safety and play are the foundations of time spent with our daughter, I'm pretty happy whoever she is left with.

Therefore, since stopping breastfeeding, my strategy has been to disappear and enjoy the time off. The benefits of rest for me while leaving her with grandparents, my friends, my siblings far outweigh the load of taking her with me. And even back when she was tiny our elderly neighbour took her for a nap-time spin in the buggy to give me some headspace; I am not sure who had a better time: me childfree for a little while or Brenda out with a baby again after all those years. When I've allowed myself to drop and go I've sat in cafes alone and read, talked to adults without a child's interruption (real adult conversations with my oldest friends will remain my most precious affair), swum in the sea, seen live music: all stuff that helps me exude that brilliant juicy good stuff and be ready and willing to be a loving Mama on my return.

Sweet FA!

I somehow ended up being excited by my first Mother's Day. Why had I hoped that my husband, complete with his new father status, would miraculously be a thoughtful creator of gifts and embracer of commercialism? Over the previous seven years we'd both nonchalantly let most commercial holidays slip through the net.

So, I am still not sure why I felt it so necessary to mark the occasion. Why was this Sunday so unique to any of the other overly commercialised, super-sensationalised, emotion-evoking day in the commercial calendar?

For six years through college and university I worked in a high-street chain of French eateries. It was a very popular place for Brummies to take their mommies on Mothering Sunday. In the quieter months of the commercial calendar management used to set incentivised challenges for who could upsell bread and olives each month. There was a chart and a winner's board up behind the bar. Luckily, I only worked weekends and the occasional evening after college but my goodness I absolutely knew at the mere age of seventeen that there was more to my life than upselling overpriced baskets of bread and marinated olives for a large corporation.

And there was a flaw to their system: one crucial element missing from the management's strategy to lure us in to selling more. An incentive! 'But there's no prize and I only work part-time,' I said when my name was bottom of the list. Again. If hashtagging had been a viable solution to this exchange when I was seventeen my response would have been simply #bothered. Aside from the upselling I loved that job. I loved being a waitress.

The way I acted, or reacted, at each and every one of those tables gave me a great sense of responsibility; I was responsible for people having a good time. Now I'm a mom and going out for a meal should be an absolute treat but I get served by seventeen-year-olds who spend too much time cooing at my child, mess up our order and then come over to the table with the wrong meal and respond with 'Ooops, my bad!'

Call me old-fashioned, or maybe it is just because I'm so acutely aware of my daughter copying everything we say right now, but I like table manners. My heart melts when my daughter says thank you to a stranger, and my tummy roars with laughter when she later repeats inappropriate words she's heard around the house.

A young, fresh-faced and usually very chatty volunteer in our local community cafe once asked her very cheerily, when we popped in for a cuppa just before closing time, what we'd been doing all day. She bent down to my daughter's height in anticipation of a magical story.

'Sweet FA!' she replied with a huge grin spreading across her face. The waitress stood up straight, not sure how to reply. I chuckled and thought, 'Chill out bab, at least she didn't say Sweet Fuck All!' I was feeling smug because I'd managed to code my crude tongue and my little legend looked up at me acknowledging her humour.

Shit shit shit

Our daughter has a tool box of toy wooden nuts and bolts topped up with a selection of real-life Rawl plugs. When she was two and a half we moved into our new building site, I mean home. She loved carting around rows of Rawl plugs; it must be really intriguing for her small fingers to twist and twiddle at those tiny bits of plastic connecting one plug to another. And probably a huge sense of satisfaction when she finally pulls one apart. Each time there was an opportunity to join in with our builders for some hard graft, there she was, accompanied by her tool box and Rawl plugs.

Six months later or so, one rainy November day, not long after her third birthday, we were playing 'decorating her room' which gave me a chance to unpack another from the stack of boxes *still* occupying the corner of her room since we moved in months earlier.

She was well and truly busy, knelt down at toddler height, talking to herself quietly about all that she was doing, totally in her zone. When toddlers talk quickly and quietly to themselves that is the voice that says *do not disturb*. There she was

267

banging away at some drawing pins holding photos, at her eye level, never to be seen by anyone taller than about 60cm.

I'd tediously downloaded them from my brother's Google+ circle (why on earth did he carry on using Google+ after 2014?), selected a few more from my sister's What's App conversation (she's one of those who sends about seven of almost the same pic because someone, usually her, has their eyes closed) and duly uploaded onto Boots photo at around 11.43pm because that discount code for the bargain of the century was going to expire at midnight. I always feel a bit smug when I meet those money-saving deadlines within at least the time it takes to make a cup of tea.

So there she was immersed, carefully selecting colourful photos of her beaming cousins against brightly clad city playgrounds with the glowing light of a cloudless day in Valencian spring. We spent a week visiting them in their new Spanish home: it simply wasn't long enough. Back in her bedroom in Blighty she was kneeling and tapping into the wall with her bright yellow 'tapper', or hammer as most adults would call it. Around three years old she developed a very sophisticated way of using onomatopoeic words to describe items or experiences. I've shown her to use the hammer gently and therefore the tender tap of a hammer has become a 'tapper', urinating is 'shi-shi', and confusingly when she holds two adults' hands and expects to be swung up in the air, she calls it a 'wee': 1-2-3 weeeee.

And as she tapped with her tapper I heard her muttering, at intervals, what could only be audible as 'shit'. My immediate response was somewhere between pure comedy and utter concern. As a bilingual family I always hoped that she'd swear in her father's tongue rather than mine so that I wouldn't have to carry the guilt of raising a foul-mouthed child. That's a lie, there would be no guilt, I swore as a child because I had heard it from adults around me. This has been a great lesson of parenthood; if what you say out loud offends your ears, then do not say it out loud because sooner or later your child will parrot you, and very possibly in embarrassing company.

For example, I made sure Little Miss Listens-A-Lot was out of earshot when I told my friend over the phone that we couldn't go swimming because I had thrush. I could just envisage us at the following trip to the leisure centre, rocking up at the reception and her announcing at that slightly-louder-than-average volume that three-year-olds know to use for really special announcements, 'We couldn't go swimming before because my mama has thrush.'

'Shit, shit, shit.' That's not hypothetical me stood in embarrassment at the hypothetical leisure-centre reception. No, that was my three-year-old daughter happily hammering wooden push pins into her bedroom wall. I continued searching my brain for a word in English or Portuguese that she could be mistakenly imitating as she tapped. It certainly wasn't 'hit' because the 'sh' sound was so obvious. 'Chita' in Portuguese is cheetah, but that was totally out of context and I wasn't even sure if she was accustomed to lesser known feline relatives. I kept searching and also trying to listen as she repeated what was getting louder and louder and finally was quite unmistakably 'SHIT'.

I calmly said 'Pardon amor, I didn't hear you?' I couldn't let this one go. It was too intriguing. I'd wonder for weeks where she'd picked it up if I didn't investigate further. Slowly, she looked up from her work place and gently laid the hammer on the floor, like she knew she was about to say something very profound and very earnest. I could see she was tired and in a very calm, controlled mood. She was mellow. My nostrils were flaring as I held back raucous laughter. In a matter-of-fact yet nonchalant tone she informed me, 'It's what Pépé says when he is tapping.'

My dearest dad, known as Pépé to his grandchildren, known for his expletives to his grown-up children, had been well and truly heard by his youngest grandchild. Thanks, Pépé.

Part 8 - We never know what women are going through

What if we use play to get us through the tough times?

The most difficult part of miscarriage is the secrecy surrounding the first trimester. We have a weird social norm in Britain that means we generally don't announce a pregnancy until twelve weeks, after the first scan offered by the NHS. But when one in four pregnancies ends in the first twelve weeks, thousands of women are left with a lonely secret to decipher.

Come to rest

I met Mr Lowprofile at 4am on a dancefloor in Lisbon. Nine years and nine weeks after that night in Lisbon I was awake at 4am, but this time it wasn't for dancing.

I raced out of bed and downstairs hoping the toilet would catch my bleed in time. It didn't. I sunk into the toilet bowl to let it curl around my midsection. I closed my eyes and dreamed of a place where I could lose my baby with dignity. Eleven weeks pregnant and I started to bleed. I knew what was happening but I wanted to cling onto every last grain of hope.

Lots of women experience spotting, I told myself. The evening before I had casually texted friends who I remembered had experienced spotting during pregnancy and went on to have healthy children. I was hanging onto their hope, I knew what was happening.

There is no dignity in miscarriage. We bleed our children onto sanitary pads and either throw or wash them away. I wanted to sit in a hot spring for weeks. A natural warm pool, way up in the Japanese Alps, far away from civilisation where I could let my body be still and quietly birth my not quite complete child.

By 7am we'd woken our daughter from peaceful slumber and dropped her with some friends so we could go to the hospital. The senior midwife confirmed that there was a 'collection' in the womb. How could such a kind soul use such awful vocabulary? I was done with clinical nonsense and was desperate to leave the hospital; I've never liked those places. Part of me wishes we'd never gone to the clinic and just let nature take her course. She handed me a booklet from an orderly but unlabelled drawer on her desk. I declined it. I didn't want to know. But I do now wonder if that booklet would have told me to rest, like really, really rest: quit my job, embark on an art therapy course, be in nature, join a choir, find comfort in the discomfort. Write a book.

I think rest is unarguably undervalued in our society and I can't think of anything better than to accept rest. Plan for rest. When I sent a message to my wise friend announcing the healthy arrival of our daughter, she simply replied 'STAY IN BED x x'. We need to be explicit about rest.

While I welcomed hibernating in the winter I gave birth, those first few weeks were far from sacred. Not that I was aiming for sacred; I had no idea that many cultures honour the first forty days after childbirth as a time of special treatment in the form of total rest. Women in the family or village see to all the needs of the mother so she can focus on rest and bonding with her newborn.

In my first forty days I got health visitors inviting me and reminding about the Healthy Baby sessions at the children's centre. Despite all the breastfeeding mayhem, I went. It was awful. I ask myself of all those pamphlets they lovingly thrust in my lap why there wasn't one that just said REST in big block letters.

When I had my second miscarriage it was summer and I just felt so fortunate to be so close to the sea. I swam a lot over those weeks that I slowly bled. Another unspoken element of baby loss is the duration of the process unfolding in our bodies. When it is all over, we say 'I had a miscarriage', but during those days and weeks the cramps and stains sporadically told me 'I am still having a miscarriage, I am still losing my baby. How long does this last?'

With each dip I allowed the waves to pound into my face and wipe away my rolling tears. On the better days I looked up to the sunlight and let the sun brighten my grey and empty expression. At moments I felt at peace, I trusted in my body that she had saved me from further complications and heartbreak.

My immediate response was relief. Relief that the humming nausea I'd felt for weeks had left my body as quickly as it had arrived. Someone had flicked the off switch, and that was that. A few hours after we had the scan that confirmed everything was off I suddenly felt foolish that I had not considered the next sensation of sickness that was about to strike my body; grief. One nauseating feeling replaced by another.

We women hide a lot. We put on a brave face and we just get on with it usually for the sake of other people's necessity of us. Our employer, our friend, our spouse, our sibling, our parent, our nephew, our neighbour, our child. They all need us. They have requirements for us to fulfil. Menstruating women fulfil an incredible number of work tasks that I am sure a man bleeding from the arse would never dream of doing. A miscarrying mother follows suit.

Another wise woman told me some weeks after I'd miscarried that grief is confusing because our society designates no time for grief. I remember one employment contract stating that one-day absence would be granted to attend the funeral of an immediate relative: no other end of life ceremonies or cherished friendships acknowledged. Empathetic employers may say 'take all the time you need' when a close one passes, but calling in 'sick' six months, 7 years or a decade later 'because grief has overcome me today' just doesn't seem viable.

I'd had a miscarriage prior to 'becoming a mom'. Did that first blue line confirm I was a mom? My mothering role didn't last long enough for me to decipher if I was indeed a mom. It was early, around 5 weeks, and I was devastated, confused and went back to work the next day and told myself it was just a really heavy period. I was an agency worker back then and if I didn't go to work I wasn't paid. More to the point I was hoping to be offered a permanent contract with them in the new year so I didn't want my employer to think I was planning to go on maternity leave anytime soon. What a shit and naive situation. I now feel a sadness for my younger self for being so unsure of myself and my rights. Not that there are any written rights for a woman in that situation, but the rights I would give myself are those of kindness and compassion to self.

So, the second time around I allowed myself to sit with my grief. Everything else had to stop. I remember sitting with those feelings while 'Mama I want a snack please', 'Mama I want to play moms and dads, you be the mom, I'll be the baby', 'Mama I've finished wipe my bum' were amplified all around me.

It's actually quite difficult to 'sit with it' when we are so unaccustomed to sitting and feeling. I was never encouraged to sit and feel at school; no mention of listening to my body in PHSE, Religious Studies or at health reviews with the school nurse. Sitting and feeling the grief felt a bit odd, to say the least. And while feeling odd is one barrier, what feelings actually come out and how to process them is a whole other mind-blowing battlefield, especially with a toddler in tow.

I had a reluctance to talk, to write, to communicate. A reluctance to eat. A reluctance to be a mother; after all my body had just rejected the process of being a mother again. I was paralysed; I really wanted our daughter close, I didn't want her out of sight but I was stuck as to what to do with her. Well-meaning friends offered to take her so I could rest, but she was my comfort and my happiness and my sorrow in one perfect little parcel of emotionally raw toddler.

We told her that her baby sister had gone away on an adventure but we don't know where exactly. Over the subsequent weeks she grieved with me declaring to friends and strangers on the bus that her 'baby sister was lost.'

Her presence embodied what I had lost and that was the most difficult part of being a miscarrying mother. I wanted to bring my baby everywhere because I could no longer bring the other baby with me; she, he, they weren't here anymore.

Two months after I miscarried I was 'still' a rollercoaster. I had tried to cheer myself up too soon. I hadn't really rested. I can see now how much I really, really needed rest. On the days I was feeling 'high' I'd embrace life fully and overdo it; a few days later I was uncontrollable: sobbing on the kitchen floor or down the phone or in bed. When the tears dried, my mind spun with desperation to be pregnant again.

My loving husband and my wonderful sister both encouraged me to get blood tests, just in case. Maybe my thyroid was playing up, or my iron was low or my adrenals weren't up to scratch. My results came back normal. In a strange way I wanted them to show something was unbalanced to give me a scientific explanation as to why I wasn't feeling better. I was blessed with a GP who could talk to me like a human rather than a medical record on a screen with a four-minute appointment slot. She let me sit for a while and offload while I stared at the Victorian trees swaying in the park outside. She told me, 'Don't underestimate what you have been through' as our parting words.

So, I stopped underestimating and started acknowledging the depth of my grief. I came across a poem by Ian Robertson with the line 'There is no grief greater than a mother's grief.' I often look at my daughter and grieve what could have been if her sibling had joined us. Then I sit thankful for her

277

health, her happiness, her wisdom and hold her lively soul
close to mine.

She held her own

In the spring before my second miscarriage, well before we
conceived, I felt an unfamiliar, heavy, burdened weight in my
body. I was nauseous but knew I wouldn't vomit. After dropping our daughter to our childminder, I pulled over my car
on the way to work; I had to let my body pause. I was on the
clifftop so I took a stroll and sat on a bench under a bright
springtime sunshine. I looked out to the horizon and listened
to the small choppy waves collapsing onto the sand below the
cliffs.

It was the day my friend held her mom's funeral. I say
she held it because I'd seen her prepare for it. My sorrow was
redirected to admiration as she held her own. I tried to distract our children while she made important phone calls. She
assured me that her relatives were helping; she didn't in any
way feel that the burden had fallen on her to organise it. She
held it, she held herself, she holds her children, her partner,
her brothers, her ageing and oblivious nanny.

After about an hour on that bench I realised I was feeling
my friend's grief. I was so terribly sad for the loss of a woman
I had not met. My boss called me as I was uncharacteristically
AWOL. I told him, 'I'm grieving and I'll be in soon.' I didn't
actually say the g-word as I hadn't then realised that grief
was what I was feeling. But he got the gist. I went to work
late. I worked through my to-do list and the world kept on
spinning. An hour out of my working day to clear my head

278

was no biggy. I was so lucky to have a boss that thought like that.

A few months later I was sat in my friend's north-facing living room escaping the heat of the day with three naked children. I used to love the sunshine and would sit out all day, slapping on the layers of suncream, but those days are long gone. Nowadays I seek shade. So, we had retreated from the midday sun and sat at her oval dining table with two mugs of Yorkshire Gold (she has a refined palate), strong, with a dash of milk. Alongside my mug was a pint of water; unsure which one would better quench my thirst.

Beyond her shoulder sat an abundant and fertile window sill. I marvelled at how much she grew on a north-facing wall. The star of the show was the most piercing blue orchid. One flower perched at the peak with a cascade of smaller ones blooming below. All my orchids were twigs; never re-flowering once the initial shop-grown petals had withered. As she spoke I was mesmerised by this natural sculpture. I wanted to stand up to take a closer look but my heat-swollen limbs had sunken into the velvety dining chair. She asked me what I was smiling at as my attention had clearly diverted from the topic of conversation.

'Oh, I'm just admiring your orchid.'

'It's Mum's,' she said proudly. And she went on to tell me how she had rescued it from her mum's flat in Pimlico when it became clear that she wasn't going to be discharged from hospital.

I have so much admiration for how she has accepted her mother's passing. Though we haven't been friends for

279

long – she's a woman I'd only recently met through motherhood – I have quickly grown to admire her greatly.

And her children are the only siblings that really, really make me pang for another child. Her son is so inquisitive, especially in nature, and holds the kindness of an older gentleman. Her daughter is feisty, independent and bold. We often say our daughters are of the same breed: born with fire in their bellies. What is it that gives these girls such remarkable strength of character? Child-led, unadulterated, gender-neutral play, of course. And great music; when we first met, a year or so previously, we quickly discovered that there are a lot of parallels on our playlists. Similar taste in music has been the foundation of a lot of my friendships.

That day, in the shade of her living room, in that early summer heatwave, she taught me a lot. Practically, she showed me how to trim the brown roots from below the orchid's bark to keep it reblooming. But emotionally, she articulated that there are days when grief is the only permissible state of being. 'I just have to sit with it; to feel it and accept other stuff has to wait.'

Weeks later I joined her in sitting with my own grief. I didn't understand what it was like to lose a mother, and she didn't understand what it was like to lose a baby from her womb, but we united in reciprocal empathy. We sat beside each other, forming a micro-circle of sisterhood, offering little encouraging thoughts, welcoming distractions and reminding each other to eat even though neither of us held much of an appetite.

From one grieving mother to another, we heavily ferried our children around local parks, trying to regain a sense of normality for our young family. Of course, some days were brighter than others. And on the darkier, foggier days, in between dishing out snacks and nursing the odd fall here and there, we spoke quietly and openly about life and death. We had both, individually, explained honestly and simply to our children why we were sad. My daughter tunes into my emotions and so I believe openness is imperative when it comes to building her emotional literacy.

There aren't really any words that help the situations we found ourselves in. Only gestures. I gave her a dress to wear to her mum's funeral and she gave me a specially curated Spotify playlist of songs to let the tears flow. On one of those days in late summer, her then nearly two-year-old who imitated my daughter had taken to calling me 'Mama', offered me a pat on my arm as I sat cross-legged on the arid grass, weeping. Her big brown succouring eyes set upon my watery pools as she said 'Mama' softly in a 'there, there' kind of tone.

Nature heals

One morning we grieving Mamas mutually agreed over What's App that we both needed a slow day in nature. So, we packed basic picnics and boarded the X3 to Ringwood. We could have squeezed into my car but actually the day was far more restful without driving. In part of my commitment to slowing down, on days when I don't want to cycle, if it is a doable journey on a bus, I choose the bus over driving.

Our ever excitable three children shared a double seat on one side of the table and we sat opposite. A bus with a table! I was astounded! Fancy. After twenty minutes of much wriggling, shrieking, exaggerated bouncing and the inevitable bashed head on the now not-so-fancy table we unloaded our herd down onto the pavement. As we made our way along the top deck, down the stairs and out the doors we apologetically smiled at our fellow passengers who I am sure were glad to see the back of us and our raucous pack.

'Thank you drivah!' I customarily sang in my broadiest, jolliest Brum.

We had bold plans that day to march deep into the forest; somewhere we could escape and avoid any sign of humans except our own. But we quickly found that reminders of the real world were not so threatening.

The buggies remained childless as our three rascals took the lead. Somehow, they knew that we were both burdened with the overwhelm of being grieving parents. So, they took it in their tiny strides and somehow declared that we could have the day off. Over about six hours we clocked no more than two kilometres as we dawdled at their pace through the woods and along a stream. We were both fragile and we let nature and our blissful children console our aching hearts. And so the buggies carried our backpacks, and our children carried our heavy souls. It was a warm day and sunlight crept through crevices in the woodland canopy. Beneath the birdsong, the damp, shaded path held the scent of Mother Earth. I inhaled and welcomed her presence.

The slow plod along the stream was enough. On these idyllic days when curiosity and play control the agenda I can step back and enjoy the view. With under-fours this is rare, I know. But I remind myself to take note and allow myself to be amazed at what these kids know and how much they don't need us.

It's so easy for us moms to get caught up in directing, in timekeeping, in fulfilling expectations, showing up, taxi-ing, cooking meals, providing care to others. Where is the care for us? We have to carve out time each and every day to care for ourselves too.

That day in the woods I'll hold close and treasure because it was so, so needed. My friend and I were unintentionally indulging in a carefree, and almost self-indulgent day. And yet it was so simple. So, so simple. We didn't see our no-longer-babies as burdens. All the love, care and guidance we instilled into our kids, we allowed them to give back to us at a time when we needed it most.

Beautiful Stranger

That same summer, one sunny day when it was hard to stay indoors with a determined two-year-old who could see and hear the park through our open windows, while I was in the middle of my miscarriage that made me want to curl up in a ball and speak to no one new, I also wanted to lie on the grass and let the days pass in stillness under the branches of old trees. Eventually we went out to the bustling playground and I pretended I was up in the mountains, or deep in the forest, on my own with only my children for company.

From the top of the tall red slide our daughter spotted a large table over the far side of the playground and wanted to take a closer look. She was fast approaching three and her internal radar for social opportunity was, as ever, fully charged as she bounded down the slide and raced over to the table where she stood and watched. I slowly followed her and found children, parents and grandparents quietly gathered and drawing a few vegetables that had been spread along the middle of two fold-out tables borrowed from the little cafe in the corner of the playground.

At the head of the table sat a local mom who I recognised but didn't know. She sorted through a huge box of pens and pencils: chucking out pens that no longer coloured into a carrier bag and leaving pencils out along the table that needed sharpening.

My daughter sat herself down and lapped up the company of the older artists. She watched with scrutiny as their pencils danced across the paper. She marvelled as familiar fruit and vegetables began to appear on the pieces of paper in front of each older child. I was thankful for a chair, the peace and the quiet.

I was reluctant to draw; since I was old enough to realise that the objects or people I was attempting to mark out on the page didn't particularly resemble what I was trying to draw, I concluded I wasn't very good at drawing. Like many I was so self-critical way too soon.

Why aren't we introducing children to abstract art before still life? Nowadays I'd tell that kid that they are drawing the wrong thing; everyone can draw, we just have to find, with tact and patience, the objects, landscapes or characters most suited to their hands.

The drawings that took shape before us in our make-do art studio in our park replicated the bright yellow of a cut-in-half pepper and the deepest greens of a courgette at its mid-summer peak. At the centre of the table sat a small half of a brazen gold kiwi and a row of the juiciest strawberries whose aroma sweetened the table. I was astonished that small hands refrained from pinching them. I doubt I would have held back when I was a kid.

All the while, I busied myself by sharpening pencils, and let my daughter be the social butterfly I usually was. As my fingers went pink from the grip of the small metal sharpener, I marvelled at the peacefulness around the table. The park was busy and full of the movement and sounds of children playing in an urban playground.

There was a welcomed breeze in the air which occasionally sent a child chasing their artwork as it flew off the table. Conversation was intermittent. There was a respectful quiet around the table as children focussed on shaping and shading their vegetables and their parents embraced a simple creative challenge.

The grandmother shipped in from abroad to help with childcare over the long holidays sat patiently with her arms crossed and her chair angled slightly away from the table. Although she looked uncomfortable being part of the group she respectfully nodded in the direction of each new person who sat down to join us. She smiled shyly as her granddaughter explained to us in that way that seven-year-olds explain things with such importance and purpose, 'She's my grandma but she doesn't speak English so I have to tell her everything in Spanish so she knows what's going on.'

I'd usually pipe up and make a bit of conversation with this Abuela, but I was worried this grandma, like many others, would harmlessly ask when I was going to have another baby which would make me burst into tears and spoil the golden calm around the table. So, I sat in as much silence as possible with a nearly three-year-old and marvelled at the meeting around the table. Young and old, frail and strong, creative and critical, all united by the simplicity of one humble woman's attempt to survive the six-week-long break from the structure that school brings her family.

'MomI'mhungry,' her youngest moaned in one syllable as we packed away the tables.

'Eat the pepper,' she replied flicking her hand towards the cotton tote she'd just filled with the still-life models. Her daughter picked out the yellow pepper which fell into the two halves. Her daughter, obviously generously spirited like her mom, asked me,

'Is she allowed this?'

I smiled and two chubby hands grabbed it from her hand before I could permit the exchange of this humble vegetable and thanked the girl for being so kind. Both girls, curls moving in the wind, took a simultaneous chomp from their half as seeds and juice sprinkled onto the concrete at their feet.

It was one of those pleasant British summer days, not too hot, just pleasant. Someone was sizzling sausages on a barbecue in the front gardens that lined the four sides of the park.

I was nauseous from the loss of my baby, and in some weird my-body-still-thought-it-was-pregnant kind of way I was still smelling what my neighbours were cooking before their produce hit the pan.

I was so grateful for that day. I sat in the company of a stranger as if she was an old friend. Something about sitting at that table reminded me of my friend Kez and the warmth of being sat around her kitchen table in the school holidays when it was her turn to look after her neighbours' kids.

I liked that this woman, my neighbour, was honest about her three offspring 'driving her mad' this summer and any excuse to bring an activity to the park made everyone happy. I learned she actually brought six children to the park that day.

'It's much easier when each one invites a friend... We all take it in turns in the holidays... You gotta. There's only so much time we can all spend together. We're human after all.'

Conclusion - Learning from my village of playful people

289

What if we reach out to humans instead of reaching out for Google?

The word 'community' comes from two Latin words – com and munos, which literally translates to 'together in gift'. I'm not trying to gather lots of people together on the village green to all sing 'kumbaya' at the same time each week, but I have been asking for gifts here and there; some to borrow, some to keep. A few hours of childcare, outgrown clothes, a slow cooker, camping kit, my neighbour's huge cardboard box as they carried it to our communal recycling bin, etc., etc. It is so easy to just pop online and buy stuff whenever we need it, but there is something so much more meaningful about reaching out and asking for stuff. And all too often my villagers are only too pleased to help.

A woman at yoga class in Camberwell had described the arrival of her sister's first baby as 'a gift to the family'. I couldn't agree more. We didn't have our immediate families close, so I saw our daughter as a gift to our villagers.

In the very early days I felt needy and unable to contribute very much back to the humans that were helping me through a treacherous time. But I realise now that there is a very unique power in sharing the gift of life. As we passed our daughter around for cuddles I saw adults melt with joy and relax into the unique peace that holding a newborn brings. You can't buy that kind of gift down the high street. As our daughter grew she gifted her villagers with her smile and a *joie de vivre*, and we gifted them with our trust as we shared out the responsibility of growing a child, and asked for little favours here and there.

I've heard many of my friends doubt their capabilities to give birth, or to be good parents, listing the reasons they feel guilty rather than listing all the incredible things the tiny human they have created is doing each day. Remember that 'I am working towards expert status' I was playing around with, back in Part 7? I am going to leave you with a few (unlikely) experts from all walks of life and all corners of the globe who have exemplified, in one way or another, ways of living that are more freely chosen, personally directed and intrinsically motivated. I value what I have seen them do, or how they share their life with others.

By learning from and calling upon our village of experts I've definitely lightened the load of motherhood, built a valued community and created more time for meaningful play. I am absolutely not poo-pooing the humans who choose to study in great depth to become experts in their fields: we need people to understand the intricacies of the world. But I would like everyday folk to value themselves and their contribution to others.

To value ourselves we need to feel all that brilliant juicy good stuff sloshing about inside of us. I am not demanding that you must go out and play in the rain (though please feel free to do so), but embarking on a life full of play with decisions that are 'freely chosen, personally directed and intrinsically motivated' is always going to be a good place to start.

Kez

I learned a lot at the kitchen table of my friend Kez. She likes her tea strong with a dash of milk and a sneaky ciggy on the back doorstep. I hate that she smokes and I tell her so every time I see her. I stole her cigarettes from her once: just to really piss her off.

She is one of five kids. They moved to the other end of our traffic-laden urban road and she joined my class in our local primary school when we were around seven. We went to different secondary schools and drifted in our teens, but reunited in our twenties when she had two sons under five. We unexpectedly revived our friendship one Friday night when I bumped into her walking along our road in between our parents' houses. I'd been out for dinner with colleagues in the town centre and was disappointed that there were no familiar faces in my local pub when I'd popped in on my way home. As I walked home feeling at a bit of a loss there was Kez ready to party because she had a night off from her boys.

She had moved to the other side of Brum, way out in East Birmingham. It was an arse to get there but it was fun to catch up on the years we'd drifted. What I loved most about being at her house was sitting at her kitchen table and taking in all the comings and goings of her neighbours. A tribe of children from their road and the adjacent cul-de-sacs roamed in between houses, front lawns and back gardens. I saw vacuum cleaners, lawn mowers and bike pumps being passed around households.

This wasn't some dreamy eco community or middle-class cooperative. The majority of her neighbours were single moms, striving to hold down poorly paid jobs to set an example to their kids even though they were probably better off living on benefits. I wasn't there often but what I did see was a group of women asking each other for help with school runs, babysitting and tins of beans. Through her unlocked door strode in bold women carrying the burden of the world on their shoulders and not afraid to show it. They may not have been your typical- parenting-guide-book-all-prim'n'proper but I learned a lot about motherhood when I sat at that kitchen table.

When I became a Mama I thought a lot about Kez's little community. Sure, a lot about their situations was not ideal; many of them were struggling in ways I will never understand. But two things stood out that I haven't experienced beyond her kitchen table. Those families were asking for help and giving help: they were all pulling up their sleeves and lending a hand.

And those new builds on the edge of a faceless housing estate in East Birmingham offered a clever little setup with garden gates and space in front of their homes for community play. It was a shame the designers of the estate hadn't thought more about diverting traffic so there were some car-free play spaces for safer play. Thankfully there wasn't much through-traffic and the bigger kids always looked out for the smaller kids' safety.

I think we should all be doing more of what I saw there: raising each other's children and demanding all new building developments keep moving traffic well out of the way of people at play. There's so much potential in building new homes so that groups of households can play together in shared spaces.

Kofi

I chose to study at the University of Leeds because the International Development course offered a semester abroad in Ghana. When I was a student on the Legon campus in Accra it was the first time I had travelled to the global south. I was engrossed with watching how closely Ghanaians lived, how much people were involved in each other's lives. There was a strong sense of togetherness that I'd never seen in the global north. I liked it; even though I was thousands of miles from my beloved Kings Heath High Street where I was always guaranteed to spot a familiar face, in Accra I was never alone.

One of my Ghanaian classmates used to refer to his family home as 'the Compound'. My only reference to a compound was a prison yard with a barbed wire fence and a watch tower. I thought it was a bit of a begrudging dig at living with his ever-scrutinous granny while the rest of us were living it up in the freedom of student halls on campus. However, when I went to visit his home, and the homes of several other friends I've made while travelling around West Africa, I have learned that compounds are not just for prisoners.

After a few months of studying the Geopolitics of West Africa together, my classmate invited me to visit his family home. I duly accepted and the Saturday thereafter, along with his cousin, we left the sprawling green campus, a pocket of calm amidst the bustling city, and caught two trotros and a short taxi ride.

Trotros are one of those quintessentially 'foreign' forms of transport that young Europeans marvel at for being adventurous. Ghana was bustling with these noisy minibus taxis where everyone including the family goat were squeezed in and the middle aisles were filled with folding seats or wooden stools so the unlucky passenger had to get up at every stop to let others off. I didn't complain because the fares ranged between 3 and 42 pence depending on the distance travelled. I noticed that many of my Ghanaian and Nigerian classmates avoided taking such transport if they had the money for a more comfortable taxi car, while we international students (it always puzzled me that the other African students weren't considered 'international') enjoyed the novelty of 1960s bus fares.

By the heat of the day the residential neighbourhood outside was still; our taxi rolled down the dirt road without a pedestrian in sight. A quiet road is a rarity in Accra so I remember it well.

'Yes boss,' Kofi called to the taxi driver as he magically stopped at the correct gate. There were lots of walls with gates in them; I was impressed the driver had halted at the correct one. I got out of the taxi sharpish and left the locals to haggle the fare. I knew only too well that having an *obruni* – white – passenger added a disproportionate tax that made voices raise with exasperated 'Eh's and 'Ah's and arms and index fingers do all sorts of exaggerated movements in disapproval.

The taxi doors slammed and the red-and-yellow car rolled off raising a trail of dust which my friends beat down with their folded cotton handkerchiefs. They both wiped their brows before turning the small handle on the doorway set within a large metal gate. As we stepped through the doorway we left the silence of the street behind us and were welcomed with the volume of family life in full swing.

'Kofi, Kofi, Kofi!' chanted some gappy-toothed seven-year-old girls with matching beads in their braids as they skipped towards their uncle.

'Obruni!' stammered a three-year-old and started to scream into the leg of his mother.

'I am soh-ry oh. He hahsn't seen soh many white folk,' she exclaimed, reaching out and holding onto the flesh above my wrist which was a gesture that I'd noticed strangers did in Ghana when they wanted to show me I was welcome and physically at their side.

There was so much hustle and bustle in that home. I was only there for about twenty minutes but I must have greeted over thirty people at the doorways of different rooms, some preparing ingredients in huge saucepans, some seated in front of a television and others just passing in the courtyard. Everyone was in house clothes, hair wraps and 'bath slippers' – a sure sign they were relaxing in the comfort of their own home and not dressed to impress as they would have been on the other side of the gate. That's what a Ghanaian compound was.

In several countries I have visited, extended families build their homes around central courtyards and share living spaces. Wealthier families build a wall around their plot so upon arrival I would step into their compound through a gate. Nuclear families occupied an individual room or a small collection of rooms and the doors between each unit were left unlocked for the flow of relatives. The responsibility of caring for the young, old, disabled, child-bearing, the sick was shared amongst all the occupants.

I find this dynamic fascinating. I've always enjoyed family get-togethers but family live-togethers wasn't something I had any experience of growing up. My parents are both only children so my immediate family was really just us six. On the contrary, my best friend Sara who I met at secondary school lived around the corner from her nan and grandad, and her uncles and aunt lived nearby. Sara's house was lively with visitors popping in and out, cousins hanging out together in school holidays and uncles coming over for her dad's delicious weekend cook-ups.

I visited her house for the first time when I was eleven and noticed that her front door was unlocked, so was her nan's; we could just let ourselves in. I loved that their front doors were always open and people would just appear in their doorway. Recently I've really yearned for that kind of home but we've always lived in flats and not had the luxury of an open-door policy.

I am sure many people would question whether it be 'a luxury' or not to have visitors, pre-planned or spontaneous, strolling into their home at any time of the day. I think it is absolutely vital when walking past a friend's door to be able to knock on and see if it is a good time for a cuppa. If they are not home, or it is not the right time, then it's no big deal; I just carry on my stroll.

Social media and mobile phones have cut out much spontaneity but I think that unplanned cups of tea are a crucial part of forming a community and vital for combatting isolation in new parents. I aspired to be timeless when our daughter was tiny; clock-watching and arriving on time was added pressure I decided I could do without.

Our generation has lost the art of rocking up on a door-step and finding each other as we are. I have no expectation of my friends to make me a meal or put on a spread; I don't even need to have milk in my tea! But I love a bit of human contact and I certainly prefer to sit and have a cuppa at my friend's kitchen table than in a cafe; especially when young children are involved. Cafes are lovely for adults: no cooking, no washing up. But all that novelty went out of the window for me once our daughter was on the move and purposefully grabbing the feet (and once even the food!) of unsuspecting cafe-goers.

Yes, cafes are lovely but kitchen tables are the heart of real life.

Rosie

The first time I visited Churchill Gardens in Bournemouth it reminded me of Montreal. It is a square garden surrounded by large Victorian houses many of which boast beautiful hig-gledy-piggledy wrought-iron balconies. I was told they were built to house the doctors working at Boscombe Hospital just around the corner. Once a middle-class utopia, like much of our neighbourhood, the square has crumbled over the years; those grand family homes chopped into flats and bedsits and the small park, and the half mile around it, have grown an unfavourable reputation for dog shit and drug addicts. On my first visit I was unaware of the reputation though the fly tipping and the drug deals in broad daylight were a giveaway.

I didn't care: the park was alive with happy humans, community arts and colourful families enjoying the late summer sunshine.

'It reminds me of Montreal,' I enthusiastically declared to Mr Lowprofile as we plonked ourselves on the grass and admired the architecture. The humans around us were nodding and skanking to the Afro-reggae band playing from the area which everyone recognised as the stage, even though it was no different from the rest of the lawn.

Five years after attending that small festival we moved into one of those first-floor flats with a wrought-iron balcony. That sixteen-year-old who cried to her mama that their Brummie high street was dull and ugly finally found her bit of Montreal on this side of the Atlantic. It was once the cricket field for a local boys' school; I'm pleased that nowadays it is a gender-neutral community play space.

Our first-floor bay frames the crown of several sycamores and one pine, all lined up, forming a boundary around our garden that we share with everyone. Predictably in springtime, familiar daffodils and crocuses sprout up around the tree trunks. And in the approach to Diwali the trees surrender their leaves and the foliage plays hopscotch around their roots. We are avid park-goers and avid stay-at-homers. On days when I am embracing rest, from the comfort of our living room I enjoy being on the periphery of a bustling community. The basketball court and the metal playground painted in primary colours brighten the green lawn, and tree-lined square and a small community cafe occupies the far corner.

Those of us who choose to grow our families here in one of the 'undesirable' neighbourhoods of Bournemouth relish the company of other non-judgemental folk who can see beyond Boscombe's ageing reputation. We escape our cramped flats by walking and cycling to playgrounds, the beach and cherished indie cafes where the owners greet us like the fondest aunty: 'Buongiorno Lovie!' 'Buongiorno Rosie!'

I can't simultaneously live anywhere else to compare if I'd have the same sense of community elsewhere but I think there is something quite unique about our neighbourhood. It is not the buildings that make a place desirable; it is the interactions between people that bring a place to life. We need spaces in between buildings to allow these vital interactions between people to happen. We need businesses where we feel like we are visiting a favourite relative's dining room, rather than faceless establishments where everyone is treated like a money machine.

Of course, there are lots of my neighbours that I do not know or exchange pleasantries with. There are though folk who are looking for community, who don't want to live alone, who value the sense of place; I have found them and we live side by side.

There's a man who coaches football to local kids on the basketball court. Come rain or shine he is there, Tuesday and Thursday evenings, and school holidays too. He gets all ages involved. There's a brother and a sister, the keenest by far, who show up about thirty minutes before the rest to secure the court. I haven't spied with binoculars or gone to make enquiries but from our window there are two things I have never noticed; I've never seen the exchange of money and I've never seen him arrive or leave with children in tow. I'll never ask if he has children of his own; the truth can be hard to hear.

El bandito

Playful adults all around the world have caught my eye. But there is one group in particular who never fail to steal a piece of my heart; the Sunday park-goers who congregate in Mount Royal on Sundays.

On my first trip to Montreal when I was eight years old I distinctly remember the gathering of hundreds of drummers and dancers around a large winged angel statue on the edge of a park next to a busy road. I don't think I had been to a music festival in nature by then so Tam-Tams was my first taste of open-air dancing on grass and beneath trees (albeit with highrise from the downtown skyline beyond the crowd). Even though we were walking along a busy boulevard with three lanes of traffic, I remember hearing the drumbeat as we approached. As we turned off the sidewalk and on to the grass I was submerged into a sea of entranced giants who were moving and shaking and I thought it was pretty funny. How could they see with their eyes closed? Why weren't they wearing shoes? How did they all know when to hit their drum? How could their hands move so fast? Who was telling them what to play?

When I returned to the Mountain (the local name for the mound of green that backdrops the city) for a spot of Tam-Tams in my late teens I was a little more used to going to gigs and the festival vibe was right up my street. In Brum I was

301

used to community arts events (probably organised by my dad and his colleagues) where I was guaranteed to see at least one adult that really let themselves go, leaping about, arms waving, ecstatic-awakening stylie amongst a crowd of otherwise pretty tame spectators.

But Tam-Tams was an unmeasurable amplification of any of those community arts gigs. What I really loved about Tam-Tams was that it wasn't all hippies. Even the most unlikely North American sports jock would find his place at Tam-Tams and let himself feel the rhythm. Sure, there were drink and drugs fuelling some adults, but I always got the impression that they were in the minority. For the most part, it was a gathering of very playful people letting themselves bounce about in all that brilliant juicy good stuff after a Sunday brunch.

The spontaneity of Tam-Tams will always hold a certain charm for its simplicity. It is a model of inclusive grassroots acoustic creativity: turn up and drum, or turn up and dance, or turn up and sell your art, or turn up and nurse your hangover, that I am yet to discover in another urban environment (though you must sip your hair of the dog discreetly from a brown paper bag).

On my last trip to Montreal, however, it wasn't the shimmying-peace-n-love-sports-jocks that caught my eye. And Mr Lowprofile would probably tease me that I had become one of those dancing hippies so it wasn't them either. Hidden beyond the drumbeat, beyond the organised sports teams and the family picnics, in a clearing amongst a wilder set of trees, were another section of society that ignited my passion for adults living playfully.

Locally known as the The Warriors of the Mountain (Les Guerriers de la Montagne), they are a group of adults that take playing very seriously. I stood bewildered as I saw grown men and women charging around with adult-sized weapons, recreating a medieval battlefield. This was Recapitulative Play in all of its glory. The grass was worn so stones and dust atmospherically bumped about the ground as foam swords were swung and polystyrene lances were launched at cardboard shields gripped firmly to protect their bodies. A few bolshy teens joined the fully grown kids who appeared to strategise and form alliances with other Knights and Warriors.

I liked these guys because much of their armour and weapons were junk modelled. At closer inspection I saw a whole lot of gaffer tape and polystyrene packaging in action. Baseball bats and washing line poles were repurposed into adult-sized loose parts for play. But it wasn't just the junk-modelled weapons; fancy dress also helped bring their role play to life. Homemade costumes bring me so much joy. I love encouraging children to create their own costumes; I find when they've been through the process of creating attire they embody their chosen character with so much more meaning, and often stay in the role for so much longer.

I overheard one dude proudly admiring another's 'pauldrons'. If old Saint George was looking for bromance he'd surely find it on the Mountain of Mont-Royal. I spotted one guy in a medieval, presumably replica, tunic, and another topless with khaki shorts and outdoorsy sandals. But the dude that really caught my eye was the one simply wearing every-day, casual clothes with a bandana over his face like a Mexican gang member. He earned the nickname of 'El Bandito' from Mr Lowprofile. I liked El Bandito most because it was his mindset that made him a warrior, not his clothing.

The borrowed bigger kid

I think it is a blessing that we didn't, still don't, have much spare cash for babysitters. Yes, sometimes me and Mr Low-profile need to go out to play together, and it feels like so much less of a burden if we know our child is off playing with her friends too. When we left her in the care of the babysit-ter the passing on of responsibility felt so much heavier. But when we drop her off for a play date so we can go play too, the whole dynamic shifts.

I also love having a big kid over. 'Borrow a big kid,' I told my friends with only-child toddlers when they were bored with the monotony of their toddler's company. The parent(s) of the bigger kid(s) will welcome the break, the older kids entertain your relentlessly lively child, the younger kid learns from the older, the older kid learns from the younger and I am yet to hear squabbling over toys or games (or loose parts!) because with the age difference come different interests and different ways to play. I find children three or five years older than our daughter to be the best match.

Other people's children are generally more polite when they are not in their own home and there's no sibling rivalry. I enjoy being part of the jovial spirit of kids having a meal together but if that is not your thing then just ask the big kid to bring a packed lunch and lay out a picnic blanket on the kitchen floor and leave them to it.

I'm not so fussed about re-paying the childcare back to the family that looks after our daughter, but I do believe in paying it forward. And anytime a friend offers to have our daughter in return for the time I've just helped them with I remind them to pay it forward too.

Sexy Man

There was a guy who regularly came to work out in the park opposite our Montreal-esque balcony. I want to claim he was about my age. I'll emphasise the 'about' because I must remind myself I'm not as young as I like to think I am. I know I am at risk of sounding like a cougar. (An insult I learned in Canada as I watched an immaculately presented woman in her forties flirt with my then twenty-something scruffy older brother in an awful sports bar after his soccer team had played a match out in the Montreal 'burbs. They lost the game but they won the prize for my worst night out in Montreal. Ever.)

So, I'm self-deprecating by putting myself in her cougar category because I would never flirtingly approach this guy (not even in a Canadian sports bar). But from my living-room window I enjoyed the view. He was hot!

He'd casually rock up with his gym bag and hang a pair of gymnastics rings from the basketball hoop and proceed to swing all about the place while replicating positions from the Kama Sutra. Maybe I was having some kind of desperate housewive-esque moment. Maybe I wanted to savour his playful flair.

Let's be honest, the sex life of new parents is probably not anywhere as racy as it was pre-pregnancy, for the most part anyway. Fantasising over beautiful kamasutra-ing strangers in the middle of the day is evidently where I am at these days.

So, I found this dude sexy. I hadn't even seen him up close, but from way up on my balcony he was sexy. He was sexy not because his youthful, muscly, bare-chested torso was exhibiting erotic positions, all gliding and glowing right in front of my window while my husband was at work. He was sexy because each time a kid stopped to watch this ninja in action, in awe of his superhero movements, he paused, lowered the hoops and helped the kid up so they too could fly and swing and flip. Dreamy. I'm not looking for a new partner, but I find men who are great with kids very attractive.

One sunny Saturday morning I went to hang the bath mat out on the balcony. I noticed an orderly line of five or six children in the basketball court. Their body language was strong and purposeful; they weren't begrudgingly stood in line. Their bodies were poised and their expressions focussed. These small but bold and determined bodies were all looking in one direction.

I followed their gaze and through the foliage there he was. Sexy Man was back. Fully clothed, explaining to a seven-year-old how to prepare to somersault mid-air. She turned her body forward and swooped with control to the ground. He clapped his hands just twice, summoning enthusiasm as the next child in line walked towards the hoops. She was the most petite by far but from watching kids train Capoeira, and

306

seeing my own petite daughter's strength develop, I was anticipating she'd be strong.

He didn't lower the hoops to accommodate her height. He knelt down and turned towards me on the balcony and cried 'Marry me?' with his arms outstretched towards me. Rose petals spontaneously burst into the air around me, a pair of doves with an ivory silk ribbon clasped in their beaks fluttered down and delivered a shining diamond ring on my finger. And the park-goers cheered, the drivers honked their horns and we all lived happily ever after... He didn't. He just knelt down giving a leg up to that little lady. His loss.

Since becoming a mom, there is nothing more sexy than seeing a man be great with his kids. I love telling Mr Low-profile that I find him sexy when he is in true Dad Mode. Anything he can do to take the emotional or physical burden from me makes me feel more attracted to him. I love him more when he is out the house with our daughter. Sometimes I sacrifice family time just so I can love him more when the two of them arrive home from a Daddy Daughter day.

I wonder if this is unfeminist of me? Why should I be doting on the dads for chipping in? I shouldn't. A meeeeeme (not a me-me) doing the rounds really pissed me off. It was of a woman with a baby in a sling, shopping bags in one hand and a toddler holding the other. It reads 'She's got her hands full.' Beside it is the same image, a man with the same baby in a sling, the same shopping bags in one hand and the same toddler holding the other. It reads 'What a great Dad!' Our park is full of great dads. It is also full of really great moms.

Vovó

'Sabes Adele, na minha terra...' When my mother-in-law starts a sentence with 'you know Adele, back home...' it is a generous warning that she is going to shed some wives' tale knowledge from her motherland upon me, even though she concedes it has no place in our twenty-first century global north.

I have always known that she means well, but in the early days of motherhood I just couldn't find much patience for her. When her first grandchild was about twelve days old she told me to fold a piece of cotton thread into a cross and place on our precious newborn's tiny forehead to cure her hiccups. I had to ask her to repeat the instructions three times because I thought we were lost in translation. Surely, she wasn't telling me to fold a piece of thread into a cross and place it on her forehead? Surely not.

Good job that my sister-in-law was in earshot to translate and duly tease her mother for the illogical nonsense she was imposing on me. Over the rhythmic 'eek' of my newborn's hiccup we agreed that most people don't have reels of cotton to hand and by the time I'd dug out a thread from the depths of my sewing tin my baby's diaphragm probably would have stopped contracting anyway. She laughed in agreement and told me to just pull a slither of thread from my clothes. Her quick wit always outplays my practical logic. Hands down she wins.

She also suggested I put my tongue in the bath water to check the temperature; probably doable in a bucket bath like she would have used back home in Cape Verde but I still

308

replay the ridiculous image of me bending over, head first into our full-size British bathtub and flicking out my cobra tongue anytime I run a bath.

I like these insights. They are often lighthearted, kind and whisk me away to her *terra*, her home, where her siblings, her nieces and nephews, her childhood comrades live simply to the Western eye. I'm fond of the simple life, even if it doesn't always seem like I'm living simply, I certainly aspire to live with less fuss. I genuinely love hearing different perspectives. There's something so magical about humans all being the same but also being so wildly different.

My Final Thoughts

It's an absolute privilege to know the things I know about children and play and higgledy-piggledy people. I hope that sharing some of what I have absorbed from other humans will make the next stage of your journey as a parent, or a playful adult, kinder on yourself. We've become so conditioned to looking for all our answers from 'experts' that we've forgotten the value of human experience. All around us there are humans with lived experiences, right under our noses, ourselves included. We can choose to listen to ourselves more. Please remember that our villagers come in all shapes and sizes, all walks of life and sometimes they offer the most unexpected of gifts. It is not always what the villager does, it is sometimes what they say. I recently learned that sometimes I need a villager to remind *me* to reach out and ask others for help. I am human: I forget my own advice.

Times might have changed, our circumstances might be different, but there is one thing we all have in common: we are all still humans. And all humans need to, you've guessed it, play. Yes, I hope you'll receive the permission to do more for yourself and let your child(ren) trail behind, lapping up the joy that comes from living with playful adults. I hope you can let go of at least some of your structured time and the pressure to entertain, teach or control your kids. They are perfectly capable of filling their own time and learning while they play so long as they have the resources to meet their own individual play preferences (stuff from around the house will often engage for longer than mass-produced toys).

I am excited that this is only the tip of the iceberg for me and I am well aware I have so much more to discover about the way children play. Please don't beat yourself up for 'not playing with your kids'. We are all learning. The past may feel unplayful but the future is not yet written.

We can all be doing more to advocate for the rights of the child by creating time at home and spaces in our community for play. Even in neighbourhoods where there are no adventure playgrounds, no play centres or other places dedicated to children and their free play, we can create spaces, albeit temporary, that scream 'play is our priority here': play streets, resident-led pocket parks and parklets, playground hacking, pop-ups in empty retail units, even simply chalking on the pavement are all examples of how humans are working together to make childhood the best it can be. And on a professional level, we can demand more playwork training within the children's workforce.

We can all play our part in exemplifying acceptance. As an example, I have made the decision to drive our daughter across town to a preschool where there are several children with disabilities. I would much prefer walking or cycling to a local provision but, despite what their bumf says, inclusion and child-led play didn't appear to be on the agenda of our local preschools: school readiness was. Until now we have been fortunate to have a culturally diverse childminder's where bilingualism is common and afro curls are a plenty, but I was innately aware that our daughter was only ever meeting and playing with neurotypical children. I know I can't dictate who she plays with at preschool but at least I can give her the opportunity to mix. This particular preschool is not a 'specialist provision' but is simply staffed by open-minded children's professionals who respect each child as an individual and don't close doors to children with complex needs. Our choice of childcare provider is a privilege afforded to us because we have a car and I have flexible working hours but I really don't think inclusion should be a privilege.

I purposely avoided writing about the pandemic – I really hope there is only one pandemic in our lifetime, because I am not being paid for product placement of everyone's favourite Mexican beer – best served cold with a slice of lime. I really wanted to keep this book about my experience of parenthood up until our little bundle of joy turned three. I could probably write another book about the year or so we were 'playing at home'; I took a distaste to 'lockdown'. But I'll say just three things about what sat with me in 2020: 1. I think the basic needs of children were starkly forgotten; our nation prioritised screen time over resilience-building play. 2. I noticed a painful divide between the suffering of England's poor families and England's wealthy families, all living with the same decision makers in one of the richest countries in the world. 3. Neighbours united, strangers spoke to each other and communities of higgledy-piggledy people popped up at rocket speed to help each other out.

In the same period in recent history that we spent isolating from each other, a darker side of being human hit me. Hit me hard. The final word of this book will not go towards play or playwork and I am sure you will appreciate why. Centuries of mistreatment and, at worst, murder of so many Black people which culminated in the murder of George Floyd on

25th May 2020 have brought a heaviness upon our home and stirred deep in many of my close friends.

The heaviness has brought some positives to light; 'finally' I am not part of an exclusive club of white people who hear the plight of brown-skinned people, I don't sound radical or out of place for explicitly talking about diversity and difference. Thanks to my liberal upbringing in Birmingham I am aware of – at least some – the daily lived injustices not-white people face. Just like not-able-bodied, not-straight, not-legally-residing or not-neurotypical people, I respect and value these humans as humans. We are all human and I really, really wish I didn't have to feel I'm in some special brand of humanitarian, able-bodied, straight, legally entitled white citizen who 'gets it'. There shouldn't be anything to 'get'. I shouldn't need to write about this but there are still, evidently, many folk around who just don't get it.

The term 'ally' was never on my radar before May 2020. I have never cared much for labels or memberships of exclusive clubs, but in the company of non-discriminatory humans, speaking out and using my privileges to raise others is where I have chosen to be and where I choose to remain. Ally is probably the only label (beside playworker!) that I'll pin upon my chest. I am grateful that white people are now having these open, often uncomfortable, dialogues and that there has been a huge wake-up call to a bigger, widely unspoken and often ignored problem. I am quite picky about what media I follow so I surround myself with positive news stories and choose to follow less-mainstream journalism, research and podcasts. Mainstream media has a huge part to play in inciting hatred

315

and often chooses not to print balanced news stories. There is plenty to be optimistic about: films like Rocks and campaigns such as the Halo Code and Choked Up led by young Black and brown-skinned people reassure me that the world will be a more equal place in the not-so-distant future.

However, no matter how liberal and open-minded our immediate circle is, no matter how broad and varied the knowledge we choose to share with our daughter, 2020 made me sit with an uncomfortable possibility that my beautiful brown-skinned child might not have the privileges of a care-free childhood that I did. It took me weeks to digest that despite all that I can give her, I can't protect her from other people's perceptions of her and I still swallow the lump that forms in my throat each time I dwell upon that.

* * *

Thanks for reading *Children don't dissolve in the rain*.

If you enjoyed this book please pass it on to a friend, neighbour or your local library. If you are feeling generous and got a few quid going spare, donations to Big Blue Play will be very much appreciated.

www.bigblueplay.org/donate